# Public Finance in Developing Countries

# Public Finance in Developing Countries

Vito Tanzi

Edward Elgar

Published by
Edward Elgar Publishing Limited
Gower House
Croft Road
Aldershot
Hants GU11 3HR
England

Edward Elgar Publishing Company
Old Post Road
Brookfield
Vermont 05036
USA

**British Library Cataloguing in Publication Data**
Tanzi, Vito
Public finance in developing countries.
1. Developing countries. Public finance
I. Title
336.0121724

**Library of Congress Cataloguing in Publication Data**
Tanzi, Vito
Public finance in developing countries / Vito Tanzi.
p.  cm.
Includes index.
1. Finance, Public–Developing countries.  2. Fiscal policy–Developing countries.  3. Developing countries–Economic policy.
I. Title.
HJ1620.T36  1990
336.09'1724–dc20                                    90-3735
                                                     CIP

ISBN 1 85278 374 5

Printed in Great Britain by
Billing & Sons Ltd, Worcester

# Contents

*v*

# Tables

# Acknowledgements

The following chapters were originally published, in different versions or languages, in the sources listed.

**Chapter 2**
*World Development* 4, 10/11, 1976: 907–17. *World Development* is published by Pergamon Journals Ltd, Oxford, United States.

**Chapter 3**
*IMF Working Paper* 88/7. An earlier version of this chapter was published in the *Asian Development Review* 5, 2, 1987.

**Chapter 5**
*The American Economic Review* 76, 2, May 1986: 88–91.

**Chapter 6**
*Public Finance and Public Debt*, Proceedings of the 40th Congress of the International Institute of Public Finance, Innsbruck, 1984: 139–52.

**Chapter 7**
*IMF Staff Papers* XXIV, 1, March 1977.

**Chapter 8**
*IMF Staff Papers*, 36, 3, September 1989.

**Chapter 9**
*External Debt, Savings, and Growth in Latin America*, IMF, 1987: 121–41.

**Chapter 10**
*Tax Administration Review* 3, January, 1987: 23–34.

**Chapter 12**
*The Relevance of Public Finance for Policy-Making*, Proceedings of the 41st Congress of the International Institute of Public Finance, Madrid, 1985: 225–36.

**Chapter 13**
*Hacienda Publica Española*, Instituto de Estudios Fiscoles, 100, Madrid, 1986.

# Introduction

Developing countries comprise at least three fourths of the world population. Still they receive relatively little attention from economists, and especially, from public finance specialists. There was a time, particularly in the 1960s, when economic development, as a major field of economics, became very popular. Several conferences were organized and various reports were written on developing countries' tax systems. Some of these reports, for example the studies by Professor Carl Shoup on Venezuela and Professor Richard Musgrave on Columbia, attracted a lot of attention and helped shape the professional thinking on the desirable tax systems for economic development. The past decade, however, has been more sceptical about the role of policy-making and more preoccupied with stabilization than with growth. Economic development, as an independent field of economics, seems to have lost out in this process.

Because of the debt crisis, and because of the implications that the debt crisis might have on the international financial system, there has been growing attention paid to developing countries in more recent years. In the public finance area the attention is either narrowly confined to public finance specialists, who seem to pay relatively little attention to the macroeconomic problems of these countries and tend to discuss tax reform or reform of public expenditure more or less in isolation, or, alternatively, it is confined to macroeconomists, who keep their analysis at a broad enough level of aggregation to make their conclusions not too useful for specific policy changes. I hope that this book will help establish a closer link between the writing of macroeconomists and that of more narrow public finance specialists. This book deals with many issues of public finance within a macroeconomic framework relevant to developing countries. At the same time there is enough discussion of specific public finance issues to make it useful, not just to academics but also to policy-makers. The book is based more on policy experiences than on theorizing.

The book is made up of 15 self-contained chapters. Because the chapters have been written independently and in some cases have appeared previously in academic and financial journals there is the inevitable danger of some repetition. Although I have done my best to keep this to a minimum, I am aware that I have not been totally successful. However, had I been totally successful, some of these chapters would have lost their self-sufficiency. The book is divided into three sections. The first three chapters deal with the general role of government in the economies of developing countries. Chapters 4–9 deal with issues of stabilization and growth, while Chapters 10–15 are predominantly orientated toward issues of taxation.

My awareness of the limitations which exist in the implementation of policies in developing countries has undoubtedly influenced much of the writing. Policy advice that is right in theory but of highly doubtful application has been pretty much ignored. Unfortunately, many of those who write on developing countries carry with them an advanced industrial countries' bias; they implicitly assume that once they have spelled out their general principles, the implementation of those principles becomes a trivial matter not deserving much attention. In developing countries, however, the situation is very different. Because of implementation problems, one can never assume that the final outcome will reflect the initial idea. This implies that the original recommendations must contemplate the limitations that will be encountered in the implementation stage. What this means is that complicated schemes should be avoided in favour of simpler schemes, and schemes that give too much discretion to policy-makers or to bureaucrats should also be avoided. If there is a philosophical thread that goes through this book, it is the need to limit to the maximum the interference of the government in the economy. This does not mean that a smaller government is necessarily best, but it does mean that simpler tax systems, for example, should be preferred to more complex ones, explicit subsidies should be preferred to implicit ones, even when on theoretical grounds the latter may be preferable and policies that are more transparent in their effects should be preferred to those which are less transparent.

Chapter 1 starts with a general discussion of the role of government and of fiscal policy in developing countries. It recognizes the three traditional functions – allocation of resources, stabilization, and redistribution of income. However it argues that in view of the low level of income of developing countries the pursuit of economic growth must also be a genuine government objective. Chapter 2 outlines the main tenets of fiscal policies in the 1960s and early 1970s, when governments were told to hold down current expenditure, increase taxes and increase growth by increasing public investment. This particular position is criticized in that chapter and, more specifically, in Chapter 3 where it is argued that many elements which prevail in these economies almost guarantee that the rate of return to public investment will be relatively low. When this public investment is financed through expensive external debt, then one must be doubly sceptical about the wisdom of this approach.

Part 2 of the book shows, in Chapter 4, how the 'stabilizing role' of government advocated by Keynesian economics has, over time, become a destabilizing one, with fiscal deficits endemic. Chapter 4 highlights the tenuous grip that, for a variety of reasons, governments have on policy instruments. In a way, it continues the theme developed in Chapters 2 and 3. Chapter 5 introduces a new key idea, an idea which is very important but which has not received as much attention as it deserves: the link which exists between the budget and the balance of payments of developing countries. The chapter argues that, on the average, almost 50 per cent of the total tax revenues of these countries are directly or indirectly derived from the external sector. While in many industrial countries what happens to the exchange rate has only a marginal influence on the budget, in developing countries what happens to the exchange rate and to foreign earnings can have fundamental consequences. Some general policy guidelines are also discussed in Chapter 5.

Chapter 6 brings out another important element of the developing countries' fiscal policies: whether there is a limit to the size of the fiscal deficit in real terms. This chapter analyses the various sources available to the government to finance its expenditure and shows that in real but not in nominal terms all financing sources have clear limitations, so that there is an upper limit to the size of the properly measured fiscal deficit expressed as a share of gross domestic products (GDP) that a developing country can have.

Chapter 7 deals with an issue which has become extremely important in countries with high inflation rates: why the ratio of taxation to GDP normally falls when the rate of inflation accelerates, and increases when the rate of inflation decelerates. This somewhat counterintuitive effect is commonly associated in the literature with the author of this book. The effect is counterintuitive because the usual assumption in industrial countries has been that inflation leads to a more than proportionate increase in tax revenue through the 'fiscal drag'. The so-called 'Tanzi effect' has played a large role in stabilization programmes in Latin America and other countries, such as Israel.

Chapter 8 picks up the theme advanced in Chapter 5 about the relationship between macroeconomic policy and the level of taxation in developing countries. When the tax revenue of a country falls precipitously in a short period of time, it is customary to argue that tax administration has deteriorated. However, the truth of the matter is that tax administrations normally do not deteriorate, or, for that matter, do not improve that quickly. There is lots of inertia in the way in which taxes are administered, and, in the absence of social upheaval, only over a period of time can major changes in tax administration come about. Therefore, the fluctuation in the ratio of tax revenue to GDP must be attributed to other factors. This chapter provides a detailed analysis of some of these other factors. It identifies especially the exchange rate, the rate of inflation, quantitative restrictions, and financial policies as the main culprits. It is argued that improvements in macroeconomic policies often bring about major increases in the ratio of taxation to GDP. Chapter 9, a key chapter raises the question of the 'quality' as compared to the quantity of fiscal policy in the design of stabilization programmes. It is argued that when a fiscal deficit needs to be reduced substantially, so that a country's economy can be stabilized, it is important that the deficit reduction be associated with good and sustainable tax and expenditure

policies, rather than with poor and temporary policies. A stabilization programme achieved through inefficient measures, or through measures that will not
last over time, is likely to be disappointing.

Part 3 focuses on issues of taxation. The first is a general chapter which,
combining some theory with a lot of practical experience, provides general
guidelines and principles to assess the tax systems of countries and to suggest
major changes. These principles are unlikely to satisfy taxation theorists who
would find them conflicting with at least some of the prevailing views, especially
those promoted by optimal taxation theory. However, it is my view that the
recommendations made in this chapter are implementable and that they result in
an effective tax system which is likely to be more efficient than the one that would
result from more sophisticated recommendations. Chapter 11, a short chapter,
deals with some common views, especially popular in the early 1980s, related to
supply-side economics. It is sceptical about the extreme importance attributed by
some supply-side economists to elements of the tax systems of the developing
countries, as, for example, the marginal tax rate of the personal income tax. The
chapter argues that implicit taxation through regulations, and perhaps foreign
trade taxes, may be more important in their negative effects on economic
behaviour than income taxes.

Chapter 12 discusses in an informal way tax reforms recommended by foreign
experts and it identifies some conditions which lead to successful or unsuccessful
tax missions. Chapter 13 has been included mainly because, although not
generally recognized, in developing countries taxes on presumptive incomes are
far more prevalent than taxes on precisely measured incomes. A theoretical
section argues that, in theory at least, it would be better to tax average potential
incomes of individuals than actual incomes; it discusses some examples in which
developing countries have tried to apply these principles. Finally, Chapters 14
and 15 discuss import and export taxes, as not much is written on these important
sources of revenue in developing countries. The book has not attempted to deal
with all the issues of public finance in developing countries. As a consequence,
it cannot be considered a textbook, or a treatise, on that subject. It has dealt with
issues which were considered important by the author and about which he felt he
had something worthwhile to say. It is hoped that this book will provide guidance
to policy-makers in many countries and will also be seen as a useful addition to
the literature by scholars and students in the field. The writing of this book has
benefited a lot from the environment in which the author has lived for the past 15
years, and perhaps even before that. In fact, it is unlikely that it could have been
written otherwise. My interest in developing countries started while, as a
university professor, I worked as a consultant with the Organization of American
States (OAS), The World Bank, and the United Nations (UN). This interest
continued as an employee of the International Monetary Fund (IMF), where I
have had the benefit of heading, first, the Tax Policy Division and then the Fiscal

Affairs Department. I want to take this opportunity to give a generalized thanks to all my colleagues, both within the Fiscal Affairs Department and the Fund, who over the years have been willing to discuss issues with me, to comment on my papers, and to provide me with much useful information and insights.

Finally, I would like to dedicate this book to my children, Vito Luigi, Alexandre and Giancarlo who, because of it, were deprived of their father's company for too many weekends during their adolescence.

# PART I

# THE ROLE OF THE GOVERNMENT

# 1 The role of fiscal policy in developing countries

## Objectives of fiscal policy

The term fiscal policy normally applies to the use of fiscal instruments to influence the working of the economic system in order to maximize economic welfare. Although the maximization of economic welfare is the obvious ultimate objective of governmental economic action, it is too vague a concept to be the focus of specific policy measures. For this reason policy-makers often concentrate on more specific objectives in the belief that there is a direct relationship between changes in those objectives and changes in economic welfare.

The activities of the fiscal authorities can be classified under four major headings, each reflecting a specific function on the part of the public sector. These are allocation, distribution, stabilization and growth.

*Allocation* is, historically, the function which has been emphasized for the longest period of time. Since the time of Adam Smith, and perhaps even earlier, it has been recognized that an organized society required the production of certain goods and services whose collective or social consumption makes unprofitable their private production. These goods, which in the modern literature have come to be called public goods, are basic to a continuation of organized social life; they include such things as defence, law and order, justice. Provision of resources for the supply of these goods and services was the original justification of taxation. Taxation was supposed to be imposed in the least painful way and was to be kept at just the level necessary to provide to the government the resources needed to produce the desired public goods.

*Redistribution* was, historically, the second function to receive attention. Redistribution is the intentional manipulation of the particular income distribution which results from the free working of the economy. Unlike allocation, redistribution of income is not basic to the existence of organized society. Societies have existed, do exist and probably will continue to exist with almost any conceivable income distribution. This, however, does not mean that redistribution is not a legitimate function of the government. Even though organized society could continue to exist if the government did not carry out this corrective function, it might be a society with characteristics which are not considered optimal by the majority of its citizens.

For developing countries, however, one can argue that redistribution should be related to the role of the government in promoting growth. Although in these countries, just as in the so-called developed countries, one can make a good case for redistribution as an end in itself, it seems more useful to relate the objective of redistribution to that of growth. It would seem sensible even to subordinate redistribution to growth, because, at the income levels which prevail now in most of the developing countries, only marginal absolute improvements in the standard of living of the masses could be achieved through income redistribution. Only through growth can these masses be lifted out of their economic backwardness.

The fact that it is argued that growth is more important than equity does not mean, of course, that a relatively more uneven distribution of income has to be preferred. In fact, apart from equity considerations, one can advance many purely economic arguments against such a preference.

One can, for example, maintain that in some cases a more even distribution of income will mean a larger market for products produced by the local industry, which will be particularly desirable if the larger market leads to a greater use of industrial capacity which was not being used and workers who were not already employed. Or it may be that those with relatively high incomes have a greater propensity to import than those with low incomes; in such case income redistribution will have beneficial effects on the balance of payments. One could easily think of several other cases in which a more even income distribution would have beneficial economic consequences. For example, an increase in the consumption of those in lower income classes made possible by a more even income distribution might increase their productivity and incentives. Consequently, such increase in consumption might be looked at as investment rather than consumption since it would lead to an acceleration in the rate of growth. Alternatively, it has even been argued that an improvement in income distribution might increase total private saving rather than decrease it (see Tanzi *et al.*)

*Stabilization* is the objective most commonly associated with fiscal policy. In terms of conscious policy it reflects a relatively recent role of the government. It is normally the most important short-run objective and is the one which has received most attention in the developed countries. For many economists, stabilization and fiscal policy are synonyms. It is in this sense that fiscal policy is generally considered the logical outgrowth of the Keynesian revolution.

In the developed countries the meaning of stabilization is relatively unambiguous. In these countries the most important economic objective of the government is to keep the actual level of national income close to the potential. Potential output can be determined with a certain degree of accuracy and its realization implies a relatively small level of frictional or structural unemployment and substantial price stability. Stabilization also does not assume any serious underemployment of labour or capital. Thus by stabilization policy is meant the manipulation of aggregate demand in order to achieve at the same time full employment and price stability. The balance of payments, although at times the object of some concern, is not generally the major objective of stabilization (or short-run fiscal) policy.

In developing countries, however, the situation is not so simple and stabilization as an objective loses the simple and well-defined nature that it exhibits in the developed countries. First of all, the concept of potential level of income is not easily definable since a substantial proportion of the labour force is underemployed rather than openly unemployed. Second, for technological reasons, there is not a clear correspondence between full employment of labour and full employment of capital. Third, the balance of payments cannot be ignored since movements toward full employment may be stopped by limitations of foreign exchange. Finally, the evidence of many countries indicates that the implicit assumption of stabilization policy – that prices will remain relatively stable as long as actual national income is lower than potential – simply does not hold.

It is the last function – that is promoting growth – which, in the case of the developing countries and at this historical junction, is probably the most important. The developed countries do not have to concern themselves excessively with growth. To them stabilization and equity may be more worthwhile pursuits. For the developing countries, however, where per capita incomes are generally very low growth must be the overriding objective.

If growth is in fact the overriding objective of governmental action, then the tools of taxation and public expenditures should be utilized to achieve an acceleration of the rate of growth. In some cases the pursuit of this particular objective will conflict with that of the others; in such cases the governments should have some ideas about the constraints that they are willing to impose. For example, is there a certain income distribution which is the least equitable that the government is willing to accept in its pursuit of growth? Or, if no such absolute levels of constraints are identified, does the government have any notion of trade-offs between growth and the other objectives? For example, what worsening in income distribution would the government be willing to accept if such change could accelerate growth by one percentage point?

Not all the countries will have the same trade-offs or the same constraints. Their economic situations, their historical backgrounds and their political realities will influence countries in different ways even when all the countries belong to the same region.

Growth has been considered the major and in many cases the only objective of economic policy in developing countries for much of the period following the end of World War II. This emphasis on growth was relatively new in economic thinking and this particular objective had been absent in much of the economic writing of the previous hundred years. The classical economists (Smith, Malthus, Ricardo) had, of course, been interested in economic growth. However, the neoclassical economists (from J.S. Mill onward) had paid little attention to it. The post-war interest in growth can be attributed to various reasons. However, an important one was that, for the first time in the late 1940s comparative statistics became available on the per capita incomes of many developing countries. These statistics, with all their shortcomings, clearly showed the tremendous gulf that existed between the standards of living of those countries and those of the industrial countries. It became obvious that only growth could reduce that gulf and growth required capital accumulation.

Capital came to be regarded as the all-important and strategic factor in the growth process. Growth models – mainly Harrod and Domar types of models – which closely linked changes in income to changes in aggregate tangible capital, became very popular and many works on developing countries dealt largely with 'capital formation'. Developing plans were greatly influenced by this thinking and the calculation of capital-output ratios became basic to the policies advocated in those plans. If a country aimed at a given increase in income, it had to have a given increase in aggregate capital input and the government had to play a role in this capital formation. During this period, fiscal experts advising developing countries followed without embarrassment the procedure of dividing the total expenditure of the government in current and capital and of praising increases in capital expenditure while castigating increases in current expenditure. Works on taxation were often concerned with the tax structure and level that would maximize capital formation. Recent years have brought about a healthy scepticism about these simple relationships. They have brought the realization that the growth process is very complex and that capital formation is only one element of that process.

## Role of government in economic development

It has been argued above that the overwhelming objective of tax and budgetary policy in developing countries must be the acceleration of economic development. In particular, the tax system must transfer resources from the private to the public sector and it must also reallocate, to the extent possible, private investment and consumption in directions which will be beneficial to the growth of the economy. Through the transfer of resources from the private to the public sector, the latter will have the capacity to carry out those functions which are basic to the role of the government – defence, police, administration, justice and so on – as well as those functions which are related to the development of the country or to the redistribution of income.

Among the growth-related expenditures, the creation of infrastructures – both economic and social – has received a great deal of attention. Taxes put resources in the hands of the government and these resources can be used to implement certain investment programmes which are supposed to be productive to the economy, especially in the long run. These investment programmes normally involve the building of roads, railroads, dams, power plants etc. Lately, much attention has been paid to expenditures for education and health, recognizing the importance that 'human capital' plays in the process of economic growth.

The traditional emphasis has been on the contribution that the government makes to capital formation through these types of infrastructures. Obviously, however, the productivity of public investment is closely related to the level and the quality of investment in the private sector. In fact, one can really think of public investment of the type outlined above as a kind of input for private investment. The direct contribution of public investment to potential output is generally very low. It is its effect on the productivity of private investment which makes public investment desirable.

It follows that, in the developing countries, the government has the responsibility not only of creating the infrastructure but also of seeing that the level and the quality of the private investment forthcoming be as high as possible. This is an aspect of fiscal policy which has not received the attention that it deserves.

The stimulation of private investment normally comes through maintenance of political stability and of a climate that encourages the internal reinvestment of saving. It comes, as was already pointed out, through the creation of the basic economic and social infrastructures which are essential to the development of a country. It comes through the creation of a sizable market which permits production at the optimal technological level. It comes through the provision of fiscal and credit incentives to those industries which need initial help. It also comes through access to foreign exchange which is essential to the purchase of equipment not locally produced. It is facilitated by conditions of price stability.

There is one additional way, however, in which the government can help in increasing the level and improving the quality of private investment in the country. It is a way that to a limited extent has been used by the governments of some developing countries, but has not received the attention that it deserves; yet it may be essential when a country has not developed a well working capital market.

If a well-working capital market does not exist it should be the responsibility of the government to try to develop one. To do so is generally a long-range enterprise. In the short run the government will only have the option (as a second-best solution) of providing a kind of proxy for the capital market.

This leads us back to the role of fiscal policy in developing countries. If the previous analysis is correct, it would provide an argument for a planned budgetary surplus in the current account in excess of what the government needs to spend itself for direct investment. In other words, the government should aim to set the tax burden at a level which would leave a surplus that could be made available to the private sector and even to the public enterprises; this would provide the government with an extremely powerful and flexible tool which would make possible, to a considerable extent, the allocation of private investment in the desired pattern.

Several surveys carried out in many developing countries have shown beyond any doubt that the inability on the part of many enterprises and individuals to obtain credit is a serious obstacle to development. It is likely that credit incentives are more important than tax incentives, especially for the creation of new enterprises. Tax incentives by increasing the liquidity of the already established enterprises may facilitate their development but normally will not help very much the potential enterprises or the individuals who do not have funds for the fixed initial investment. Credit incentives, on the other hand, will have an impact in both areas.

Thus, credit incentives financed by surpluses in the government budget are an integral part of fiscal policy. But, unlike tax incentives, they put in the hands of the government an instrument which is exceedingly flexible. Through the use of this instrument resources can be channelled toward investments which are considered to have high social significance. In this way the government would in fact be acting as a proxy for the capital market; it would, in addition to increasing the level of savings, affect the quality of investment.

One objection that can be easily anticipated to the previous scheme is that the capacity on the part of many governments actually to use extra tax revenue for the purpose indicated is often limited. Given extra revenues, the political pressure on the government would be such that nonproductive budgetary expenditure would be the type to increase, that is the increase in tax revenue would be absorbed by increases in non-productive government expenditures. The scheme suggested above is discussed in more detail in the following chapter. Korea is one country that has made much use of credit incentives. Of course the possibility that credit incentives will be abused must be kept in mind.

## Fiscal policy for stabilization

As already stated, the complex of fiscal measures that governments use to influence the working of the economy is traditionally called fiscal policy. The objective of fiscal policy may be the correction of temporary disequilibria or the stimulation of economic growth or income redistribution. Correspondingly, we have short-run, or stabilization, fiscal policy and long-run policy.

In reality most short-run measures have long-run consequences in the same way that long-run policies have short-run implications. However, at least in a formal sense, one can think of certain measures as being mainly for one or for another purpose. Changes in the level of taxation and/or public expenditures aimed at influencing the level of aggregate demand constitute one example of short-run fiscal policy. Another example would be the manipulation of import and export taxes to rescue the country from a serious disequilibrium in the balance of payments.

Fiscal measures which can be supposed to be aimed at longer-run objectives include those dealing with tax incentives for the development of certain industries, the restructuring of the tax system to influence growth by increasing the supply of savings and even the stimulation of demand for certain types of locally-produced products when the enlargement of the market will bring about significant reductions in the average cost of production. The discussion which follows will emphasize short-run measures.

Even a superficial analysis of the role of short-run fiscal policy in the developing countries reveals two things: first, in many countries this type of policy has not been explicitly used; second, when it has been used the results have often been disappointing. This raises the obvious question of why it is so. Why do developed countries, by and large, find easier and more effective the use of fiscal policy than do the developing countries?

The answer that has often been given to the question has emphasized differences in the structural characteristics of the developed and the developing economies. On one hand, some writers (e.g. MacBean) have pointed out that the types of disturbances which upset the equilibrium in the developing countries are different from those which upset the equilibrium in the industrial countries. They argue that while in the industrial countries the economic disturbances are caused by fluctuations in private investment, in the developing countries they are caused by fluctuations in the value of exports due either to reduced agricultural output or to a fall in export prices.

Other fiscal experts (see Rao), on the other hand, have stressed the role that the elasticity of supply plays in the two types of economies. In the developing countries, because of various bottlenecks and because of the structure of demand and the composition of the output, the response of the private sector to increases in aggregate demand is limited; consequently, economic policies of a fiscal and monetary nature remain relatively ineffective. These structural limitations on fiscal policy are important but they have been extensively discussed in the literature. I shall, therefore, deal with limitations of the fiscal instruments themselves rather than of the economy. Chapter 4 deals in greater detail with the same issues.

Let us assume, for the sake of argument, that the objective or structural conditions of the economy are the same in developed and developing countries and inquire as to the characteristics that the instruments of fiscal policy must have if fiscal policy is to have a chance of success. Stabilization policy may be pursued through changes in government expenditures or in tax revenues or in both.

One could argue that, from a social point of view, the change in tax revenues is to be preferred to the change in expenditures on grounds that the government of a country should establish and maintain the level and the structure of public expenditures which is assumed to be optimal. If it should become desirable to change the impact of the budget on the economy, the government then should ideally change revenues. In reality governments have normally changed both; however, it seems that the developing countries have often changed expenditure rather than taxation. Why is this so?

There are many reasons why the tax instrument has not been used to a greater extent in developing countries. Here I shall outline some of the most important although of course the reasons given below will not be valid in equal degree for all developing countries.

First of all it is self-evident that the higher the tax burden the greater will be the impact of the tax system on the economy. If the tax burden is low, a given percentage increase or decrease in total taxes will not affect the economy in the same way as when the tax burden is high. For example, if the tax burden of a country is 30 per cent of GNP, a 10 per cent change in total taxes will be equivalent to 3 per cent of the GNP; on the other hand, if the tax burden is only 10 per cent of GNP, a 10 per cent increase in taxes will be equivalent to only 1 per cent of GNP.

If one makes the assumption that, in the short-run, it is equally difficult to change the tax burden by a given percentage, regardless of the initial level of that burden, then it is obvious that a country with a high tax burden will, *ceteris paribus,* be able to use fiscal policy more effectively than one with a low tax burden.

The existence of a heavy tax burden, even though it would appear to be a necessary condition for effectively pursuing an active stabilization policy, is not a sufficient condition; a second condition necessary is the existence of a centralized public sector – for the collection of revenues and disbursing of expenditures. We have here a classical conflict of objectives since there may be many reasons why a country might be better off with a decentralized government regardless of the demands of effective fiscal policy.

The reason for the importance of the centralized public sector is simply that the government of a centralized country with a tax burden which is only 10 per cent of GNP may have an equal or even greater potential for control over the economy than does the government of a highly decentralized country with a much heavier tax burden. Decentralization of the public sector normally increases the difficulties encountered in trying to make use of fiscal policy and normally decreases the policy's effectiveness. This factor is particularly important when the local governments and the autonomous enterprises follow their own programmes without any concern for the policy being pursued at the national level – a situation that has often been a cause for fiscal crises in some

Latin American countries. In some cases the local governments and the autonomous enterprises increased their expenditures at the very time that the central government was trying to reduce its expenditures. In other cases the central government was unable to induce the rest of the public sector to increase (or decrease) taxes in accordance with action of the central government. The problem is that only the central government could have the welfare of the whole country in mind in making its policy decisions; other governments (and entities) will not have any interest in looking beyond their immediate areas of concern.

Obstacles to an effective use of fiscal policy may also be imposed by a lack of concentration of tax revenues at the central government level. Fiscal policy has normally been most effective in those countries where a few taxes provide most of the revenues of the government. In most of the industrialized countries one finds that two or three taxes provide more that half of total government revenues. If two taxes yield 50 per cent or more of total revenues, and if total revenues are a substantial share of national income, the manipulation of those two taxes will bring about important effects on the economy.

One of the characteristics of most of the tax systems of the developing countries is the tremendous number of taxes in existence. Proliferation of taxes not only complicates their administration, confuses the tax payers and facilitates or even invites tax evasion, but it renders very difficult the use of an active fiscal policy because if the government wants to raise more revenues for stabilization purposes it must change the nominal rates of many taxes. In other words, it needs to study each of the many taxes, decide on the changes desired and then go to the legislative body where, ideally, each tax would be discussed and voted upon – a rather obvious source of complications and difficulties.

Short-run fiscal policy is made difficult also by the lack of synchronization between the time when an action becomes legally taxable (for example, the moment when income is earned) and the time when the tax obligation to the authority is met. The longer this lag, the more difficult becomes the use of fiscal policy. If the lag is long enough, fiscal policy may even become destabilizing. This problem is more serious with some taxes than with others. In developed countries the principle of PAYE (pay as you earn) brings about desired synchronization. On the other hand, in most developing countries there is normally a long delay between earning of income and paying of taxes.

The same problem, though perhaps not as serious, seems to exist with respect to public expenditures when, because of faulty or old-fashioned budgetary procedure, it is at times difficult to tell what part of cash payments made in a given year actually reflects claims against resources made by the government in that same year.

One last problem which seems to be common to many developing countries and which also contributes to the ineffectiveness of fiscal policy for stabilization is the existence of fiscal evasion. The problem of evasion has received much attention for its implication for revenues and for equity but it has not been discussed with respect to short-run fiscal policy although it is obvious that the problem is quite relevant.

An effective fiscal policy requires that the authorities be able to estimate first what change in revenue would be required to correct the disequilibrium and second, what changes in the legal or nominal structure of the tax system will bring about the desired increase or decrease in revenues. To do this the authority needs a lot of statistical information that it often may not have, but it also needs to assume that evasion is either nonexistent or that it will continue at a constant rate. Otherwise there will not be any possibility of relating a given change in nominal rates to a given increase or decrease in revenues. Since the government can directly manipulate only the legal structure of the taxes, if it cannot assume a direct relationship between that structure and the size of tax revenues it will not be able to pursue a successful fiscal policy. It has often happened in some developing countries that the government would push through some tax reform in the hope of raising a given amount of additional revenue only to find that its projections were highly unrealistic.

A somewhat similar result can be expected when an acute inflationary situation reduces that availability of credit to such an extent that people declare their taxes but abstain from paying them. In this situation, too, the expectations of tax authorities would not be met and the effectiveness of fiscal policy would be reduced.

**Concluding remarks**
Fiscal policy can play a significant role in the economic development of the relatively backward countries. It can generate the means to create the social and economic infrastructures which are basic to economic growth. It can be used as a proxy for a still non-existing capital market and thereby stimulate private investment and lead to a better use of scarce entrepreneurial ability. It can also be used to stabilize the economy, although this particular role is made difficult by the present tax structure existing in many developing countries. So far, however, only a few developing countries have used fully this very useful and flexible instrument.

This chapter has discussed some of the traditional roles of fiscal policy. These roles are still generally accepted by many economists and are justified in relatively well functioning developing countries. However, large fiscal imbalances, debt problems, and the existence of policymakers not fully committed to the public interest make some of the policies suggested in this chapter of limited application in some developing countries.

## References

Hirschman, Albert O., *The Strategy of Economic Development,* New Haven, 1958.
MacBean, Alasdair I., *Export Instability and Economic Development,* Cambridge, 1966.
Myint, Hla, *The Economics of the Developing Countries,* New York, 1965.
Rao, V.K.R.V., 'Investment, income and the multiplier in an underdeveloped economy', *Indian Economic Review* February 1952.
Schumpeter, Joseph Alois, *The Theory of Economic Development,* New York, Oxford University Press, 1961.
Tanzi, Vito, and Ascheim, Joseph, 'Saving, investment, and taxation in underdeveloped countries', *Kyklos* XVIII, 1965.

## 2 Fiscal policy, Keynesian economics and the mobilization of savings in developing countries

**Fiscal policy and the new thinking on development economics**

It has now become commonplace to believe that the economic welfare of a nation depends on the level of national income, on the way that income is distributed, on the employment opportunities associated with it, and on the stability of employment, income and prices. If an economy is growing but the income distribution becomes or remains very uneven, if jobs are difficult to find and many people willing to work remain unemployed, and if stability is lacking, one cannot be sure that economic welfare is rising. This means that a rapid growth rate *per se* is not a panacea as it will not necessarily be accompanied by a reduction in unemployment and underemployment and by a more even income distribution.[1] In fact it may even exacerbate social frictions and lead to political instability.

This, of course, does not mean that growth should be ignored, as some writers have suggested. The abandonment of growth as an important objective would be a tragic mistake that might condemn a large proportion of the population of the developing countries to a life of misery even if that were accompanied by full employment, stable prices and income, and an even income distribution. Only growth can create, if not the certainty at least the option of a more comfortable life for the masses.

Fiscal policy, alone or with the help of other policy instruments, can promote growth in a variety of ways. It can, for example:

(i)     increase the rate of savings of the country;
(ii)    channel these savings into more socially productive uses;
(iii)   increase what has been called productive consumption,[2] i.e. education, health;
(iv)    discourage non-productive and extravagant consumption and investment such as expensive cars and luxury housing;
(v)     reduce inefficiency throughout the economy and particularly in the public sector;
(vi)    maintain a climate of economic stability;
(vii)   remove bottlenecks of various kinds;

(viii)   reduce or eliminate growth-retarding distortions introduced by the tax system and other public policies; and

(ix)   eliminate or at least reduce distortions in the relative prices of the factors of production.

In past discussions of the role of fiscal policy *vis-à-vis* growth, the emphasis has generally been on the tax structure that would be the least damaging (or the most favourable) to growth, the role of the government in providing the basic economic and social infrastructures for development, and the role of the government in 'mobilizing' savings. In this chapter emphasis is mainly on the third, namely, the mobilization of savings.

## Keynesian economics and role of government in mobilizing saving

The role that over the past two or three decades was assigned to the government with respect to the mobilization of savings – a role which we shall characterize as the orthodox one – was a direct outcome of the economic thinking that prevailed over much of that period. That thinking was heavily influenced by the set of ideas, concepts and theories that is often, and perhaps a bit loosely, referred to as the Keynesian Revolution. It was also influenced by growth models of the Harrod and Domar types.

What Keynes did first, and the Keynesian Revolution later, was essentially to pull together various strands of theories and ideas, which may have been to a certain extent already around, and to make them the building blocks of a novel framework for approaching and analysing macroeconomic questions. The consumption function, the marginal efficiency of investment, the liquidity preference function and the multiplier were some of these building blocks for the new framework. Whether some of these blocks did or did not originate with Keynes is of importance as far as the history of economic thought is concerned but, once they were incorporated into his framework, they became 'Keynesian' and played a fundamental role in so-called Keynesian economics. It is in this sense that Keynesian economics is referred to in this chapter. And it was Keynesian economics, so defined, that was influential in the past two or three decades in the economic policy of the developing countries. As growth was assumed to be the direct result of capital accumulation, and as the latter was assumed to depend to a large extent on the country's rate of saving, fiscal policy was aimed at increasing the latter. Saving can be private and/or public and the government was, consequently, expected then to add to those savings with its 'mobilization'.

Private saving is often thought to be negatively affected by the use of progressive taxes. The argument that a redistribution of income, through progressive taxation, will lead to a decline in the proportion of total income saved depends on the acceptance of a specific hypothesis of the consumption function. Such a hypothesis was implicitly but vaguely accepted in some neo-classical literature.[3] It is in Keynes's work, however, that what was a vague possibility becomes a well specified, though not necessarily valid, theory.[4] And as such it becomes very influential in policy decisions. The result of this was a general wariness in the use of progressive taxation. Policy-makers and economists alike came to believe that progressive taxes should not be used in developing countries, or, at least, that their progressivity should be limited.[5] There was also a proliferation of tax incentives and easy credit measures which by reducing the private cost of investments or by increasing the private rate of return to investments in certain lines of activity, were supposed to stimulate the accumulation of capital. For these, too, a case can be made that the Keynesian framework may not have been without influence.

In the Keynesian system, investment depends, *inter alia,* on the price of capital goods and on the cost of investible funds which is generally assumed to be, but need not be, the rate of interest. The propensity to save of households, on the other hand, is made to depend, as it was seen above, on the level of their income alone and not, as it was assumed by many classical or neo-classical economists, on (or also on) the rate of interest.[6] The tax incentives policies outlined above are consistent with the Keynesian system; they attempt to increase investment by lowering the private cost of capital goods and/or by increasing the after-tax private rate of return. Within the Keynesian context this would amount to a rightward shift of the point of intersection between the marginal efficiency of  investment schedule and the cost-of-capital schedule. Furthermore, while they emphasize the rate of return to the investors, they de-emphasize the rate of return to the savers. As saving is assumed to depend on income and not on the rate of interest, why worry about the rate of interest except, of course, in so far as it affects real investors?

Perhaps the Keynesian influence was also present in the belief that the developing countries, if they depended only on the actions of the private sector, would not be able to save much,[7] and would not be able to invest much. Governments were thus urged to take over part of the function of mobilization of saving, by themselves contributing to the increase in the saving rate. While in the developed countries, governments had been urged to stimulate spending, in the developing countries they were urged to stimulate saving. An additional justification for this function was also the belief, advanced by Nurkse,[8] that international demonstration effects were at work which would make it hard for developing countries to keep down their consumption standards.

The governments of the developing countries were urged to increase their countries' saving rates in current accounts, by increasing the tax burdens (i.e. the share of all taxes in gross national product) while limiting their own current expenditures. This became a standard recommendation in reports prepared by experts. The total tax burden of a country and the government current account saving became indices of good performance, which in many instances were used as a rationale or justification for asking, or for giving, larger external assistance or loans to particular countries.

In addition to being urged to increase their current account savings, the governments of the developing countries were urged to increase public investment. There were at least three reasons for this policy recommendation: first, it was believed that public investment would almost always be productive as the economic infrastructures of these countries needed to be created and modernized; second, there was a belief that the private sector was basically lacking in economic entrepreneurship so that this function should be taken over by the government; third, there was a widespread feeling of pessimism about the ability of the private sector to invest sufficiently.

This thinking had a substantial effect on the policies of developing countries. In most of them and especially during the decades of the 1960s and 1970s, public investment rose substantially. During the 1960s there was a great effort to finance this investment through higher taxes. During the 1970s public investment was financed largely through foreign borrowing. As we shall argue in the following chapter, when the investment proved largely unproductive and the foreign borrowing became costly, the countries got into serious economic difficulties.

### Shortcomings of orthodox role

The role described in the previous section has serious shortcomings. In particular one can characterize it as too aggregate, too simple, politically naive, and too oblivious to important inter-relationships among macro-variables. In this section we elaborate on some of these aspects.

First of all, in stressing the need for increasing the level of taxation, which taxes ought to be increased is not specified; the choice has often been left to the government and the assumption has been that basically it does not make much difference, except for the impact of different taxes on private saving. However, all taxes have some disincentive effects and some taxes (as, for example, those on exports and imports) may so distort the structure of production that the economic growth of a country may, in some extreme cases, be seriously affected. As the ability of countries to raise particular taxes depends on their level of economic development, on their degree of administrative sophistication, and on their internal political structure, they may often be unable to raise 'good' taxes and may thus be compelled to raise very inefficient ones in order to increase their tax burden. This means that even if the country succeeded in generating a higher saving rate, that rate might well be associated with a lower-than-expected growth in income. Furthermore, an increase in the tax burden under poor administrative conditions is likely to widen the inequity of the tax system, almost regardless of the taxes that are used.

Second, that approach is also too aggregative with respect to the rate of saving and investment. It emphasizes macro-elements without putting enough emphasis on the quality of those elements. In particular, does growth depend more on the rate of capital formation than on its quality? Or, looking at it from a different perspective, does it depend more on total saving than on how that saving is used? How important is the allocation of investment? Given the nature of the developing economies, or for that matter, of any economy, is not some investment spending likely to be more productive than another? Can one ever ask the question of how much a country needs to raise its investment rate in order to increase the growth rate by a certain percentage? A high rate of capital formation may be a necessary condition for a fast rate of growth but it surely is not a sufficient condition. We have the example of countries that have invested a high share of their GNP without experiencing much of an increase in the rate of growth, and that of other countries that have grown at satisfactory rates with relatively small investment rates.[9] In this connection, it is enlightening to quote Schumpeter who, in a book first published over 70 years ago, wrote:

> The slow and continuous increase in time of the national supply of productive means and savings is obviously an important factor in explaining the course of economic history through the centuries, but it is completely overshadowed by the fact that development consists primarily in employing existing resources in a different way, in doing new things with them, irrespective of whether those resources increase or not.[10]

Furthermore, if total investment depends on total saving, the composition of that investment in the absence of a well-working capital market is also likely to depend on the composition of that total saving. As one cannot assume the existence of a perfect or even of a good capital market, in reality funds will often be invested in the areas where they are generated. If saving takes place in the social security institutions it will be invested in activities of immediate interest to these institutions or to those who are able to obtain access to those funds. If if is in the public utilities, it will most likely be invested in that sector. Thus, as long as the capital market is not what it should be, the place of origin or saving is also an important question for public policy. This is true also in the private sector, where, in most countries, household savings generally go to finance housing while savings by enterprises are generally reinvested in the manufacturing sector.

Third, the particular role for the government described above ignores the relationship between the tax burden, the rate of saving, and the balance of payments. In fact, if taxes are increased and capital formation increases accordingly, much of the additional capital has to be imported.[11] As the short-run exports will not grow, the country's balance of payments will worsen. Thus, to the extent that a relationship exists between investment and growth and between tax burden and investment, there may be a level of tax burden beyond which it is useless to go as the bottleneck in the foreign sector would prevent the additional savings from being productively used in capital formation.[12] Of course, if the tax system creates distortions and thus decreases the ability of a country to earn foreign exchange, this limit would be reached with lower taxes.

This particular point is related to the broader issue of what has been called the absorptive capacity of the developing countries with respect to investment. That concept is difficult to define precisely without getting into the details of social cost–benefit analysis but it relates to the ability of a country, at a particular moment, to absorb investment productively from a social – and not a private – point of view. Putting it differently it refers to the quantity of capital that can be invested in projects with social rates of return high enough to justify the investment. Within the context of this discussion, absorptive capacity is the ability of the country to absorb its own savings into productive investments. Quite apart from the limitations imposed by the scarcity of foreign exchange, public savings may in some instances exceed the absorptive capacity – as defined above – of the public sector. Then, if these savings cannot be channelled to the private sector as suggested below, a tax increase cannot be justified on the grounds that it will promote capital formation.[13]

In the fourth place, it is assumed that the government will be willing and able to resist the pressures to increase expenditure for politically attractive but economically unproductive types of expenditure. At least one economist has argued that the increase in taxes will often be accompanied by an increase in the current expenditure of the government so that current account savings will not rise.[14] There has been some controversy over whether this will or will not happen with statistical support on both sides. However, the issue is not whether the increase in total taxes will bring about an increase in current expenditure or in savings. The more important issue is rather whether increased taxation will be consistent with greater economic welfare when such welfare depends on the four economic objectives stated above. In other words, will it lead to a faster rate of growth, to a more even income distribution, to more employment and to greater stability? And, if not, what are the trade-offs? Even if we limit our discussion to growth alone, the quotation from Schumpeter makes clear that the issue is not whether current or capital expenditure will increase but which expenditure in particular? The problem is again one of excessive aggregation.

This then brings us to the final and, perhaps, most important issue with the traditional role of the public sector with respect to capital formation. The fact is that, as T.W. Schultz reminded us more than two decades ago, 'much of what we call consumption constitutes investment in human capital',[15] and, one could add, a good deal of what we call public investment is really public consumption. The excessive emphasis on investment and capital formation may be completely misplaced.[16] The assumption that consumption has no impact on growth may be wrong. We can no longer make a sharp distinction between the supposedly growth-inducing and, thus, desirable capital expenditures (whether private or public) and the supposedly growth-retarding consumption expenditures. As S.R. Lewis put it: 'Investment in plant and equipment, social overhead capital, etc., is not the only source of economic development. The matter of skilled manpower, managerial ability, business acumen is also important...'[17] And, of course, skilled manpower etc. depends on consumption, be this in the form of proper nutrition, proper education, proper health care and so forth. It makes little sense to praise the building of a road (a capital expenditure) more than the upkeep of that road (a current expenditure).

The basic and almost tautological conclusion that can be drawn from the above discussion is that if the government is to be helpful in bringing about a faster rate of growth, it has to do this by discouraging the allocation of resources in unproductive uses, be these of a capital or a consumption type, and by encouraging the allocation of resources to productive uses. And, perhaps more importantly, the government must always be on guard not to be, itself, a major source of misallocation.

### Capital markets and the allocation of savings

The productivity of public investments is closely related to both the level and the quality of investment in the private sector. In fact, one can think of public investment as a kind of input for private investment (and, of course, for private consumption). Generally, one can argue that, with the exception of investment in public enterprises, the direct contribution of most public investment to potential output is not high. It is generally its effect on the productivity of private investment that makes public investment worthwhile.[18] Consequently, fiscal policy in developing countries should not be limited to creating the economic and social infrastructures, although this is a very important function, but should be extended to insuring that the level as well as the quality of private investment be as high as needed. This is an aspect of fiscal policy that, during the past, did not receive the degree of attention it deserved, except for the analysis of tax incentives for investments.

Private investment is normally stimulated by the maintenance of political and economic stability and by a climate that is conducive to the internal reinvestment of saving. This process is obviously aided by the parallel creation of the essential economic and social infrastructures and by the creation of a market large enough to permit production at optimal technological levels. During the next decade only few developing countries will have well-working capital markets in spite of efforts made to develop such markets in the past few years. Without an efficient capital market, a government must aim at improving other mechanisms for channelling saving to productive investment.

Financial deepening – that is the accumulation of financial assets at a pace faster that that of non-financial wealth – may be very important as several contributions have maintained.[19] The careful reading of these works should convince many readers that improving the working of the capital market may very well be necessary for economic development. In fact, it may not be an exaggeration to define economic development as 'the reduction of the great dispersion in social rates of return to existing and new investments under domestic entrepreneurial control'.[20] We have, thus, come a long way from Joan Robinson's view that 'by and large, it seems to be the case that where enterprise leads finance follows'.[21]

It would certainly be desirable for the developing countries to have financial institutions that worked smoothly and efficiently to promote economic development. Unfortunately, many developing countries do not have the benefits of such institutions. There is then a particular and rather obvious role that the government of these countries can perform to alleviate some of the shortcomings associated with the absence of a capital market.

The main task of a well-working capital market is the transfer of claims on resources from some economic units (the surplus units) to others (the deficit ones). This transfer of resources is generally indirect in the sense that the savers, or surplus units, lend their savings to financial institutions, which then, acting as intermediaries, lend the funds to the investors. In this process there is no need for savers and investors to be acquainted with one another nor do they also need to come in direct contact. Once the investors have received control over these resources, they invest them in opportunities or projects from which they expect rates of return high enough to pay back the loans and the interest charges and, in addition, to make a profit.

In the process of acting as an intermediary between surplus and deficit units, a well-working capital market will perform some very important and, perhaps, not so obvious functions. These can ultimately be expected to raise the overall rate of saving for the country and, what is perhaps more important, the rate of return to investment thus leading to faster economic growth.

In the first place, the capital market provides an easy and normally relatively safe investment opportunity to both large and small savers. This is especially important for small savers who, when financial investment opportunities are absent, may be discouraged from saving. If such an opportunity is accompanied by an attractive real rate of interest, it is likely to result in higher savings. This stimulation of savings in response to high interest rates has been reported in a few countries where reform aimed at raising those rates (from often negative real levels to positive ones) has been followed by increases in savings.

One dramatic example of the impact that high real rates of interest can have on savings was provided by Korea, where a sharp increase in the real rate of return on time deposits (from negative rates of 6 per cent in 1963 and 16 per cent in 1964, to positive rates of more that 10 per cent in 1965 and following years) was followed by an equally sharp increase in the national saving rates (from 6.9 per cent in 1963 to 16.5 per cent in 1970). Similar, even if less dramatic, results have been reported for Taiwan and Indonesia.[22] These results are worthy of mention because of the widespread belief that interest rates are not important in the determination of saving propensities.[23] In any case even if in fact high positive interest rates were not successful in bringing about a higher rate of savings, there is now overwhelming evidence that they are successful in reallocating savings toward those financial assets which have a higher rate of return. This 'financialization' of savings is itself very important since it is likely to permit a better use of savings.

Second, a well-working capital market will bring together in a common pool the savings of thousands or millions of individuals. This pooling of resources is very important as the nature of modern technology is such that many investment opportunities require financing that may often exceed the financial capacity of any one individual or of any small group of individuals, especially in countries with relatively low per capita incomes. Without this pooling, some very productive but relatively large investment would not be made, while the resources saved might be fragmented in many less productive investments.

As a digression to the above paragraph one might point out that in poor countries, where capital markets are not well developed and where governments do not exercise this pooling of savings' function, only the rich may be able to amass the resources needed to take advantage of investment opportunities. In these particular circumstances one could make the case that the rich may be viewed as a substitute for this pooling-of-resources function of the capital market. It could even be hypothesized that income redistribution may affect growth more by bringing about an atomization of savings than by the alleged reduction of total savings, which some argue would result from reducing the income of those who, supposedly, have a greater marginal propensity to save. In other words, under such circumstances, $1 million of savings in the hands of one person might be more productive than an equivalent amount scattered among thousands.[24]

If the argument outlined above is correct, it implies that a well-working capital market will eliminate the need for this pooling function on the part of the rich. Or, putting it in stronger terms, it will make the rich less socially useful, or less needed, than they might be assumed to be in an economy without such a market. This argument is reinforced if, by allowing the payment of higher rates of interest to savers, such a market does in fact bring about additional savings on the part of the masses.

Third, by replacing the debt of the deficit units (the real investors) with that of the intermediaries, the capital market increases the liquidity of the assets held by the surplus units while at the same time the savings are made available to the deficit units for longer periods of time. In other words, it converts short-term into longer-term debt, and relatively illiquid debt into relatively liquid debt. Also important in this context is the fact that the savers can now continuously convert their savings into financial assets rather than accumulate large amounts to be invested into real assets. Quite apart from what happens to the rate of returns on savings, the availability of safe financial assets in small denominations will facilitate the saving process.

Fourth, by averaging the risk, the capital market will decrease the possibility of loss to any one saver and will thus increase the willingness to lend. When there is no market '[The economic agents] cannot relieve themselves of risk bearing. Hence, any unwillingness or inability to bear risks will give rise to a non-optimal allocation of resource...'[25]

Fifth, if the capital market is fairly well-working, it will guarantee that the investors who succeed in getting the funds are also the most productive; in other words, it would not only transfer savings from savers to investors, but from savers to the potentially most productive investors, i.e. those with the greatest entrepreneurial ability. As McKinnon has argued, when the economy is fragmented 'firms and households are so isolated that they face different effective prices for land, labour, capital and produced commodities and do not have access to the same technologies'.[26] In particular 'fragmentation in the capital market...causes the misuse of labour and land, suppresses entrepreneurial development and condemns important sectors of the economy to inferior technology'.[27] In these circumstances:

> One farmer may save by hoarding rice inventories, part of which is eaten by mice so the return on his saving is negative. Another may foresee an annual return of over 60% in drilling a new tube well for irrigation, but the local moneylender wants 100% interest on any loan he provides. The operator of a small domestic machine shop may find it impossible to get bank credit to finance his inventories of finished goods and accounts receivable, whereas an exclusively licensed importer of competitive machine parts has easy access to foreign trade credit at a subsidized rate of 6%.[28]

The basic point is that when the capital market is too fragmented and the rate of interest that a saver can expect from lending is too low, savers will have the incentive to use their funds directly even when the rate of return that can be expected from their own investments is too low. Thus, a low rate of interest will not only discourage people from saving but will also stimulate many unproductive uses for existing savings.[29] In this case, those who have entrepreneurial ability and who are able to direct savings toward more productive uses may not be able to do so for lack of investible funds.

Entrepreneurial ability is the capacity to foresee investment opportunities, to put together a team that will produce a commodity at a competitive cost, and to organize all those other functions connected with production, distribution and marketing processes. This is an extremely important and scarce quality, especially in developing countries. Some economists have, in fact, gone so far as to argue that the lack of this quality in satisfactory supply is the main obstacle to economic development. Myint,[30] for example, has written about the need for mobilizing the brain power of the people from the developing countries while Hirschman[31] has stressed the role of the entrepreneur just as Schumpeter did long before him.

As the supply of entrepreneurial ability is very scarce in most countries, and in the developing countries in particular, it is obvious that it should be fully utilized and not wasted. The degree to which available entrepreneurial ability is utilized determines to a large extent the quality of investment and, in some cases, even its quantity; the government has the responsibility to see that this scarce resource be utilized to the fullest degree. This is where fiscal policy comes in.

An interesting aspect of this ability is that it is most likely not very strongly concentrated in any particular income group of the population. There is, in fact, no particularly strong reason to assume that those with high incomes also possess a monopoly of those qualities that Schumpeter associated with the successful investor, especially when those incomes are generated by inherited wealth. It is likely that often those who have financial resources do not know what to do with them except perhaps spend them, or invest in land and residential construction, or take them out of the country. On the other hand, many people who, because of their mental qualities and their general aptitudes, could be successful entrepreneurs often have neither personal wealth nor access to resources through the capital market. An important function for fiscal policy would then be that of making financial resources available to these people.

A final point that is worth making and that has not, apparently, been made before concerns the relationship between the capital market and protection policy. In an important paper, Robert E. Baldwin convincingly argued that the theoretical case for infant-industry protection had been oversold.[32] The details of Baldwin's arguments cannot be discussed here, but what he has done is essentially to show that four principal infant-industry cases are invalid. However, Baldwin's own argument against infant-industry tariff protection depends largely and critically on the ability of affected firms or workers to obtain access to credit – to make up for temporary losses for the former and to survive on very low wages 'or even pay the firm with these borrowed funds to provide on-the-job training'[33] for the latter. What is implicit in Baldwin's argument is that the case for infant-industry protection may be largely a case for a well-working capital market. Or, what is the same, the argument for protection becomes stronger the less developed is the capital market and the more difficult it is to get credit.

## Fiscal policy and the generation and allocation of savings

If a country does not have a centralized economy and if it does not have a well-working capital market, it should be the responsibility of government to try to develop one. This, however, is a difficult task which requires rather a long time to be accomplished. In the intervening period, the government can follow two alternative, second-best solutions.

First, it can itself invest a rather substantial share of total savings, as has been done in developing countries in recent decades. There the share of total investment carried out by the public sector has often exceeded 50 per cent. This is the route that was supported over the years in much of the writing on the role of government in economic development. This support was based on the assumption that the government should supply the entrepreneurial function that supposedly was missing in the private sector;[34] and the need for the creation of infrastructures discussed above and on the implied assumption of high productivity for public investment.

Second, it can itself provide a kind of proxy for this function of the capital market. This leads back to the role of fiscal policy in the developing countries. If the reasoning through much of this paper is valid, it would provide an argument *for a planned budgetary surplus.* In other words, the government should aim to set its total tax revenues and, what is the basic point here, its *total* expenditure (both current *and* capital) at a level that would yield an overall surplus, which could then be made available *on a competitive and non-concessionary* basis to the private sector, as well as to public enterprises. This would provide the government with a powerful and flexible tool that would facilitate, to a considerable extent, the allocation of private investment along more efficient lines.[35]

That such an approach is possible is shown by the Japanese example in the decade after the Meiji Restoration (1868) and in the period following World War II. In a very interesting paper[36] Koichi Emi described how during these periods 'the function of public finance was extended to set up a new saving-investment scheme for the national economy...' and how during the first of these periods this function was 'gradually switched to the private banking system'.[37] He went on to state that 'at this stage, the purpose of government loans and investments shifted from the establishment of private enterprises to the proper function of creating public works and other social overhead capital'.[38] The basic conclusion of this author is worth quoting:

> the role of public finance is not only to perform its own saving and investment, but also to establish the initial saving and investment channels for private industries, taking the place of the banking system.[39]

Surveys carried out in some Latin American countries have shown that the inability on the part of many enterprises and individuals to obtain credit is, perhaps, the most serious obstacle to investment and development. In these countries those who obtain the credit available get it, often, at concessionary or even at negative real rates of interest. On the other hand, many who would gladly have paid high positive rates are not able to obtain any credit. It is likely that the availability of credit is far more important than all the incentive schemes, especially for the creation of new enterprises. Tax incentives, for example, by increasing the liquidity of the already established enterprises may facilitate their expansion but normally will not help very much the potential enterprises or the individuals who do not have funds for the fixed initial investment. Credit availability, on the other hand, will have an impact in both areas.[40]

Thus, the availability of credit financed by surpluses in the government budget is an integral part of fiscal policy. But, unlike incentives and controls it puts in the hands of the government an instrument that is exceedingly flexible. Through the use of this instrument, resources can be directed toward productive investments carried out by private entrepreneurs and toward those with high social significance. In this way the government would, in fact, be acting as a proxy for the capital market; in addition to increasing the level of savings, it would stimulate entrepreneurship and thus affect the quality and not just the quantity of investment.[41]

The objection to this scheme that can be easily anticipated concerns the capacity of many governments to actually use these funds for the purposes indicated: as already discussed, given extra revenues, the political pressure on the government may lead to increases in non-productive budgetary expenditure or to politically motivated loans. Thus, it is clear that 'generation of "public savings"...would require some very deliberate efforts on the part of the governments to economize on their administration and other current [and one should add capital] expenditures'.[42] The basic point made here is that we cannot assume that public capital expenditure is always productive. Funds can be wasted in non-productive capital expenditure as well as in current expenditure.

In fact many developing countries have had substantial deficits that have generally been financed either by borrowing from the public (and more often from foreign institutions) or by borrowing from their central banks. This action has reduced the availability of resources for investment in the private sectors and often has had inflationary consequences that have distorted the financial structure of the countries, generated serious balance-of-payments difficulties, and retarded the development of a capital market. A relatively tight fiscal policy, together with a liberal monetary or credit policy, is likely to create the most favourable atmosphere for economic development.[43]

## Notes

1.  I. Adelman and C.T. Morris have argued that economic growth may in fact even lead to a fall in the *absolute* income of the poorer segments of the population. See their *Economic Growth and Social Equity in Developing Countries*, Stanford, Stanford University Press, 1973.

2.  Carl S. Shoup, 'Production from consumption', *Public Finance*, XX, 1–2, 1965: 173–98. Richard Goode has called my attention to the fact that Alfred Marshall, long before Shoup, had introduced the idea and even the terminology of 'productive consumption'. See Alfred Marshall, *Principles of Economics*, 8th ed, London, Macmillan, 1948. The relevant citation can be found in Richard Goode, 'Taxing of savings and consumption in underdeveloped countries', in Richard Bird and Oliver Oldman (eds) *Readings on Taxation in Developing Countries*, 3rd edn, Baltimore, Johns Hopkins University Press, 1975: 281. Although Goode's article has a different emphasis and objective than the present one, many of the points there made are relevant for this chapter.

3.  See Alfred Marshall, op. cit. p.229.

4.  In Keynes's words: 'The fundamental psychological law...is that men are disposed, as a rule and on the average, to increase their consumption as their income increases but not by as much as the increase in their income', and '...a greater *proportion* of income being...saved as real income increases', *The General Theory of Employment, Interest and Money*, New York, Harcourt, Brace, 1936: 96 and 97.

5.  See, for example, B. Higgins, *Economic Development: Principles, Problems and Policies*, New York, W.W. Norton and Company, 1959: 481–2; A. Lewis, *The Theory of Economic Growth*, Homewood, Ill., Richard D. Irwin, 1959: 225–44; Ragnar Nurkse, *Problems of Capital Formation in Underdeveloped Countries*, New York, Oxford University Press, 1962: 146. In time, the (Keynesian) absolute income theory of the consumption function was subjected to sharp criticism. New theories – J. Dusenberry's relative income, M. Friedman's permanent income, F. Modigliani's life-cycle – with different policy implications were put forward.

6.  As Goode has pointed out, even among classical or neo-classical economists 'there seems (to be) a growing tendency toward scepticism' about the existence of a positive interest elasticity of saving. He cites Wicksell and Knight as having expressed such a scepticism. See Goode, op. cit., p.275, n. 2. What the Keynesian Revolution did for most economists was to change this scepticism into a certainty about no relationship at all.

7.  This follows from the Keynesian theory of the consumption function but, of course, it reverses the more general Keynesian conclusion about the tendency for savings to be too high in industrialized countries.

8.  Ragnar Nurkse, op. cit., Chapter 3.

9.  See in relation to this point, Edward F. Denison (assisted by Jean-Pierre Poullier), *Why Growth Rates Differ*, Washington DC, The Brookings Institution, 1967; and H.J. Bruton, 'Productivity growth in Latin America', *The American Economic Review* LVII, 5, December 1967: 1099–116.

10. Joseph A. Schumpeter, *The Theory of Economic Development*, New York, Oxford University Press, 1961; 68.

11. In developing countries the import content of investment is generally much higher than that of consumption.

12. One corollary of this is that foreign borrowing may raise the level of the tax burden that can be productively used.

13. Hla Myint, *The Economics of the Developing Countries*, New York, Praeger, 1965; 126.

14. See Stanley Please, 'Saving through taxation: reality or mirage?' in *Finance and Development* 4, March 1967; 24–32.

15. T.W. Schultz, 'Investment in human capital', *The American Economic Review*, March 1961: 1.

16. For the industrialized countries there is now much evidence that the growth of capital stock has contributed relatively little to the growth of per capita national income thus supporting Schumpeter's view.

17. S.R. Lewis, Jr, 'Aspects of fiscal policy and resource mobilization in Pakistan', *The Pakistan Development Review* IV, 2, Summer 1964: 262.

18. A road built in the middle of nowhere does not contribute to potential output. One built on potentially very productive land does.

19. Ronald I. McKinnon, *Money and Capital in Economic Development,* Washington; The Brookings Institution, 1973; Edward S. Shaw, *Financial Deepening in Economic Development,* New York; Oxford University Press, 1973; Raymond W. Goldsmith, *Financial Structure and Development,* New Haven, Yale University Press, 1969. For a more agnostic view, see Rattan J. Bhatia and Deena R. Khatkhate, 'Financial intermediation, savings mobilization and entrepreneurial development: the African experience', *IMF Staff Papers* 22, March 1975: 132–58.

20. R.I. McKinnon, op. cit., p.9.

21. Quoted by Anand C. Chandavarkar, 'How relevant is finance for development?', in *Finance and Development* 10, September 1973: 14.

22. See Robert F. Emery, 'The use of interest rate policies as a stimulus to economic growth', Board of Governors of the Federal Reserve System, *Staff Economic Studies* 65, mimeo 1971; Gilbert T. Brown, 'The impact of Korea's 1965 interest rate reform' mimeo, 1971; U Tun Wai, *Financial Intermediaries and National Savings in Developing Countries,* New York, Praeger, 1972; Anand G. Chandavarkar, 'Some aspects of interest rate policies in less developed economies: the experience of selected Asian countries', *IMF Staff Papers* 18, March 1971: 48–110.

23. For the United States a significant positive relationship between saving and the rate of interest was found by Colin Wright. See his study, 'Saving and the rate of interest' in Arnold C. Harberger and Martin J. Bailey (eds) *The Taxation of Income from Capital,* Washington, The Brookings Institution, 1969: 275–300.

24. Obviously, this assumes that the person will use that million in the most productive investment rather than in the most prestigious or conspicuous one.

25. K.J. Arrow, 'Economic welfare and allocation of resources for invention', in National Bureau of Economic Research, *The Role and Direction of Inventive Activity: Economic and Social Factors,* Princeton, Princeton University Press, 1962: 611-12.

26. Ronald I. McKinnon, op. cit., p.5.

27. Ibid., p.8.

28. Ibid., pp.8–9.

29. One example of this misuse is the building of houses over several (or even many) years. Normally, these individuals spend their savings on the construction of their houses and then stop the work. A few months later (or even years later) when more savings have been accumulated the work is continued; for these countries, that must have very high rates of discount; this process is very wasteful.

30. Hla Myint, op. cit.

31. Albert O. Hirschman, *The Strategy of Economic Development,* New Haven: Yale University Press, 1958.

32. Robert E. Baldwin, 'The case against infant-industry tariff protection', *Journal of Political Economy* 77, 3, May/June 1969: 295–305.

33. Ibid., p.301.

34. An obvious question is: if entrepreneurial ability is missing among the population that constitutes the private sector, why should it not be missing among the supposedly similar population that makes up the public sector?

35. The implication of this choice is that public capital expenditure and not only current expenditure should be limited in order to generate the needed budgetary surplus to be made available to the private sector. Thus, the basic policy recommendation is not necessarily a higher tax burden for the countries.

36. Koichi Emi, 'Saving and investment through the government budget', in David Krivine (ed.) *Fiscal and Monetary Problems in Developing States: Proceedings of the Third Rehoboth Conference,* New York, Praeger, 1967: 138.

37. Ibid., p.142.

38. Ibid.

39. Ibid., p.147.

40. Obviously some tax incentives do reduce the need for initial capital.

41. And it would, as shown above, also have implications for protective policy.
42. Ved P. Gandhi, 'Are there economies of size in government current expenditures in developing countries?' *The Nigerian Journal of Economic and Social Studies* 12, 2 (July 1970): 173.
43. Richard Bird has called my attention to the fact that this conclusion for developing countries is consistent with Musgrave's policy prescription for developed countries. See Richard Musgrave, 'Growth with equity', *American Economic Review* 1960.

# 3 The role of the public sector in the market economies of developing Asia: general lessons for the current debt strategy

## Introduction

Discussions on the role of the public sector tend to focus on what the public sector ought to do on the basis of theoretical assumptions about the existence of public goods and externalities, the need to mobilize resources and to create infrastructures, and the need to redistribute income and to stabilize the economy. These discussions are inevitably influenced by ideological considerations and by an implicit concept of the public sector as an all-knowing entity that makes few if any mistakes and that always aims at maximizing the 'general' welfare. These normative discussions, that fill the pages of public finance textbooks, are useful for providing a framework for reference.[1] However, more attention must be directed toward the positive role of the public sector recognizing that governments are run by real, and not fictional, individuals who have biases just like everyone else and who make their share of mistakes, and recognizing that public sectors are not monolithic institutions but are generally made up of hundreds of separate and, to some extent, independent entities.[2] Thus, it may be more useful to reverse the normal question by focusing on what governments should *not* have done rather than what they should have done.

To limit the scope of this chapter I shall deal only with the following nine countries: Bangladesh, India, Indonesia, Korea, Malaysia, Pakistan, Philippines, Sri Lanka and Thailand. These countries contain about a fourth of the world's population.

## A sketch of a positive theory of public sector intervention

The market economies of Asia have assembled in recent decades an economic record that, in many ways, is the envy of policy-makers in other regions of the so-called developing world. Whether the performance of these economies is assessed by the rate of growth, by the rate of inflation, by the growth of exports, or by the fact that by and large most of these economies have managed to avoid the economic crises that have afflicted other regions, the basic conclusion must be that the performance of these countries, taken as a group, has been quite good.[3] Given this performance, and the fact that the public sector has played a major role in these economies, there must be a presumption that that role must have contributed importantly to these results; or, at a minimum, that it must not have been an obstacle to economic development.

In theory at least there are two polar roles that could be assigned to the public sector: an all-embracing one, derived broadly from the work of Karl Marx, and a far more limited one, derived from the work of Adam Smith and his followers. Since we are dealing with market economies, there is a presumption that the optimal role for the public sector would be closer to the one envisaged by Smith than by Marx. However, that role must depend on the weights that the policy-makers assign to objectives such as income distribution and stabilization, objectives that were not taken into account by market-oriented classical economists. These other objectives may take several forms. For example, income distribution may refer to distribution by size of income, or between urban and rural dwellers, or between wage earners and those who receive other forms of income, or between the workers and the pensioners, or between the very poor (say, the bottom 10 per cent of the income distribution) and the rest. Stabilization may refer to stabilization of output, prices, balance of payments, employment, and so forth.

The greater is the concern of policy-makers for these other objectives, the greater the role of the government would be expected to be.[4] Furthermore, even within the purely allocative, or efficiency-enhancing role emphasized by *laissez-faire* economists, one could argue that, given the nature of the developing economies and the need to create infrastructures (both social and tangible), given the widespread quantity and quality of information available to private economic agents than in advanced countries, the optimal role of the public sector must be greater in developing countries than in more advanced economies. Here, however, an important distinction must be made between an optimal 'normative' role and an optimal 'positive' role.

If governments were made up of policy-makers who did not have any objectives other than those consistent with 'the public interest', had all the information needed to conduct good economic policy, did not make mistakes, and had enough control over the public sector's bureaucracy (tax administrators, employees of public enterprises etc.) to ensure that no gaps developed between the laws and the effective implementation of those laws, then the relevant role for the public sector would be the 'normative' one. In other words the government should intervene in all those cases where there would be a theoretical presumption, on the basis of available knowledge and of rational forecasts, that this intervention would bring results that maximize the public welfare given the resource constraints.[5]

The governments of the Asian countries, as with all governments, are not made up of all-knowing saints but of real-life individuals who, to varying extents, have personal objectives that may at times take precedence over national objectives; and, of course, the national objectives are not always definable or defined. These personal objectives may reflect pressures created by political affiliations, racial, demographic or regional characteristics, class affiliations, friendships, family connections and personal ambitions or greed. When these special interests play a significant role, the results of economic policy and/or the costs of carrying out those policies are likely to differ from those that would have prevailed in the absence of these special interests. More specifically, desirable changes in the national objectives would come at higher, and sometimes at much higher, cost than in the ideal situation. In such cases the optimal 'positive' role of the public sector is likely to be somewhat smaller than, and different from, the optimal 'normative' role. In other words it would be desirable to reduce the role and, thus, the discretion that policy-makers have. Especially in these circumstances, policies ought to be judged by results rather than by declarations of intent.

Governments can pursue their economic objectives through the budget or through regulations. For example, assistance to a producer can be given through a direct subsidy, which requires higher public expenditure, and, thus, higher levels of taxation or borrowing, or, indirectly, by limiting or forbidding the importation of the product produced by this producer. Other types of subsidies can be given through the credit mechanism, through overvalued exchange rates, through so-called tax expenditures, through special permissions for particular activities (permissions denied to other activities).[6] Therefore, the role of the public sector in the economy cannot be assessed only by the ratios of taxes or public spending to GDP as is often done, although these ratios are important. That role should be assessed also by the many regulatory policies that exist in all countries. These regulatory policies may not be correlated (or may even be negatively correlated) with traditional measures of the public sector (share of total taxes or total public expenditure in national income). Unfortunately these regulatory policies are not quantifiable in the same way as tax revenue or public spending so that countries cannot be objectively ranked on this basis.

In most developing countries, the government attempts to determine among other things:

(i)     who can import, what can be imported, and how much;
(ii)    the domestic prices at which goods can be imported or exported;
(iii)   what can be produced domestically and where;
(iv)    the cost of domestic credit;
(v)     who gets bank credit, how much, and for what purpose;
(vi)    who can borrow abroad; and
(vii)   the prices at which many goods and services can be sold.

When all these controls are taken into account, it can be safely stated that the impact of public sector intervention on the economy is generally far greater in

developing countries than in developed countries, in spite of their lower tax and
expenditure ratios.

There is a fundamental difference between policies that control the economy
through the tax-expenditure process and those associated with the regulatory
route. There is generally a limit (political or administrative) to taxation and
public spending, but there is none to regulations since these can be introduced
with very little direct costs.[7] These can be multiplied *ad infinitum* and can be
extended to all areas of economic activities. Therefore, the potential for economic inefficiency in the use of regulations can, in principle, be far greater than
in the use of taxes and public spending.[8] The efficiency costs to an economy from
import quotas, high and differentiated import duties, unrealistic exchange rates,
negative interest rates, uneconomic pricing policies, and over-regulated economic activities could, under particular circumstances, exceed those associated
with inefficient and burdensome tax systems and expenditure programmes even
though the latter can be very high.

Figure 3.1 provides a stylized version of the point that I wish to make. The
horizontal axis measures the net economic benefit (that is net of economic costs)
that the country derives from public sector intervention. Here intervention refers
to both regulations as well as the tax and spending process. These benefits are
positive for some level of intervention and become negative when intervention

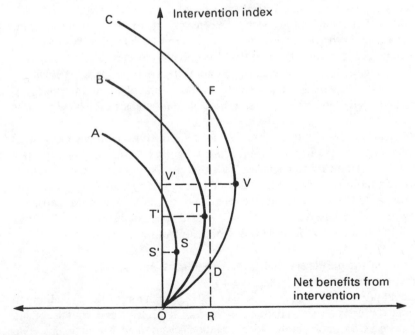

*Figure 3.1*

is carried too far, when it serves special rather than general interest, or when it is based on wrong information, wrong expectations, or wrong policies. The vertical axis measures the degree of public sector intervention, assuming that somehow we have an index that properly measures it.[9] The curves OA, OB, and OC show how countries can benefit from various degrees of intervention. At points S, T, and V the degree of intervention is optimal given the quality of that intervention.[10] In other words, at those points the countries derive the maximum net benefit from governmental intervention.

Each curve represents a given country at a given moment in time – that is with a given need for public sector intervention and a given set of policy-makers.[11] In the country represented by curve OC the beneficial effect of each level of public sector intervention is much greater than in the country represented by curve OA. This may be due to differences in the efficiency of the private sector in allocating resources and in distributing income; or, it may be due to the fact that the policy-makers in country OC would predominantly pursue the public interest while those in country OA would promote policies that ultimately benefit them and their clienteles more than the country at large.[12] Of course, both of these groups of policy-makers will declare that the policies that they are promoting are for the benefit of the country. When intervention is carried beyond the optimal levels represented by S, T, and V, the welfare provision of the country begins to fall.[13] Eventually public sector policies may do more economic damage than good (when the curves cross the vertical axis).

Although it is difficult to specify the determinants of the optimal role of the public sector in the real world, they are likely to be related to how well the government is pursuing the traditional economic objectives of allocation of resources, redistribution of income and stabilization of the economy.[14] Basically the optimal role will depend not only on the results of economic policy, as measured by the objectives pursued, but also on the costs of achieving these objectives.

My basic, and admittedly impressionistic, conclusions about the market economies of developing Asia are the following. By and large economic policy has been better in these countries, taken as a group, than in other regions. However, the relatively good results were achieved at higher costs than was necessary. Putting it differently, intervention by the public sector was carried to a degree somewhat beyond the optimum. This chapter emphasizes the allocative role of redistribution of income and stabilization of the economy.

## The role of the public sector in resource allocation
*Public spending: level and composition*
Table 3.1 provides information, for the 1981–5 period, for public expenditure in the nine countries considered. Some of the data in this table and in all the others may not be strictly comparable so that caution is warranted. The main objective

*Table 3.1:   Public expenditure (in per cent of GDP)*

|  | 1981 | 1982 | 1983 | 1984 | 1985 |
|---|---|---|---|---|---|
| Bangaladesh | 17.4 | 19.9 | 17.3 | 16.1 | 16.4 |
| Current | ... | 6.7 | 6.6 | 6.6 | 7.4 |
| Developmental | ... | 13.2 | 10.7 | 9.5 | 9.0 |
| India | 29.7 | 32.3 | 31.1 | 33.6 | 33.3 |
| Current | 10.1 | 12.1 | 10.9 | 11.4 | 12.0 |
| Developmental | 19.6 | 20.1 | 20.2 | 22.2 | 21.3 |
| Indonesia | 23.7 | 23.9 | 23.5 | 20.0 | 22.8 |
| Current | 12.9 | 11.8 | 11.5 | 11.0 | 11.7 |
| Developmental | 10.8 | 12.1 | 12.0 | 9.0 | 11.1 |
| Korea | ... | 22.5 | 20.9 | 20.6 | 20.6 |
| Current | ... | 16.0 | 15.7 | 15.6 | 16.0 |
| Developmental | ... | 6.5 | 5.2 | 5.0 | 4.6 |
| Malaysia | 44.3 | 45.1 | 38.8 | 34.2 | 35.3 |
| Current | 24.4 | 26.5 | 24.5 | 23.4 | 26.0 |
| Developmental | 19.9 | 18.6 | 14.3 | 10.8 | 9.3 |
| Pakistan | 22.5 | 22.0 | 24.1 | 23.9 | 24.4 |
| Current | 14.3 | 14.4 | 16.5 | 17.8 | 17.8 |
| Developmental | 8.2 | 7.6 | 7.6 | 6.1 | 6.6 |
| Philippines | 19.6 | 19.7 | 17.8 | 12.9 | 13.2 |
| Current | 9.7 | 10.2 | 10.0 | 8.4 | 9.7 |
| Developmental | 9.9 | 9.5 | 7.8 | 4.5 | 3.5 |
| Sri Lanka | 33.1 | 33.7 | 32.6 | 30.8 | 32.9 |
| Current | 17.2 | 18.3 | 17.8 | 15.7 | 17.1 |
| Developmental | 15.9 | 15.4 | 14.8 | 15.1 | 15.8 |
| Thailand | 22.5 | 23.6 | 23.2 | 23.3 | 24.7 |
| Current | 14.6 | 15.5 | 15.8 | 16.3 | 16.9 |
| Developmental | 7.9 | 8.1 | 7.4 | 7.0 | 7.8 |

Source: Various IMF, and IBRD and national sources.

here is to provide broad impressions rather than precise statistical information. There is a wide range between the almost 45 per cent of GDP reached by total public expenditure in Malaysia in 1982 and the level (about 13 per cent of GDP) shown by the Philippines in 1984–5. It does not take special expertise to conclude that, from an allocative point of view but not necessarily from a stabilization point of view, public expenditure was probably excessive in the former and too low in the latter.[15] The levels shown by India and Sri Lanka appear to be relatively high by the criterion of Indonesia, Pakistan, and Thailand. The validity of these conclusions, however, depends on whether the countries could easily and cheaply finance that level of expenditure, and whether it was efficiently spent. For example, there is nothing wrong with a high level of public expenditure if it is financed by cheap resources (that is, efficient taxes and low-cost loans) and if it is spent in a highly efficient way. When these considerations are taken into account, the above conclusions may have to be revised. We shall pay some attention to these issues; however, it is important to emphasize that precise answers are just not possible.

Table 3.1 provides also a breakdown of total public expenditure between current and developmental. From a stabilization point of view this distinction is generally not useful since all expenditures contribute to demand pressure and affect the balance of payments.[16] That distinction is considered useful by many economists and policy-makers who believe that a large share of developmental expenditure in total public expenditure is a sign of an economic policy that contributes to growth. However, there is no standardized way of classifying expenditure as current or capital so that what is classified as current in one country may be classified as developmental in another. Furthermore, since it is easier to obtain foreign grants and concessional credit for developmental expenditure than for current expenditure, there is an incentive for countries to make this category look larger than it might be in reality by reclassifying some current expenditure as developmental.

Some aspects of Table 3.1 merit comment. First, a very large proportion of total public spending is classified as developmental. In India and Bangladesh developmental expenditure far exceeded that for current expenditure; in India it was twice as large. Second, a substantial change over the years characterizes this category compared with current expenditure. Current expenditure is more rigid because it is associated with wages and entitlements that are difficult to change in the short run. Therefore, the impact of financing difficulties often falls on the developmental part of the total. For example, in Malaysia developmental public expenditure dropped from almost 20 per cent of GDP in 1981 to about 9 per cent in 1985. In Bangladesh it dropped from 13.2 per cent in 1982 to 9 per cent in 1985. In Indonesia it dropped from 12.1 per cent in 1982 to 9 per cent in 1984 and rose again to over 11 per cent in 1985. In the Philippines it dropped from 9.9 per cent in 1981 to 3.5 per cent in 1985. Financing difficulties were often behind these reductions. Third, there was a very low level of developmental expenditure in Korea, which was – ironically – the country with the highest rate of growth.

Although developmental expenditure is not the same as public investment, it is closely related to it.[17] Table 3.2 shows total gross investment (gross capital formation) as a per cent of GDP. It also shows a breakdown of gross investment into public and private for the nine countries. The large role played by the public sector in the capital accumulation of many of these countries is highlighted by this table. In Bangladesh, India, Malaysia, Pakistan, and Sri Lanka the public sector accounted for about half or more than half of total gross investment. In the

Table 3.2    Gross investment (in per cent of GDP)

| | 1981 | 1982 | 1983 | 1984 | 1985 |
|---|---|---|---|---|---|
| Bangaladesh | 15.1 | 13.6 | 12.3 | 13.2 | 13.0 |
| Public | 6.2 | 6.2 | 5.6 | 6.1 | 5.9 |
| Private | 8.9 | 7.4 | 6.7 | 7.1 | 7.1 |
| India | 23.9 | 24.4 | 23.5 | 24.4 | 25.4 |
| Public | 11.8 | 12.2 | 11.2 | 12.1 | 11.9 |
| Private | 12.1 | 12.2 | 12.3 | 12.3 | 13.5 |
| Indonesia | 27.1 | 25.8 | 24.8 | 20.3 | 19.1 |
| Public | 5.8 | 9.1 | 9.5 | 6.3 | 6.9 |
| Private* | 21.3 | 16.7 | 15.3 | 14.0 | 12.2 |
| Korea | 30.3 | 28.6 | 29.9 | 31.9 | 31.1 |
| Public | 4.3 | 4.6 | 4.7 | 4.8 | 4.7 |
| Private | 26.0 | 24.0 | 25.2 | 27.1 | 26.4 |
| Malaysia | 37.2 | 38.0 | 37.4 | 34.2 | 32.7 |
| Public | 16.7 | 19.0 | 19.1 | 1.2 | 16.2 |
| Private | 20.5 | 19.0 | 18.3 | 18.0 | 16.5 |
| Pakistan | 15.2 | 15.3 | 15.7 | 15.1 | 15.0 |
| Public | 9.2 | 9.7 | 9.7 | 9.0 | 8.8 |
| Private | 6.0 | 5.6 | 6.0 | 6.1 | 6.2 |
| Philippines | 26.1 | 25.6 | 25.2 | 20.1 | 16.5 |
| Public | 9.9 | 9.5 | 7.4 | 4.5 | 3.5 |
| Private | 16.2 | 16.1 | 17.8 | 15.6 | 13.0 |
| Sri Lanka | 27.4 | 30.5 | 29.0 | 25.7 | 24.8 |
| Public | 13.3 | 15.5 | 13.0 | 12.1 | 11.8 |
| Private | 14.1 | 15.0 | 16.0 | 13.6 | 13.0 |
| Thailand | 24.7 | 21.1 | 23.0 | 22.1 | 21.3 |
| Public | 8.7 | 7.9 | 7.9 | 7.9 | 8.6 |
| Private | 16.0 | 13.2 | 15.1 | 14.2 | 12.7 |

Source: Various IMF, IBRD and national sources.
* Includes the investment of public enterprises.

Philippines and in Thailand the proportion was somewhat lower. In Korea public investment was only about 20 per cent of total investment. In many of the countries considered the ratio of gross investment to GDP was high, partly explaining the good growth performance of these countries.[18]

The magnitude of the public sector's gross investment as a share of GDP raises several questions. First, was the investment of the public sector in areas of genuine government concerns such as transportation, irrigation, education, and health; or was it in areas such as manufacturing, and agriculture that, according to the normative theory of public sector intervention, should have been left to the private sector?[19] Second, was the allocation of public sector investment made on the basis of efficiency criteria or on the basis of other criteria reflecting the social, political, or private objectives of some policy-makers or public sector employees? Third, how much impact did the cost of raising capital, often from foreign sources, have on the determination of the size of the investment budget and on the choice of specific projects?[20] Fourth, how much impact did the borrowing to finance this expenditure have on the government's future bill for interest payments?

## *The efficiency of public enterprises*

In several of these countries, historical factors or social considerations contributed or were mainly responsible for the fact that public enterprises were often engaged in activities that are normally left to the private sector in market economies.[21] For example, in Bangladesh public sector involvement was necessitated by a mass exodus of owners and managers at the time of the break-up of Pakistan into two countries in 1971. However, in some of them government involvement reflected policy decisions and was perhaps encouraged by the availability of cheap credit to the government or by windfalls from high commodity prices in some periods. More recently there has been a change of attitude that has resulted in movement towards the privatization of some of these enterprises. In Bangladesh, for example, the share of public investment in manufacturing declined from about 66 per cent of total investment in 1980 to less than 40 per cent in 1984–5. The trend toward privatization is also apparent in several of the other countries. However, in most of them government involvement in areas in which it does not have an obvious role to play remains large.

On the basis of available information, it is realistic to conclude that often public sector investment has not followed efficiency criteria. There are too many examples of 'white elephants' that have come into existence for reasons that had little to do with efficiency.[22] In many cases these projects have contributed significantly to the foreign indebtedness of these countries and are likely to reduce their future standards of living. The information available on rates of return to public sector investments, though limited and not strictly comparable, indicates that, although in these countries the public enterprises (taken as a group) were often not the major drains on the budget as in countries in other regions, the financial rates of return were often very low, especially when the enterprises engaged in oil production are excluded.[23]

According to available information, the recent financial performance of public sector industrial enterprises in Bangladesh shows an overall rate of return of 0.4 per cent on the book value of assets in 1985–6.[24] For the non-financial public enterprises taken as a whole, the rate of return on assets was higher at 3.7 per cent in 1984–5. However, much of the profits came from enterprises engaged in the extraction of gas.

For India, net profit as a percentage of capital employed in the public manufacturing and service enterprises of the central government was 2.3 per cent in 1982–3 and 2.8 per cent in 1985–6. However, all the profits came from the 12 enterprises engaged in oil production. As a group, non-oil enterprises have been making losses. State government enterprises have also been running losses. According to a recent World Bank study: 'In India...the financial performance of public enterprises has been significantly worse than that of private enterprises in the same industry...'[25]

In Malaysia the number of public enterprises increased rapidly in the period 1980–4. Most of these relied on the government for capital or for guaranteeing external loans. These public enterprises have been running large losses in recent years, in part as a consequence of the fall in commodity prices. Recently steps have been taken to privatize some of them.

In the Philippines the rate of return on equity investment in 15 major public enterprises was estimated at 2.8 per cent for the years 1980–4.

In Indonesia the after-tax rate of return on total assets for a sample of 135 non-financial public enterprises (excluding Pertamina, the national oil company) was about 1 per cent in 1982–3. For the enterprises in the industrial sector the rate of return was close to zero. For all public enterprises the share of profits before tax to total assets was 3.0 per cent in 1985. However, much of the profits came from financial enterprises and from Pertamina. The after-tax rate of return to Pertamina was 3.5 per cent for the 1982–5 period. Losses were particularly significant in enterprises engaged in industry and communications.

In Sri Lanka the returns on many of the massive budgetary capital projects carried out since 1978 have been disappointing. In Pakistan 'the returns on capital averaged about 2 per cent during the 1970s and slightly over 4 per cent during 1980–3, compared to an average rate of inflation over the whole period of about 12 per cent'.[26]

When considering these financial rates of return of public enterprises, some factors ought to be kept in mind. First, these are *nominal* rates of return. Since all of these countries had positive rates of inflation, the real rates of return were often negative. Second, these rates are often inflated by factors such as:

(i)     subsidized credit;
(ii)    cash grants from the government;
(iii)   special tax treatments especially in connection with imports;
(iv)    government implicit or explicit guarantees for foreign borrowing;
(v)     the provision of monopoly status to public enterprises; and
(vi)    the fact that in many cases no deduction from profits is made for depreciation.

Several factors have contributed to the low productivity of public investment. These include:

(i)   the choice of unprofitable investment projects for political or other reasons;

(ii)   the lower emphasis given to efficiency than to objectives such as employment, redistribution of income, regional development, and so forth;

(iii)   low capacity utilization;

(iv)   poor pricing policies;

(v)   managerial staffing at times based more on political considerations than on managerial ability;

(vi)   the absence of incentives imposed by competition and by the profit motive; and

(vii)   for some of them in recent years, the fall in commodity prices.

Whatever the reasons, the net result has been that while the rates of growth of many of these countries have been relatively high, they have been lower than they should have been considering the high level of total investment. In other words, the incremental capital output ratios (ICOR) in several of these countries have been very high. In India, for example, the ICOR has ranged between 3 and 7 in the first half of the 1980s and was about 5 more recently; in Malaysia it has ranged from a low of about 5 in 1982 to a high of above 12 in 1986; in the Philippines it was 9.8 in 1980–3; and in Thailand it was 4.6 in 1980–3. These figures refer to the economy as a whole and thus apply to total investment. However, since public investment has been a relatively large share of total investment in many of these countries, and since private sector investment has probably been more productive than public sector investment, these figures provide a broad indication of the contribution of public investment to growth.[27]

*Public spending and the growth of foreign debt*
In many of these countries, a good part of investment was financed by foreign borrowing. When, as in Korea, the borrowed capital was used to finance investment projects with high rates of return and high potential for earning foreign exchange, it could be argued that the borrowing was fully justified on allocative grounds. In other words, when the marginal productivity of capital exceeds the marginal cost of borrowing, the country is justified in contracting foreign debt.[28] However, in several of these countries investments that would generate low or even negative rates of return were often financed by foreign loans obtained at financing costs higher than the projects' expected rates of return.[29] This is an important aspect that deserves further attention.

For the nine countries combined the foreign debt rose from about US$44 billion in 1975 to US$109 billion in 1980 and to US$203 billion in 1986 (see Appendix Table 3.A–1). Interest payments on this debt rose from US$1.4 billion in 1975 to US$13 billion in 1986 (see Appendix Table 3.A–2). Dividing the interest payments by the stock of foreign debt provides a measure of the average cost of foreign borrowing for the region as the whole. This cost was 3.3 per cent in 1975, rose to 7.3 per cent in 1981, and remained relatively high in the 1981–6 period. The yearly average costs were as follows:

|      | %   |      | %   |      | %   |
|------|-----|------|-----|------|-----|
| 1975 | 3.3 | 1979 | 5.3 | 1983 | 6.4 |
| 1976 | 3.7 | 1980 | 6.4 | 1984 | 7.1 |
| 1977 | 4.0 | 1981 | 7.3 | 1985 | 6.3 |
| 1978 | 4.5 | 1982 | 7.0 | 1986 | 6.4 |

These are average costs for the whole group. They are, therefore, biased downward by concessional loans which are very important for some countries such as Bangladesh, India, and others (see Appendix Table 3.A–3). The terms on commercially obtained debt were much higher, in some cases as high as 15 per cent or more.

A comparison of these costs with the rates of returns that the public enterprises were obtaining on their investment suggests that the allocation of these foreign resources has been far from optimal.[30] In order for countries to avoid long-term difficulties on their external borrowing, the uses to which foreign loans are put must generate financial rates of return which, in real terms, are at least equal to the real cost of borrowing. This has not been the case for investments by public enterprises and, as we shall argue below, it is unlikely to have been the case for investments in infrastructures or for those private investments that benefited from generous tax incentives.

The consequence has been a considerable increase in the ratios of external debt (public plus private) to GDP for the majority of these countries (see Table 3.3). In other words, the stock of external debt has grown much faster than the economy. In some of these countries the external debt to GDP ratio has become disturbingly high. It is not surprising that the ratio of debt service to export

*Table 3.3    Ratio of external debt to GDP or GNP (in per cent)*

|            | 1981 | 1982 | 1983 | 1984 | 1985 | 1986 |
|------------|------|------|------|------|------|------|
| Bangaladesh | ...  | 35.3 | 42.2 | 39.8 | 37.8 | 45.0 |
| India      | 12.3 | 14.3 | 15.5 | 17.2 | 18.7 | 19.5 |
| Indonesia  | 21.1 | 23.0 | 31.0 | 31.1 | 35.3 | 45.8 |
| Korea      | 49.0 | 53.5 | 53.1 | 52.3 | 55.8 | 46.9 |
| Malaysia   | 34.0 | 47.3 | 59.4 | 56.5 | 69.6 | 85.3 |
| Pakistan   | 38.2 | 37.2 | 43.8 | 41.0 | 40.7 | 44.1 |
| Philippines | 54.4 | 61.6 | 72.7 | 80.7 | 82.1 | 95.0 |
| Sri Lanka  | 52.3 | 56.2 | 58.6 | 52.0 | 55.7 | 60.7 |
| Thailand   | 30.6 | 33.3 | 34.7 | 37.4 | 45.3 | 43.2 |

Source: Various IMF, IBRD and national sources.

Table 3.4   Debt–service ratio (in per cent of exports of goods and services)

|  | 1981 | 1982 | 1983 | 1984 | 1985 | 1986 |
|---|---|---|---|---|---|---|
| Bangaladesh | ... | 24.5 | 28.7 | 25.7 | 34.0 | 43.5 |
| India | 9.9 | 12.1 | 14.0 | 16.1 | 18.0 | 19.6 |
| Indonesia | 11.8 | 15.0 | 15.5 | 18.9 | 23.4 | 37.3 |
| Korea | 21.2 | 22.6 | 20.9 | 22.9 | 23.9 | 24.7 |
| Malaysia | 8.0 | 10.2 | 11.1 | 13.3 | 17.4 | 18.8 |
| Pakistan | 23.5 | 25.4 | 25.2 | 31.7 | 36.6 | 43.7 |
| Philippines* | 24.9 | 36.6 | 32.7 | 35.0 | 33.0 | 33.0 |
| Sri Lanka | 19.3 | 22.3 | 24.4 | 17.5 ` | 22.3 | 27.6 |
| Thailand | 19.0 | 20.9 | 23.2 | 24.0 | 27.4 | 27.0 |

Source: Various IMF, IBRD and national sources.
* The figures for the Philippines for the more recent years are biased downward by the rescheduling of the debt. Without rescheduling the debt–service ratio of that country would have increased more than shown here.

earnings of goods and services has been growing in all these countries except Korea (see Table 3.4).[31] Since a large proportion of the foreign debt is held or guaranteed by the public sector and since much of this debt was contracted to finance investment projects, it is obvious that the role of the public sector in allocating investment has left much to be desired. Foreign borrowing may have created jobs and incomes in the short run but at the cost of reductions in the future disposable incomes of these countries. The servicing of the foreign debts must be seen as a tax that will reduce for years to come the net income available for domestic uses in these countries.[32]

### Public expenditure for operation and maintenance
The current expenditure of the public sector has not been as high as the developmental expenditure in the majority of these countries. It was, for example, relatively low in Bangladesh, India, Indonesia, and the Philippines. However, it was high in Malaysia and it was not particularly low in Korea (see Table 3.1). These levels of current expenditure were achieved in spite of: high expenditure for defence in several of these countries (India, Korea, Pakistan, and Thailand); fast growing expenditure for interest payments on both domestic and foreign debt;[33] and relatively high levels of spending for education in several of these countries.

The market economies of developing Asia have preferred indirect measures for redistributing income; as a consequence, the public sector's expenditure for social security, direct welfare payments and subsidies has been low by international standards. For example, this expenditure has been less than 10 per cent of total expenditure compared with about 25 per cent in Latin America. The level of expenditure on operations and maintenance has also been low in most of these countries.

From much of the evidence available, it can be concluded that these countries have been more successful at building infrastructure than at its adequate maintenance or use.[34] Pressures of various kinds have induced the policy-makers to give high priority to new investment projects rather than to ensuring that the existing infrastructure is kept in good working conditions and is fully utilized. These pressures have included:

(i)   the more benevolent international attitude toward 'capital' spending compared with 'current' spending;[35]

(ii)   the greater availability of loans for investment projects than for mainte-nance expenditure;

(iii)   the political benefits associated with the opening of new infrastructures or new enterprises;[36]

(iv)   the greater facility of planning for investment than for recurrent costs;

(v)   the traditional attitude of many economists and policy-makers that invest-ment is the basic ingredient of growth (see Harrod and Domar models); and, finally,

(vi)   the possibility that some of those who arrange contracts may at times receive personal pecuniary benefits.[37]

Given the very large sums involved, and the potential benefits to the firms who receive the contracts, there are likely to be greater attempts at bribery associated with the capital expenditure part of public spending than with the current expenditure part. When these attempts succeed, as they occasionally do, part of the capital expenditure is *de facto* transformed into what could be called a transfer payment. This diversion of investment expenditure benefits those who receive these payments but, by inflating the costs of the investment projects, reduces the rate of return to investment. Often these payments are not referred to as bribes but have acquired more colourful and more neutral names such as 'oiling the mechanism', 'tangents', 'under the table payments', and so on.

Inadequate resources for the operation and maintenance of infrastructures and for the operation of public services have resulted in both deterioration and underutilization of existing capital assets.[38] A majority of these countries has suffered to varying degrees from this shortcoming. Financial difficulties in some of them have contributed to this problem but cannot be completely blamed for it. At least part of the explanation must be found in the differential benefits that those who make these decisions receive from capital spending as compared with spending on operation and maintenance. One important effect has been a deterioration in the existing public sector capital stock.[39] Another has been the less-than-full capacity use of existing capital stock.

In the Philippines, for example, in 1985 operation and maintenance expenditures in real terms were 60 per cent of their 1977 levels. In Indonesia much of the infrastructure built over the past two decades is reported to be deteriorating and in need of costly rehabilitation. For example, only 40 per cent of national and provincial roads are considered in a stable condition. The situation for irrigation canals is similar. Equivalent results have been reported for some of the other countries. A recent study has included Sri Lanka, the Philippines, Pakistan, Thailand, India, and Indonesia among the group of countries perceived as having significant recurrent cost problems.[40]

This erosion and/or underutilization of the capital stock of these countries must again be seen in the context of the rapid rise in the stock of foreign debt. It must be recalled that the foreign debt was acquired largely in the process of building (or adding to) that capital stock. Thus, while the foreign debt must be serviced in the future, regardless of what happens to the country's capital stock, the ability of that capital to generate future income will depend on how well it is maintained and how fully it is used.[41] In the absence of adequate planning and budgeting for operation and maintenance, borrowing for new investment is not likely to be cost-effective and the increase in the countries' earning power to repay the accumulated debt will be less rapid than it could have been.

*The tax systems, the foreign debt, and the rate of return to private investment*
One of the major instruments available to policy-makers for pursuing their social and economic objectives is the tax system. Tables 3.5 and 3.6 provide information on the structure of the tax systems of the countries under consideration.

*Table 3.5    Selected Asian countries: tax revenue by type of tax, three-year averages (in per cent of GDP)*

| Countries | Years | Total Taxes | Total | Income Taxes Indiv- idual | Corpo- rate | Other | Domestic Taxes General Sales Turnover Total | VAT |
|---|---|---|---|---|---|---|---|---|
| Bangladesh | 1981–3 | 7.09 | 1.23 | 1.23 | – | – | 2.95 | 1.22 |
| India[1] | 1981–3 | 16.26 | 2.40 | 0.94 | 1.32 | 0.14 | 10.14 | 0.13 |
| Indonesia[1] | 1982–4 | 18.54 | 14.95 | 0.50 | 13.75 | 0.70 | 2.27 | 1.07 |
| Korea | 1983–5 | 16.79 | 4.48 | 2.39 | 2.09 | – | 8.45 | 4.11 |
| Malaysia | 1982–4 | 21.81 | 10.03 | 2.41 | 7.61 | – | 4.79 | 1.59 |
| Pakistan | 1982–4 | 12.92 | 2.35 | – | – | – | 5.42 | 1.02 |
| Philippines[2] | 1983–5 | 10.29 | 2.49 | 0.90 | 1.37 | 0.22 | 4.26 | 1.05 |
| Sri Lanka | 1982–4 | 17.71 | 3.06 | 0.89 | 2.17 | – | 7.81 | 4.79 |
| Thailand[2] | 1983–5 | 15.02 | 3.13 | 1.70 | 1.44 | – | 7.98 | 2.87 |

Sources: IMF, Government Finance Statistics Yearbook X, 1986.
1. State tax revenues are included.
2. Local tax revenues are included.

Unfortunately the statistics are not up to date. However, these statistics do not change much over the short run so that the tables are likely to be fairly representative of the current situation.

A few features of the statistics merit attention. First, the level of corporate income tax revenue in Indonesia and Malaysia is high. These are essentially taxes on mineral exports and especially on oil. They are an unstable source of revenue as both of these countries have recently witnessed. Second, the revenue from income taxes on individuals is relatively low. Third, the contribution of excise taxes to total revenue is higher than that of general sales taxes. This partly reflects historical factors and partly the desire of policy-makers to influence the pattern of consumption of the citizens. Fourth, foreign trade taxes still play an important role which may reflect to some extent the desire of policy-makers to influence the pattern of imports. Finally, the low level of social security contributions is very low.

Table 3.7 provides more recent estimates of the ratio of tax revenue to GDP.[42] No particular trend is noticeable in the ratios shown in the table. These countries cannot be considered overtaxed especially when it is realized that the high tax ratios for Indonesia and Malaysia are largely the result of taxes on the 'rent' that these countries receive from their mineral deposits. Comparison of the data in Table 3.7 with those in Table 3.1 shows that in several of these countries tax revenue covers only a relatively small fraction of total public expenditure. The difference is, of course, covered by borrowing, grants, and non-tax revenue. For many of the countries considered, tax revenue covers broadly the level of current public expenditure.

There are two aspects that merit consideration as they are linked with the earlier discussion in this chapter. These are the elasticity of these tax systems and

on Goods and Services

| Excises | Other | Total | Foreign Trade | | | Social Security | Wealth and Property | Other |
|---|---|---|---|---|---|---|---|---|
| | | | Import Duties | Export Duties | Other | | | |
| 1.70 | 0.03 | 3.34 | 2.90 | 0.12 | 0.31 | – | 0.19 | – |
| 5.11 | 4.90 | 3.06 | 2.93 | 0.04 | 0.09 | – | 0.18 | 0.14 |
| 1.00 | 0.20 | 0.84 | 0.72 | 0.12 | – | – | 0.34 | 0.70 |
| 2.53 | 1.81 | 2.86 | 2.86 | - | – | 0.25 | 0.14 | – |
| 1.80 | 1.39 | 6.27 | 3.58 | 2.69 | – | 0.14 | 0.14 | – |
| 4.40 | – | 5.10 | 4.84 | 0.11 | 0.15 | – | 0.05 | – |
| 2.10 | 1.10 | 2.96 | 2.63 | 0.18 | 0.12 | – | 0.36 | 0.22 |
| 2.88 | 0.14 | 6.52 | 4.09 | 2.43 | – | – | 0.06 | – |
| 3.77 | 1.35 | 3.42 | 3.06 | 0.34 | 0.03 | – | 0.37 | – |

Table 3.6   Selected Asian countries: tax revenue by type of tax, three-year
averages (in per cent of total tax revenue)

| Countries | Years | Total Taxes | Total | Income Taxes Indiv-idual | Corpo-rate | Other | Domestic Taxes Total | General Sales Turnover VAT |
|---|---|---|---|---|---|---|---|---|
| Bangladesh | 1981–3 | 100.00 | 15.64 | 15.64 | – | – | 37.37 | 15.47 |
| India[1] | 1981–3 | 100.00 | 14.75 | 5.80 | 8.10 | 0.85 | 62.37 | 0.83 |
| Indonesia[1] | 1981–4 | 100.00 | 80.61 | 2.69 | 74.18 | 3.74 | 12.24 | 5.76 |
| Korea | 1983–5 | 100.00 | 26.72 | 14.25 | 12.47 | – | 50.33 | 24.48 |
| Malaysia | 1982–4 | 100.00 | 45.98 | 11.06 | 34.91 | – | 21.92 | 7.26 |
| Pakistan | 1982–4 | 100.00 | 18.22 | – | – | – | 41.92 | 7.90 |
| Philippines[2] | 1983–5 | 100.00 | 24.24 | 8.76 | 13.36 | 2.11 | 41.30 | 10.11 |
| Sri Lanka | 1982–4 | 100.00 | 17.34 | 4.99 | 12.35 | – | 43.96 | 27.08 |
| Thailand[2] | 1983–5 | 100.00 | 20.89 | 11.32 | 9.57 | – | 53.13 | 19.11 |

Sources: IMF, Government Finance Statistics Yearbook X, 1986.
1. State tax revenues are included.
2. Local tax revenues are included.

Table 3.7   Tax revenue (in per cent of GDP)

| | 1981 | 1982 | 1983 | 1984 | 1985 |
|---|---|---|---|---|---|
| Bangladesh | – | 7.3 | 6.8 | 6.9 | 7.1 |
| India | 16.4 | 16.7 | 16.1 | 16.5 | 16.7 |
| Indonesia | 21.1 | 19.0 | 20.8 | 20.7 | 19.8 |
| Korea | 18.1 | 18.8 | 19.4 | 18.7 | 18.6 |
| Malaysia | 23.4 | 22.0 | 24.3 | 23.2 | 24.4 |
| Pakistan | 13.7 | 13.3 | 13.5 | 13.9 | 12.8 |
| Philippines | 10.3 | 10.1 | 10.5 | 9.3 | 10.1 |
| Sri Lanka | 16.7 | 15.5 | 16.2 | 19.4 | 18.9 |
| Thailand | 12.8 | 12.4 | 13.3 | 13.7 | 13.6 |

Source: IMF, IBRD and national sources.

their role in encouraging capital accumulation. Table 3.7 implies that the
buoyancy of these tax systems was around 1.0 since the tax ratios do not show
any particular trend.[43] However, Table 3.7 does not show that these relatively
constant ratios were often achieved at great political cost, due to the many
discretionary changes that some of these countries needed to make over the years
to prevent the level of taxation from falling as a share of GDP, since the elasticity
of these tax systems was in many cases much lower than 1.0.[44] For example, in
unpublished studies covering the period under consideration the elasticity has
been estimated at 0.7 for Bangladesh, 0.5 for the Philippines, 0.73 for Sri Lanka,
and 0.92 for Thailand.

on Goods and Services

| Excises | Other | Total | Foreign Trade Import Duties | Export Duties | Other | Social Security | Wealth and Property | Other |
|---------|-------|-------|--------|--------|-------|-----------------|---------------------|-------|
| 21.54 | 0.36 | 42.35 | 36.82 | 1.50 | 4.03 | – | 2.40 | – |
| 31.42 | 30.12 | 18.83 | 18.00 | 0.26 | 0.57 | – | 1.13 | 0.85 |
| 5.38 | 1.09 | 4.54 | 3.87 | 0.67 | – | – | 1.82 | 3.74 |
| 15.05 | 10.79 | 17.02 | 17.02 | – | – | 1.47 | 0.86 | – |
| 8.27 | 6.39 | 28.78 | 16.44 | 12.35 | – | 0.65 | 0.62 | – |
| 34.02 | – | 39.49 | 37.47 | 0.88 | 1.14 | – | 0.35 | – |
| 20.50 | 10.69 | 28.85 | 25.58 | 1.84 | 1.44 | – | 3.46 | 2.11 |
| 16.06 | 0.81 | 36.88 | 22.91 | 13.97 | – | – | 0.37 | – |
| 25.07 | 8.96 | 22.79 | 20.37 | 2.24 | 0.17 | – | 2.45 | – |

As discussed earlier these countries have borrowed on a large scale to finance their capital expenditure. In the process they have accumulated sizable foreign debts. For some of these countries the external debt is largely public debt. At some point, when the stock of foreign debt reaches a given share of GDP, the net flow of resources between the countries and the rest of the world is likely to change direction.[45] The higher is the rate of interest, and the more reluctant are lenders to keep lending, the more quickly will this point be reached. While in the earlier period the net flow of resources had been from the foreign lenders to the countries, in the later period it must be from the governments to the foreign creditors. This occurs when the interest payments exceed the difference between new borrowing and amortization for existing debts. When this happens, in the absence of a contraction in non-interest government spending, the ratio of tax revenue to GDP will need to rise to generate the fiscal resources needed to make these payments.[46] This is the fiscal counterpart of the external debt problem. To make the foreign payment the country must also run a surplus in its trade account.

Countries with low elasticity of their tax systems will face greater difficulties in generating this fiscal surplus through automatic tax increases. They will, thus, have a greater chance of running into financial difficulties, especially if political constraints limit their action on the expenditure side or if these constraints prevent the introduction of discretionary measures of sufficient magnitude to raise taxes to the needed level. As a consequence, it would be desirable for these countries to reform their tax systems to make them acquire a higher built-in elasticity. The desirable size of the elasticity would itself depend to some extent on the rate at which the public debt is to be serviced.

The low elasticity of the tax systems of these countries is not an accident but is, at least in part, the result of explicit policy actions. More specifically, in several of the countries considered, it is the consequence of the erosion of tax bases due to the proliferation of tax incentives granted to many activities. In some of these countries the tax bases have been reduced over the years to small fractions of their potential values. Many of these incentives were granted to private investment and resulted in large subsidies to capital accumulation. A study of these tax incentives concluded that:

> giving large subsidies to capital to the extent of an overall net subsidy might be questioned on efficiency grounds. The net subsidy drives the required rate of return on capital below the investors' subjective rate of time preference, thereby creating incentives to overinvestment....[47]

Another study has calculated the effects of these tax incentives on the cost of capital faced by enterprises in seven of these countries. The results are reported in Table 3.8. These show that in Indonesia and Malaysia firms might have found an investment profitable even when its before-tax rate of return was negative. It is worth noticing that the country that has been most successful in the use of its capital – Korea – is also that with the lowest subsidies. The cost of capital for private investors in this country was much higher than in the other countries; this factor is likely to have brought about a better allocation of private investment and a better use of borrowed funds.

*Table 3.8   Cost of capital at zero or actual rates of inflation (in per cent)*

| Country | At Zero Rate of Inflation | At Actual Rate of Inflation | |
|---|---|---|---|
| | | Ongoing Firms | Pioneer Firms |
| India | 3.59 | 3.34 | 2.53 |
| Indonesia | 2.40 | −1.80 | 2.60 |
| Korea | 2.91 | 7.82 | 6.60 |
| Malaysia | 1.50 | −0.30 | 0.85 |
| Pakistan | 1.92 | 4.53 | 4.53 |
| Philippines | 1.90 | 0.88 | 0.98 |
| Thailand | 2.00 | 1.60 | 1.11 |

Source: Liam Ebrill, 'Taxes and the cost of capital: some estimates for developing countries', mimeo, 5 March 1984, Table 18.

Once again we find that the role of the public sector has been an ambiguous one. On one hand it has contributed to a high level of capital accumulation and thus to a high rate of growth; on the other it has led to inefficient use of costly resources. The long-run implications of these policies for the ability of these countries to service their foreign debt without encountering difficulties are, thus, less good than they would have been if the capital had been productively invested and used at full capacity.

Before closing this section it should be mentioned that several of these countries (India, Indonesia, Thailand) have recently carried out tax reforms or are in the process of doing so. These reforms should increase the elasticity of the tax system and should reduce the role of these incentives in misallocating investment and in inducing firms to overinvest.

## The role of the public sector in redistributing income and in stabilizing the economies

I cannot deal in any systematic fashion with the role of the public sector in redistributing income and in stabilizing the economies. I shall thus limit myself to a few general observations.

### Redistribution

Table 3.9 provides available statistics on income distribution for six of these countries. Notice that these statistics refer to different years. Korea has the most even distribution although it should be noticed that the data for this country refer only to the urban population so that they are not strictly comparable with the others. In Korea the highest 10 per cent had average incomes only 2.5 times the country's average, while the bottom 20 per cent had incomes about 40 per cent of the country's average. In the Philippines, on the other hand, the average income of the highest 10 per cent was more than four times the country's average, while the average income of the bottom 20 per cent was only about one fifth of the country's average.

In most of these countries the redistribution of income has been an objective that has received considerable attention on the part of policy-makers. Little attempt, however, has been made to use the tax system to promote it. For example, the role of personal income taxes and of taxes on wealth and property has been limited. In general these governments have preferred to pursue the objective of redistribution through the expenditure side of the budget and through the regulatory route. To their credit they have paid much more attention to the agricultural sectors than has been the case in other developing countries.

One problem with the instruments used (such as rationing of basic products, subsidies to consumers, subsidies to producers, controlled prices of public utilities, public employment, credit subsidies) is that it is difficult to target them efficiently. Therefore, in many cases the main beneficiaries have not been the very poor but individuals from higher deciles of the income distribution. In fact this seems to be the main thread that one finds in discussions of these programmes.[48] The truly poor have benefited much less than they could have with better targeted programmes. But, of course, to achieve this better targeting is always difficult or expensive administratively.

*Table 3.9  Income distribution statistics for selected countries*

| | Year | Source | Coverage of Population | Concept | 1 | Quartile Distribution 2 | 3 | 4 | 5 | Highest 10% |
|---|---|---|---|---|---|---|---|---|---|---|
| Bangladesh | 1976–7 | Survey | 100% | Household | 6.2 | 10.9 | 15.0 | 21.0 | 46.9 | 32.0 |
| India | 1975–6 | Survey | 99% | Family | 5.0 | 9.6 | 14.1 | 20.9 | 50.4 | 34.9 |
| Philippines | 1971 | Survey | 100% | Family | 3.5 | 7.8 | 12.4 | 19.8 | 56.5 | 40.9 |
| Korea | 1981 | Survey | Urban | Household | 8.0 | 13.0 | 17.0 | 22.4 | 39.6 | 24.5 |
| Sri Lanka | 1980–1 | Survey | 100% | Household | 5.9 | 10.3 | 14.1 | 19.9 | 49.8 | 35.2 |
| Thailand | 1975–6 | Survey | 100% | Household | 5.1 | 8.2 | 11.7 | 17.9 | 57.1 | 42.8 |

Source: United Nations, *National Accounts Statistics: Compendium of Income Distribution Statistics*, Statistical Papers, 79, United Nations, New York, 1985.

*Stabilization*
There have been implications for the stabilization of these economies associated with both the large public spending on capital projects and the expenditure and other policies associated with the attempts to redistribute income. One implication already discussed has been the accumulation of public debt, especially the one owed to foreigners.[49] The other has been the creation of fiscal imbalances that have in some cases grown very large and have forced the countries to rely on foreign borrowing in the absence of sufficient non-inflationary domestic sources. In some cases (India) domestic savings have been mobilized to finance, in a non-inflationary manner and without excessive recourse to foreign sources, relatively large fiscal deficits. This mobilization of a large share of domestic saving to finance the fiscal deficit raises the inevitable questions of whether private sector activities are crowded out. In the absence of the action by the government, would domestic saving have been the same? And would domestic saving have been invested in higher yielding private sector investments? The response to the first of these two questions depends in part on whether or not private saving rises to accommodate the larger fiscal deficit. That rise could either be a consequence of the so-called Ricardian equivalence, or of the fact that the government may have created a possibility for many individuals to get a good rate of return to their financial saving. In India, for example, the opening of branches of banks in villages may have facilitated financial saving for individuals who might not have saved otherwise. The answer to the second question depends largely on the relative rate of return to private as compared with public investment. Table 3.10 provides some estimates of the fiscal balances of these countries.[50] For many countries the recent levels of fiscal deficits may not be sustainable over the long run. Once again Korea stands apart from the rest for having by far the lowest fiscal deficit and for having succeeded in reducing it over the years.

**Concluding remarks on the Asian countries**
This chapter has dealt with selected aspects of the role of the public sector in nine important market economies of Asia. In recent years, these were, with some exceptions, fairly successful economies when measured against standard criteria such as growth, inflation and so forth. It may thus seem presumptuous especially for an outsider to pass judgement on the actions of their governments. Furthermore, there have been important recent changes in various areas in some of them. For example, several countries have introduced major tax reforms, have begun to liberalize their financial markets, and have begun to privatize their publicly-held industrial enterprises. These changes are particularly desirable because, in spite of their diversity and levels of per capita income, all these countries have dynamic private sectors and significant portions of their workforce are highly skilled and market oriented. The idea that in these countries the government can

*Table 3.10    Fiscal balance (in per cent of GDP)*

| | 1976 | 1977 | 1978 | 1979 | 1980 | 1981 | 1982 | 1983 | 1984 | 1985 | 1986[p] |
|---|---|---|---|---|---|---|---|---|---|---|---|
| Bangladesh | ... | ... | ... | ... | ... | -8.7 | -11.2 | -9.2 | -7.5 | -7.3 | -8.2 |
| India | -4.6 | -4.2 | -5.9 | -6.0 | -6.5 | -5.9 | -7.6 | -7.1 | -8.3 | -10.5 | -9.3 |
| Indonesia | n.a | n.a | n.a | 1.2 | 2.1 | -2.3 | -4.9 | -2.6 | 0.9 | -2.9 | -5.6 |
| Korea | -1.4 | -1.7 | -1.3 | -1.4 | -3.2 | -4.7 | -4.4 | -1.6 | -1.4 | -1.0 | -1.6 |
| Malaysia | -6.8 | -7.1 | -6.2 | -3.2 | -6.2 | -14.9 | -16.9 | -10.6 | -6.6 | -5.9 | -10.9 |
| Pakistan | -9.5 | -8.6 | -8.0 | -8.8 | -6.2 | -5.2 | -5.3 | -7.1 | -6.0 | -7.7 | -7.8 |
| Philippines | -1.7 | -1.8 | -1.2 | -0.1 | -1.3 | -4.0 | -4.3 | -2.0 | -1.8 | -1.9 | -4.7 |
| Sri Lanka | -9.7 | -9.9 | -12.1 | -11.9 | -18.2 | -12.4 | -14.2 | -10.8 | -6.7 | -9.6 | -10.0 |
| Thailand | -3.2 | -3.1 | -3.4 | -3.4 | -4.7 | -3.2 | -5.8 | -4.1 | -3.7 | -5.1 | -4.6 |

Source: IMF, IBRD and national sources. These figures are strictly not comparable across countries as they may refer to more or less comprehensive definitions of government.

p = preliminary

do better than the private sector in providing entrepreneurial talent must be met with scepticism.

In spite of the important changes that have taken place, much remains to be done. At the risk of stating the obvious, I shall list, in general terms, actions that in my judgement the governments of these countries could take to bring their role closer to an optimum.

1.  As in all countries, it is important that governments provide stable laws and institutions. The 'rules of the game' should be clear to all citizens. When these rules are clear, there is less scope for corruption and for their arbitrary application to benefit particular groups or individuals.

2.  As economies develop there is progressively less need for intervention in, and regulations of, economic activities. Excessive intervention increases the cost of doing business and generates parallel or underground markets for such things as goods, credit, imports. Thus, a progressive and orderly dismantling of the many regulations that apply to investments, imports, credits and so forth should take place.

    The governments of these countries have been particularly active in regulating the allocation of credit. For example, government lending reached almost 5 per cent of GDP in Korea in 1981 (before starting to fall), it reached almost 7 per cent of GDP in Malaysia in 1982, and was 2.1 per cent of GDP in Sri Lanka in 1984. Also, through its credit policies, incentive legislation and regulation of investments, the government has played too large a role in determining the area where investment should go, and too large a role in determining the composition of imports and even the users of these imports. Quotas and high tariffs should give way to adjustments in the balance of payments that come from changes in the exchange rate and changes in the macroeconomic policies of the countries. Equally important, government controls on domestic prices should be reduced to the minimum.

3.  Tax systems should be simplified in all of these countries. They should reduce, if not eliminate, the incentives that have been provided to particular investments. Broader bases with lower rates should be the objective.

4.  The various factors that have brought about low returns to investment should be corrected. In particular, a concerted effort should be made to maintain the existing infrastructure in good condition and to utilize fully the existing capital structure. It is not desirable to add to capital while the existing capital is not fully or efficiently utilized. The privatization of public enterprises which are not in areas of natural monopolies should continue. If these changes bring about a lower capital accumulation, but a better use of existing capital, the countries will benefit from the change

since the rapid capital accumulation that has taken place has brought about a rapid accumulation of foreign debt and increasing interest payments.

## General lessons for the current debt strategy
*The current debt strategy*
This chapter has discussed the role of the pubic sector in nine market economies of developing Asia. Although some of these countries ran into financial difficulties in the 1980s, as a group they were relatively successful in pursuing the main objectives of economic policy (growth, low inflation and so forth). However, it was shown that there were considerable costs associated with that success, costs that would become progressively more important with the passing of time in the absence of a change in policies. Using the experience of these countries as a background, I should now like to draw some general lessons for the current debt strategy for developing countries.

That strategy is postulated on the assumption that, in the absence of a political solution, the debt crisis will become more manageable if countries can maintain high investment levels that would promote a high rate of growth; if foreign creditors make this possible by extending additional loans; and if the countries commit themselves to major structural reforms. In this strategy the maintenance of high investment rates seems to acquire a central role. It is recognised that structural reforms take time but, regardless of the speed at which these reforms are (or can be) phased in, it is assumed that a high investment rate must be maintained.

The major gauge of the external debt situation of a country is, perhaps, the ratio of foreign debt to gross domestic product, D/GDP.[51] Success in dealing with the debt crisis must result, hopefully in a declining or, at least, in a constant D/GDP ratio. Such a behaviour of the debt/GDP ratio would be a necessary but not a sufficient condition since the decline in the ratio should be brought about by an increase in the denominator (GDP) rather than just by a fall in the numerator (D). Furthermore a strategy that, in attempting to increase the rate of growth of GDP, increased D by an even larger percentage would not be conducive to a solution of the debt crisis. Yet this is, implicitly, the strategy that is followed when foreign borrowing is maintained while the major economic reforms necessary to increase the efficiency of the economy are postponed or are carried out in a half-hearted manner.

The reforms should aim to achieve at least three inter-related objectives. They should make possible a far better screening of investment projects than has been the case in many countries; a far better utilization of the existing capital stock; and a better allocation of the total resources available to the countries, including labour, capital, land and so forth.

*Investment and growth*

It was argued earlier in this chapter (see pp.40–55) that in many countries there are strong social, political and other kinds of pressures that often bring about a project selection, and thus an allocation of the investment budget, that is far from optimal. The wrong projects are chosen and are built at excessive costs or with the wrong technology. This obviously reduces the rate of return on new capital which may have been obtained through expensive foreign borrowing. It is, thus, imperative that a good international debt strategy must be associated with stringent criteria for project selection and execution. Somehow, and perhaps with the assistance of international institutions, countries should develop mechanisms that would, to the extent possible, insulate investment decisions from the pressures mentioned earlier. These mechanisms should ensure that only projects with expected (and properly measured) rates of return at least equal and hopefully higher than the marginal cost of borrowing are approved.

If a convincing case cannot be made that a project will generate a higher rate of return than the costs of capital, then there would be no reason to carry out the project. The traditional arguments often made to defend unprofitable investments – that they generate unquantifiable social returns in the form of better income distribution, employment, self-sufficiency and so forth – should not be allowed to carry much weight, especially when the investments are financed with borrowed capital that must be serviced and repaid. When public investments are financed by domestic taxes, perhaps an argument could be made on political grounds in favour of taking these social objectives into consideration, especially when more direct and better-targeted redistributive measures are not feasible. In that case some investment would be seen as a substitute for direct redistributive measures.

While the problem of poor project selection is particularly relevant for public investment (including that of public enterprises), it exists also for private investment but for different reasons. The reasons for poor project selection in the private sector, apart from the normal ones – lack of information, incompetence and so forth – are found in tax laws that implicitly subsidize certain kinds of capital accumulation especially in the presence of inflation; in fragmented capital markets that, for some borrowers, may provide credit at lower than market costs; in overvalued exchange rates that may artificially lower the cost of imported machineries and equipment for certain investments; and, finally, in policies, such as import restrictions, that may give *de facto* monopoly status to some activities. Thus, the efficiency of private investment can be increased mainly by structural reforms that bring domestic prices more in line with their true scarcity values. The argument often made – that shifting investment from the public to the private sector will automatically increase the rate of return to investment – while likely to have some validity, in the absence of major changes in the economy is less strong than it is generally believed.

A rigorous process of investment selection that followed the above rule for public investment, if accompanied by reforms that remove the distortions to private investment, might, possibly, reduce the level of net investment in some countries. This reduction should not be cause for concern but, on the contrary, should be welcomed since over the longer run, countries can only gain if they do not have to service a debt that has financed unproductive activities and that has been associated with a negative net present value.

At least since the time when W.W. Rostow wrote his influential book, there has been a prevalent view that a minimum amount of investment is essential for growth.[52] A recent expression of his view is the concept of the 'investment core' used by the World Bank, which purports to indicate the minimum investment level consistent with growth. While few would deny that there is a connection between investment and growth, especially over the longer run, and there is the circumstantial evidence that high-growth countries generally have a high investment rate, in practice the connection between investment and growth is tenuous at best.[53] As Peter T. Bauer has put it: 'it is clear from much and varied evidence that investment spending is not the primary, much less the decisive determinant of economic performance'.[54] An important reason for this is likely to be the inefficient way in which the investment budget is allocated. In conclusion, a reduction in the expenditure for those investments with low rates of return must be seen as good news.

### The utilization of the existing capital stock

Assume that the capital stock of a country has not been properly maintained and is not fully used, and that the allocation of the investment budget is unduly influenced by political and other considerations. Then the country's total output could increase considerably if its capital stock could be used more fully and more productively, even when the investment rate falls. One of the conclusions of this paper with respect to the nine countries analysed has been that the preoccupation with new investment has, in a way, distracted the countries from maintaining in good working condition the infrastructure already in place. Often funds are diverted to the building of new roads while the existing road network was allowed to deteriorate. New vehicles were acquired while many of those already on hand were unutilized because of needed repairs or lack of spare parts. The same is true for hospitals, power plants, schools and other infrastructures. In some countries new power plants were built when the existing ones were working at only a small fraction of their full capacity.

This problem seems to be a universal one as various examples mentioned in the World Bank's *World Development Report* of 1983 indicate. For example, discussing irrigation the WDR states:

> Public and private investments in irrigation in developing countries have increased dramatically over the past 20 years, reaching about $15 billion in 1980. But the returns

are much below their potential: one recent estimate for South and Southeast Asia suggested that an additional 20 million tons of rice, enough to provide the minimum food requirements of 90 million people, could be produced every year with inexpensive improvements in water distributions. (WDR, 1983, p.45)

Discussing roads, the WDR writes:

The worldwide road-building boom of the 1960s and 1970s threatens to become the road-maintenance crisis of the 1980s and 1990s. Over the past ten years, roads in many developing countries have been allowed to deteriorate beyond the point where normal maintenance could be effective...*Funds budgeted for highways have been mostly absorbed in expanding rather than maintaining the network.* (Ibid., italics added)

Still citing that report:

Because of inadequate maintenance budgets, public sector assets are often run down much faster than they would be if routine maintenance were correctly carried out. For example, in Brazil it is estimated that a significant proportion of the federal highway network built in the past ten years already needs major rehabilitation, while in Nigeria most of the roads built in the 1970s had to be rebuilt three to five years later. (Ibid., pp. 45–6)

As mentioned above (pp.40–55) these infrastructures that are allowed to deteriorate at a very rapid pace, and that are often not fully used, were at times largely financed by foreign borrowing.[55] They represent the assets that the countries bought with the foreign debts. As the rate of return on those assets falls below the interest rates that must be paid on the debts, the countries inevitably run into difficulties. Thus, assuming that the rate of interest on the debt cannot be reduced, or that the debts cannot be cancelled, an improvement in the debt situation can only come if, somehow, a larger rate of return can be squeezed out of the existing capital stock. This will be possible if the funds are redirected away from new investment and toward a concerted action to maintain and upgrade the existing capital stock. This rather obvious and innocent-sounding conclusion would require profound changes in the way countries operate, in the way political decisions are made, and in the way the international community looks at categories such as current and capital expenditures. Perhaps for a while the international community should encourage some kind of moratorium (or at least a slowdown) in new projects while reforms are made that would raise the level of efficiency and the use of the stock of capital accumulated with past investments. The moratorium would eventually create bottlenecks which, as Albert Hirschman argued a long time ago, would send the clearest signals of which new investments would be the most productive to make.[56]

*Structural reforms*

Two general lessons came out of our discussion of the nine Asian countries: first, the need to scrutinize much more rigorously than in the past new investment projects and even to look at them with suspicion. If there is any doubt about the high productivity of a new project, it would be wise not to proceed with it; second, the need to consciously insure that the capital stock available is properly maintained and efficiently used. In the previous paragraph the need to shift resources from new projects (capital expenditure) to operation and maintenance (a current expenditure) has been emphasized. In the early part of this chapter (pp. 48–50) it was argued that operation and maintenance expenses often do not have any strong constituencies in the way that capital expenditure has. Thus the proposed shift in emphasis is not likely to happen automatically. It must be pushed by policy-makers who keep the public interest predominantly in mind. In this shift they should be assisted by a change in attitude on the part of the international community. However, that change would be only a part of what is necessary. As Kuznets so eloquently put it two decades ago:

> the effectiveness of a given stock of resources, embodied in physical capital, in increasing total output is partly a matter of its uses in combination with other resources and partly a matter of availability of such other resources and of the organizational arrangements for bringing them together...the very choice of particular forms of physical capital, of quality rather than quantity of capital formation, depends upon the existence of institutions that can assure the most effective flow of savings so that they will reach those foci in the productive economy in which additions to capital stock will yield the greatest contribution to long-run growth. Without such an organization some part of saving may be stagnant and lead to no capital formation...or some may be invested in ways that are far from optimal for economic growth.[57]

This takes us to the issue of structural reforms. Reducing the amount of money wasted on unproductive capital expenditure and maintaining the existing capital stock in good working condition will be important steps in the right direction. However, these steps by themselves are not enough to make an economy achieve its full potential given its total resources (including labour, land and capital). For this it is important that the factors of production move to the uses where they can produce the highest values, measured at world prices. If government policies have introduced obstacles that have prevented resources from going to the most productive uses (and from producing at their full potential) then those policies need to be changed. There are literally thousands of examples available of such distortions but I will mention only one, and not even an extreme one. In one important country with serious external difficulties, a high tax on the production of the crop in which the country had the highest comparative advantage (cotton) progressively induced a shift in the use of the land toward low-yield but untaxed subsistence crops. It should not have been a surprise that the country's exports suffered.

Distortions abound in the use of credit, in the use of foreign exchange, in the use of labour, in the use of land, in the use of capital and so forth. These are introduced by various controls, by taxes and by other government instruments. Structural reform essentially means reducing, if not eliminating, these distortions. Major dividends are likely to be obtained from these reforms but, as the author has argued elsewhere, each distortion is tied to a vested interest. Thus, structural reforms are not likely to come easily and, as the theory of the second-best should have made clear by now, removing piecemeal some of these distortions, while leaving others in place, is no guarantee that much good will come from the change.[58] Thus, the sequencing of structural reforms is an area that requires careful attention.

Because of the theme of this chapter, I have emphasized changes that could be made by the developing countries to help solve, or at least alleviate, the debt problem. This emphasis should not be interpreted as implying that only the developing countries should contribute to the solution of the debt problem. There is much that the industrial countries can do to make that problem manageable. As a minimum they must keep their markets open to the exports of the developing countries; they must keep interest rates low and their economies growing through sensible economic policies; they must continue to provide financial assistance while insuring that it is productively used; they must encourage private creditors to show as much flexibility as possible; and they must continue supporting the functions of those international institutions that are at the forefront of the attempt to find a permanent and widely accepted solution to the debt problem.

## Notes

1.    For basic references to the normative approach see Richard Musgrave, *The Theory of Public Finance*, New York, McGraw-Hill, 1959; and A.B. Atkinson and J.E. Stiglitz, *Lectures on Public Economics*, New York, McGraw-Hill, 1980.
2.    For an earlier attempt by this author to outline a positive theory of public sector behaviour, see Vito Tanzi, 'Toward a positive theory of public sector behavior: An interpretation of some Italian contributions', *FAD Working Paper*, 1980.
3.    Of course, given their diversity, one must be aware of the fact that there was considerable diversity of performance among them.
4.    Unless the objectives conflict with each other. Conflicting objectives may imply a lesser role for the government than non-conflicting objectives. I owe this point to Professor Nicholas Stern.
5.    Many decisions that are correct (or 'rational') on the basis of the information available at the time they are made may prove wrong if the environment changes. Our definition of a policy mistake would not extend to these cases.
6.    For example, a zoning regulation that permits a particular use of land for a given activity but denies the use of that land to other activities is a form of hidden subsidy.
7.    For the limits to public spending, see Vito Tanzi, 'Is there a limit to the size of fiscal deficits in developing countries?' in *Public Finance and Public Debt*, Bernard Herber (ed.), Proceedings of the 40th Congress of the International Institute of Public Finance, Innsbruck, 1984, Detroit, Wayne State University Press, 1986: 139–52; for the limits to taxation, see

Richard Goode, *Government Finance in Developing Countries*, Washington DC, The Brookings Institution, 1984: 95–100.

8.   A more ideological discussion would also emphasize the *political* costs of regulations.

9.   The World Bank's *World Development Report* of 1983 has estimated indices of price distortions for many developing countries, including several from our sample.

10.  It will be noted that, except for the points where intervention is optimal, for each attainable net benefit, say *OR*, there will be two points on the curves at which that net benefit is attained (*D* and *F*). These two points will be consistent with a higher (*F*) or lower (*D*) degree of intervention. As the net *economic* benefits at these two points are the same, one cannot choose between these two levels of intervention on purely economic grounds. The choice between, say, *D* and *F* must be made on political grounds. Those who assign a positive weight to economic freedom would prefer option *D* over option *F*. But the choice would be a political rather than an economic one.

11.  The need for intervention is likely to depend on the efficiency of private markets in achieving given objectives.

12.  In this theoretical discussion, we assume that there is a social welfare function that indicates how the public interest is affected by public sector intervention.

13.  Of course, when the level of intervention is less than the optimal, the welfare provision of the country will also be less than possible.

14.  Of course the fundamental *political* objective of any government is the maintenance of law and order enforced by an honest executive and judiciary.

15.  This statement should not be understood to imply that the Philippines should have increased the level of its public spending regardless of any other consideration. It only means that the economic performance of that country would have improved if it had raised its productive public expenditure by a given amount while financing it by, say, taxes with the lowest distortive effects. The reverse might be true for Malaysia, which could have reduced the lowest priority spending while reducing its use of the most expensive borrowing.

16.  In this connection a more meaningful distinction would be that between real expenditure and transfers.

17.  In some countries developmental expenditure includes some development lending and some current expenditure. Also in some countries, no distinction is made between developmental expenditure and public investment.

18.  See Mario Blejer and Mohsin Khan, 'Private investment in developing countries', *Finance and Development*, June 1984, for the relationship between the level of investment and growth. See also Simon Kuznets, *Toward a Theory of Economic Growth*, New York, Norton and Company Inc., 1968. The issue of the relationship between investment and growth is taken up below.

19.  For a review of the normative theory of public sector intervention, see Musgrave, 1959, op. cit., or Atkinson and Stiglitz, 1980, op. cit. Basically, this theory would justify government investment in public goods or in activities with important externalities.

20.  One would expect that the higher the cost of financing, the lower the level of investment, and the more biased the investment budget would be toward projects with a shorter-time horizon.

21.  See Mahmood Ali Ayub and Sven Olaf Hegstad, *Public Industrial Enterprises, Determinants of Performance*, Washington, The World Bank, 1986, Annex I: 56 – 60.

22.  In some cases these investments were justified on the basis of *social* cost–benefit analysis that assigned heavy weights to the creation of employment or the redistribution of income.

23.  On the role of public enterprises in developing countries see Robert H. Floyd, Clive S. Gray, and R.P. Short, *Public Enterprise in Mixed Economies*, Washington, DC, IMF, 1984. One could argue that the social, as distinguished from the financial, rates of return may not have been as low since these enterprises were often required to engage in activities aimed at achieving other objectives (such as employment, income redistribution etc.).

24.  Please note that the estimates of the rate of return to public enterprises reported in this section are not strictly comparable.

25.  Ayub and Hegstad, op. cit., p. 15.

26.  See Ayub and Hegstad, op. cit., pp. 12–13.

27. For a discussion of the relative efficiency of public and private enterprises, see Bela Balassa, '*Public enterprise in developing countries: issues of privatization*', *DRD Discussion Paper*, World Bank, May 1987: 9–14; and Ayub and Hegstad, op. cit., pp. 12–17. Both of these studies suggest that public enterprises have been less efficient than private enterprises.

28. Even in this case prudence is required. Since the capital market is not perfect, to avoid financial difficulties, the country must pay attention to the time profile of the expected returns to the investment and to the time profile of the expected future payments.

29. At times the borrowing was done by the central government and the resources were transferred to the enterprises as loans or grants. In other cases the government guaranteed the loans.

30. This comparison minimizes the problem since the rates of return to enterprises were distorted by inflation more than the average costs of foreign borrowing.

31. Some of this increase was accounted for by the fall in commodity prices and some by changes in the real exchange rates. On the other hand, interest rates generally fell over the period shown by Table 3.4.

32. An argument can be made that the financial returns from infrastructure projects take a long time to materialize. The trouble with this is that the time may just be too long and the benefits to the present must be discounted at high rates.

33. Total public debt – that is, external plus domestic public sector debt – has been rising rapidly in some of these countries (India, Malaysia, Pakistan, Sri Lanka, Thailand) and it has reached very high levels in a few of them.

34. This is a rather general problem in developing countries. There are too many examples of hospitals or schools that have been built but that have remained unutilized for long periods because of lack of resources for operation and maintenance. And there are examples of new roads being built while old roads are not properly maintained. Furthermore, often additional capacity was being built while existing capacity was not being fully utilized. In many cases such infrastructure was built with borrowed external funds.

35. Countries have been generally praised when a larger share of their budget is allocated to 'capital' rather than to 'current' expenditure.

36. These openings are in all countries often accompanied by well-advertised public ceremonies which bring political benefits to those involved. On the other hand, the routine repairing of roads and the provision of basic materials that make hospitals or schools function adequately rarely attract any attention.

37. In these cases, the contracting firms (domestic or foreign) are likely to simply inflate the costs of the projects.

38. Often plants are not fully utilized because no provision has been made for inevitable breakdowns. Vehicles remain idle because of lack of spare parts; hospitals remain closed because money for nurses or medicines is not available and so on. These are general problems in developing countries but they exist in most countries.

39. All this means that the investment figures overstate net investment since depreciation is very high.

40. See Peter S. Heller and Joan E. Aghevli, 'The recurrent cost problem: an international overview', in *Recurrent Costs and Agricultural Development*, John Howell, (ed.) London, Overseas Development Institute, 1985: 2249.

41. Unlike equity, debt financing comes associated with a future servicing that is not reduced by the poor performance of the investment for which the capital was used.

42. The sources of Table 3.7 are different from those for Tables 3.5 and 3.6.

43. The buoyancy is the ratio of the actual percentage change in tax revenue to the percentage change in GDP. This ratio reflects the automatic response of revenue to changes in GDP as well as changes due to discretionary actions by the government.

44. The elasticity would measure the responsiveness of tax revenue to changes in GDP in the absence of discretionary (policy) changes.

45. The net flow of resources is the difference between foreign borrowing and interest payment and amortization of foreign debt.

46. In other words, either government spending or private spending must go down.

47. See Nils J. Agell, 'Subsidy to capital through tax incentives in the Asian countries', mimeo, 1982: 32.

48.   See, for example, Eugenio Namor, 'Issues in the targeting of good subsidies for the poor: a survey of the literature', *IMF Working Paper* 87/75, 28 October 1987.

49.   In some of these countries total debt (domestic plus foreign) has reached very high levels.

50.   Again, these data are not strictly comparable since they may refer to different definitions of the public sector or of the fiscal deficit. They should be used only to observe trends over time.

51.   A close competitor would be the debt–service ratio.

52.   W.W. Rostow, *The Stages of Economic Growth*, Cambridge, Cambridge University Press, 1960.

53.   For a good discussion of the relationship between growth and investment, see Dennis Anderson, 'Economic growth and the returns to investment', *World Bank Discussion Papers* 12 June 1987. See also Simon Kuznets, *Toward a Theory of Economic Growth*, New York, W.W. Norton and Company, Inc., 1965.

54.   Peter T. Bauer, *Reality and Rhetoric: Studies in the Economics of Development*, Cambridge, MA, Harvard University Press, 1981.

55.   As the WDR stated 'use of plants and equipment is often extremely low, sometimes only a quarter or a third of the rates achieved by the best maintenance organizations... The lack of spare parts and fuel is often to blame for poor plan utilization' (ibid., p. 45).

56.   See Albert O. Hirschman, *The Strategy of Economic Development*, New Haven, Yale University Press, 1958. See especially Chapters 4 and 5.

57.   Kuznets, op. cit., pp. 37–8.

58.   See Vito Tanzi, 'Fiscal policy, growth, and design of stabilization programs', in *External Debt, Savings, and Growth in Latin America*, Ana Maria Mortirena-Mantel (ed.), International Monetary Fund and Istituto Torcuato di Tella, 1987.

Table 3.A-1  Foreign debt (in millions of $US)

| | 1975 | 1976 | 1977 | 1978 | 1979 | 1980 | 1981 | 1982 | 1983 | 1984 | 1985 | 1986 |
|---|---|---|---|---|---|---|---|---|---|---|---|---|
| Bangladesh | 1,611 | 1,938 | 2,294 | 2,767 | 2,955 | 3,733 | 4,490 | 5,070 | 5,099 | 5,844 | 6,497 | 7,538 |
| India | 12,345 | 13,412 | 14,789 | 15,620 | 15,948 | 17,670 | 19,328 | 20,970 | 23,049 | 24,875 | 28,507 | 31,292 |
| Indonesia | 10,363 | 12,626 | 14,940 | 15,729 | 16,568 | 18,241 | 20,452 | 25,854 | 30,070 | 31,621 | 37,316 | 42,028 |
| Korea | 6,030 | 9,544 | 13,372 | 15,442 | 20,271 | 26,632 | 29,274 | 35,901 | 38,923 | 40,619 | 45,747 | 42,905 |
| Malaysia | 1,948 | 2,710 | 3,349 | 3,762 | 4,716 | 5,730 | 8,250 | 11,899 | 16,279 | 17,754 | 19,150 | 20,565 |
| Pakistan | 5,900 | 6,875 | 7,483 | 8,436 | 9,097 | 9,943 | 10,924 | 11,334 | 12,485 | 12,731 | 12,837 | 14,758 |
| Philippines | 3,411 | 4,618 | 5,888 | 10,969 | 13,419 | 17,533 | 21,130 | 24,751 | 24,237 | 24,574 | 25,137 | 23,041 |
| Sri Lanka | 602 | 701 | 796 | 1,046 | 1,143 | 1,569 | 1,899 | 2,300 | 2,641 | 2,808 | 2,953 | 3,746 |
| Thailand | 1,696 | 2,419 | 3,393 | 4,871 | 6,681 | 8,193 | 10,358 | 11,548 | 12,937 | 14,812 | 16,364 | 17,114 |
| Total | 43,906 | 55,843 | 66,304 | 78,642 | 88,798 | 109,244 | 126,105 | 149,627 | 165,720 | 175,638 | 194,508 | 202,987 |

Source: Various IMF IBRD and national sources.

Table 3.A-2  Interest payments on foreign debt (in millions $US)

| | 1975 | 1976 | 1977 | 1978 | 1979 | 1980 | 1981 | 1982 | 1983 | 1984 | 1985 | 1986 |
|---|---|---|---|---|---|---|---|---|---|---|---|---|
| Bangladesh | 35 | 46 | 57 | 61 | 69 | 72 | 96 | 120 | 119 | 121 | 138 | 138 |
| India | 299 | 345 | 412 | 461 | 487 | 497 | 450 | 609 | 904 | 909 | 778 | 799 |
| Indonesia | 460 | 691 | 814 | 787 | 1,164 | 1,332 | 1,671 | 1,918 | 1,979 | 2,493 | 2,558 | 2,904 |
| Korea | 225 | 339 | 552 | 931 | 1,154 | 2,609 | 3,536 | 3,632 | 3,067 | 3,688 | 3,546 | 3,589 |
| Malaysia | 81 | 180 | 204 | 238 | 304 | 406 | 641 | 808 | 1,104 | 1,218 | 1,329 | 1,465 |
| Pakistan | 115 | 138 | 197 | 262 | 285 | 329 | 362 | 421 | 584 | 528 | 592 | 661 |
| Philippines | 104 | 158 | 257 | 440 | 626 | 975 | 1,374 | 1,850 | 1,789 | 2,238 | 1,982 | 1,933 |
| Sri Lanka | 29 | 32 | 35 | 42 | 48 | 58 | 121 | 128 | 162 | 149 | 171 | 175 |
| Thailand | 93 | 106 | 137 | 307 | 551 | 680 | 987 | 1,006 | 952 | 1,108 | 1,152 | 1,286 |
| Total | 1,441 | 2,035 | 2,665 | 3,529 | 4,688 | 6,958 | 9,238 | 10,492 | 10,660 | 12,452 | 12,246 | 12,950 |

Source: As Table 3.A-1.

*Table 3.A–3  Effective interest rate[1]*

| | 1975 | 1976 | 1977 | 1978 | 1979 | 1980 | 1981 | 1982 | 1983 | 1984 | 1985 | 1986 |
|---|---|---|---|---|---|---|---|---|---|---|---|---|
| Bangladesh | 2.2 | 2.4 | 2.5 | 2.2 | 2.3 | 1.9 | 2.1 | 2.4 | 2.3 | 2.1 | 2.1 | 1.8 |
| India | 2.4 | 2.6 | 2.8 | 3.0 | 3.1 | 2.8 | 2.3 | 2.9 | 3.9 | 3.7 | 2.7 | 2.6 |
| Indonesia | 4.4 | 5.5 | 5.4 | 5.0 | 7.0 | 7.3 | 8.2 | 7.4 | 6.6 | 7.9 | 6.9 | 6.9 |
| Korea | 3.7 | 3.6 | 4.1 | 6.0 | 5.7 | 9.8 | 12.1 | 10.1 | 7.9 | 9.1 | 7.8 | 8.4 |
| Malaysia | 4.2 | 6.6 | 6.1 | 6.3 | 6.4 | 7.1 | 7.8 | 6.8 | 6.8 | 6.9 | 6.9 | 7.1 |
| Pakistan | 2.1 | 2.2 | 2.6 | 3.1 | 3.1 | 3.3 | 3.3 | 3.7 | 4.7 | 4.1 | 4.6 | 4.5 |
| Philippines | 3.0 | 3.4 | 4.4 | 4.0 | 4.7 | 5.6 | 6.5 | 7.5 | 7.4 | 9.1 | 7.9 | 8.4 |
| Sri Lanka | 4.8 | 4.6 | 4.4 | 4.0 | 4.2 | 3.7 | 6.4 | 5.6 | 6.1 | 5.3 | 5.8 | 4.7 |
| Thailand | 5.5 | 4.4 | 4.0 | 6.3 | 8.2 | 8.3 | 9.5 | 8.7 | 7.4 | 7.5 | 7.0 | 7.5 |
| Total | 3.3 | 3.7 | 4.0 | 4.5 | 5.3 | 6.4 | 7.3 | 7.0 | 6.4 | 7.1 | 6.3 | 6.4 |

Source: As Tables 3.A–1 and 3.A–2.

1. Effective interest rate defined as interest payment/total debt.

# PART 2

# STABILIZATION AND GROWTH

# 4. Fiscal disequilibrium in developing countries: from cyclical instrument to structural problem

## Concept of fiscal disequilibrium

Of all the instruments available to the governments of the developing countries in the pursuit of their economic and social objectives, fiscal policy had until recent years been considered as one of the most, if not the most, important. Fiscal policy, alone or with the help of other policy instruments, can promote social and economic objectives in a variety of ways. It can, for example:

(i)   increase the rate of saving of a country;
(ii)  channel savings into socially productive uses;
(iii) increase what has been called productive consumption (that is, education and health);
(iv)  discourage non-productive and extravagant consumption and investment (such as expensive cars, and luxury housing);
(v)   remove inefficiency throughout the economy by eliminating or reducing the distortions in the relative prices of the factors of productions; and
(vi)  maintain a climate of economic stability by the judicious use of fiscal disequilibrium.

In this chapter I shall concentrate on the last of these objectives. In other words, I shall discuss the feasibility of using fiscal disequilibrium as the 'balancing factor' in the economy as advocated by Keynes and his followers. The discussion will, however, focus on developing countries. I shall begin by addressing the question of the precise meaning of fiscal disequilibrium. (See also Tanzi, 1982.) Although all prices are relevant to the determination of a true equilibrium in an economy, some prices are far more important than others. These prices are the exchange rate, the rate of interest, the wage rate, the prices of a few key commodities (such as fuel) and, finally, the implicit price for the activity of the public sector. When the normal revenue of the public sector covers the total public sector expenditure, it can be said that the price of the public sector activity is, in a macro sense, an equilibrium one. A gap between revenue and expenditure brings about a fiscal disequilibrium.

When considering the issue of the gap between expenditure and revenue, there are various questions that must be considered:

1.   First is the question of whether the existing gap is the result of policies aimed explicitly at bringing it about, or whether it is the result of forces beyond the control of the policy-makers. Is the gap planned and welcome; or is it accidental and unwanted? Only in the first case can the fiscal gap be defined as a policy instrument. It would be hard in today's world to find too many countries where the existing fiscal disequilibrium can be said to be precisely equal to the level desired by the policy-makers. In most cases it can be assumed that, given the choice, the policy-makers would wish to have a lower deficit.

2.   A second question that has received little attention relates to the proper time horizon over which the fiscal gap should be defined or measured. This horizon could extend from a period as short as a day to one as long as eternity. As taxes and expenditures are not collected or disbursed smoothly over time, it would be unrealistic to expect that fiscal disequilibrium could be continually maintained. As budgets normally refer to 12-month periods, the year is often taken as the proper unit of measurement. There are cases where a longer time horizon might be appropriate. For example, a country that could determine the size of its fiscal balance over the longer run, and that experienced business or commodity cycles might, under appropriate circumstances, gain by running surpluses during booms and deficits during recessions, just as recommended by Keynesian economics. In such case the budget would be balanced over the cycle and not annually. A country that discovered sizable mineral deposits that a few years down the road would substantially increase its national income might be justified in running a fiscal deficit during the early years in order to raise private consumption to the permanent level justified by the country's new wealth (Buiter, 1983).

3.   A third question concerns the need to remove the transitory elements from the fiscal balance before the appropriateness of its fiscal policy can be assessed. The issue here is similar to one that received some attention in the United States in the 1960s. At that time economists became aware of the fact that the business cycle is both affected by, but also affects, tax revenue and public expenditure. Therefore, part of a deficit may be cycle-induced, or is endogenous in the technical parlance. It was thus argued that one should neutralize the effect of the cycle on the deficit in order to have a better measure of the tightness of the fiscal policy being pursued. Thus, the idea of the full-employment budget surplus (FEBS) was developed. The FEBS aimed at measuring the size of the deficit under the assumption of full employment.

For a developing country the same issue arises but in a much more complex way. Here, one important factor in determining the fiscal balance is the value of key exports; and this is largely determined by the level of economic activity in the rest of the world rather than by domestic activity. The reason is that the level of tax revenue is often, directly or indirectly, closely linked to the value of exports. Several other factors may also bring the level of revenue and expenditure, and that of the fiscal balance, away from its trend. They may thus obscure that trend. For example, the domestic price level may have fluctuated dramatically, affecting tax revenue; the exchange rate may have been devalued thus again affecting revenue; the country may have introduced temporary taxes (say, on exports) which will soon expire; wage adjustments may have been pushed into the following year and unusually large capital projects may have been initiated or terminated. All of these factors may bring about a fiscal balance for the current year that may bear little relation with what could be called the 'core' or the trend deficit; and, if one judges that fiscal policy on the basis of the current balance, the underlying or core disequilibrium may be missed.

Consider, for example, Figure 4.1 which measures the fiscal deficit (as a percentage of GDP) on the vertical axis and time on the horizontal axis. Suppose that under normal circumstances the (core) deficit for two countries A and B would have been the same and equal to OD. However, assume that temporary factors have sharply increased the revenue of A (and/or sharply decreased its expenditure) thus reducing its deficit, for the particular year, $t_o$, to $D_A$. Assume

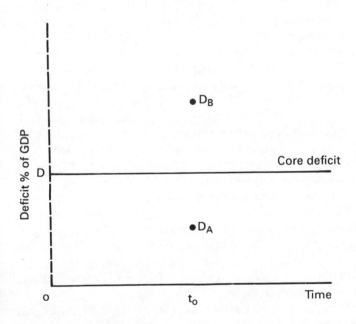

*Figure 4.1*

that the reverse has happened to B so that its deficit has risen to $D_B$. A casual observer would conclude that the fiscal situation in A is far better than in B and could, perhaps, recommend very different policies for the two countries when, in fact, over the medium run, there could be little difference in the seriousness of their fiscal disequilibrium so that similar policies would be justified.

In conclusion, it is essential to remove the transitory elements from the fiscal balance in order to assess the underlying core deficit (or surplus) and to propose correct stabilizing measures. The assessment of the fiscal situation of a country should not be based exclusively on the revenue and expenditure of that year as this may lead to serious policy mistakes. A budget that is kept in balance by unusual circumstances or actions (such as temporary taxes, postponement of inevitable wage increases, building up of arrears and so on) could not be said to reflect an equilibrium situation.

Another difficulty with the concept of fiscal balance or fiscal equilibrium has to do with the fact that the public sector is not represented by a monolithic entity with one budget and one decision-making centre. Rather, the public sector is fragmented, composed of parts such as the central government, the local governments, the social security institutions, nationalized public enterprises, marketing boards, special funds, the central bank. This fragmentation raises the question of whether revenue and expenditure should be equal in a macro or overall sense, or whether each important part of the government should be in equilibrium. If capital markets (domestic and international) were perfect, and the budgetary process worked optimally, then perhaps only broad equality would matter. In this particular case, deficits in any one part of the government could be covered by surpluses in other parts, so that the overall picture would be the relevant one. Unfortunately, in most countries the capital markets are far from perfect and the budgetary process is not well-functioning. Therefore, a surplus that originated in one part of the public sector would not automatically find its way to the part where there is a deficit. As a result, there could be serious distortions within the economy. To take an extreme example, suppose that the surpluses of the local governments are not automatically made available to the central government due to limitations in capital markets or to political decisions; suppose that the central government deficit is financed by net borrowing from the central bank. In such a situation, monetary disequilibrium could exist even in the presence of an overall balance in the fiscal sector. Of greater significance is the fact that the part of the government that has the capacity to develop a surplus might have an incentive to spend that surplus in relatively unproductive activities rather than make it available to the other parts. A common example of this occurs when profit-generating public enterprises over-invest or pay higher salaries rather than transfer the profits to the central government.

It is possible for a government to show overall budgetary equilibrium (even within each of its parts) but, nevertheless, to have allocated public expenditure in such an inefficient way that marginal social cost could be very different from marginal social benefit for each line of activity. This consideration is, of course, important also on the revenue side, whereby if taxes are inefficiently raised, the cost of the last dollar raised from each group or each activity could be, at the margin, very different from that raised from other groups or other activities. Over the long run a dynamically efficient economy would require that all resources, both private and public, be efficiently utilized. Therefore, although allocative equilibrium may seem inconsequential for short-run stabilization, it is clearly essential for long-run performance.

Just as allocative considerations cannot be totally ignored in a discussion of fiscal equilibrium, the same is true for distributional considerations. The promotion of an equitable income distribution is one of the fundamental objectives of public policy. Therefore, no true equilibrium will be possible over the long run if there is a widespread perception that the incidence of taxes and of public expenditure does not conform with prevalent social norms.

## Fiscal disequilibrium as a policy instrument for short-run stabilization

The idea that fiscal disequilibrium can be the balancing factor that would maintain the level of economic activity on a steady path was first advanced by Keynes in his seminal work during the Great Depression. Keynes theorized that, for a variety of reasons, private investment would be inherently unstable in a market economy. Fluctuations in capital spending would be magnified by a multiplier process and would affect the behaviour of the whole economy. If the government had the knowledge and the policy tools to neutralize the fluctuations in private investment through its own action – say, by increasing its own spending or cutting taxes when private investment fell – then it could truly be the 'balancing factor' in the economy. Of course Keynes was concerned with mature industrial economies rather than with developing countries. Our interest here is with the latter.

Various conditions must exist if this stabilizing role on the part of fiscal policy has a chance of being successful. Some of these have received attention in the literature; others have been largely ignored. By and large there is not an extensive literature that has focused on fiscal policy as a tool of short-run stabilization in developing countries. Our discussion will conclude that the pursuit of a counter-cyclical fiscal policy is never easy and is particularly difficult in open developing countries. It has been made even more difficult by the structural disequilibrium that now characterizes so many countries. In the following comments I shall pay particular attention to those aspects that have been largely ignored in previous discussions.

*Underlying theory of inflation.* A short-run stabilization policy of the Keynesian type was based on a specific notion of how the price level and the level of economic activity interact. An economy that is in recession is not supposed to have inflation; thus, fiscal policy can stimulate aggregate demand (through a deficit) without leading to inflation. But, as even the most casual observer of the developing world (and in recent years even that of the developed one) would soon realize, low levels of economic activity often co-exist with high rates of inflation.[1] Attempts at stimulating output can be defeated by accelerating inflation.

*Method of financing of deficit.*   Traditional Keynesian economics was not too concerned with whether the fiscal deficit is financed by monetary expansion or by borrowing. For sure, it ignored the possibility that, when a country decides to borrow, it might go abroad. In Keynesian economics monetary expansion becomes inflationary only *after* full employment is reached. Up to that point a change in the money supply would bring about a change in output without necessarily upsetting the overall relationship between money and output. The problem with this analysis, when it is applied to developing countries, is that as the 'pump is being primed' bottlenecks develop. These may be related to the availability of energy, to the transportation system, to some basic commodity or simply to foreign exchange. There are many examples of countries where monetary expansion to finance a deficit led to serious falls in economic activity when foreign exchange became so scarce that it sharply reduced the importation of basic raw materials and intermediate inputs. The monetary approach to the balance of payments has emphasized the connection between excessive money creation (to finance a deficit) and deterioration in the balance of payments.

   The alternative of financing a significant fiscal deficit through the domestic sale of government bonds to the private sector is greatly limited by both the size of the domestic financial markets and the interest rate policies pursued by many developing countries. Given the size of the domestic financial market, the higher is the interest rate that the government is willing to pay on its bonds, the larger is the size of the deficit that it could finance domestically. But even under the best circumstances, this would be a limited amount. This amount becomes even smaller when interest rates are kept artificially low and even negative in real terms. Furthermore, if the rate of inflation is already high – part of the deficit may be financed by monetary expansion – and interest rates are kept positive in real terms, the share of public expenditure that would need to be allocated to the financing of the deficit would grow rapidly. In this case the interest payments that the government makes are to a varying extent (that depends on the rate of inflation) amortization of the public debt.[2] In other words the government finds itself forced to raise funds not only for the payment of the genuine interest but also for the repayment of the principal itself. As this leads to an increase on the expenditure side of the budget, the fiscal deficit, as conventionally measured, is likely to widen. The deficit comes to feed upon itself leading to greater monetary expansion.

There is a further element, and one that has not received the attention it deserves, that contributes to and often accelerates the process of fiscal deterioration connected with the use of inflationary finance. This element is related to the impact of inflation on the revenue side of the budget. As public sector revenues in many developing countries are very much dependent on

(i) taxes that are specific (not *ad valorem*);
(ii) taxes that depend on customs valuations that do not keep up with inflation, perhaps because of the failure of the exchange rate to adjust to the rate of inflation;
(iii) taxes that are collected with considerable lags; and
(iv) revenue for public enterprises that tend to fall as the prices for their services are not fully and automatically adjusted in line with the rate of inflation

a policy of monetary expansion often reduces the ratio of public sector gains (in terms of control over resources) from monetary expansion (see Chapter 7).

When all the above is taken into account, the considerable advantages to the policy-makers associated with foreign financing of the public sector deficit appear obvious. First, foreign borrowing, by making foreign exchange available, increases the total resources available to the country. Thus, the fiscal deficit is not associated with a necessary and often painful redistribution of a cake whose size has not changed. As foreign borrowing increases the size of the cake, nobody needs to suffer in the short run. Second, the interest rate policy of the government is not constrained by the need to sell bonds domestically. A policy of 'financial repression', often associated with highly negative interest rates, can be pursued, often in the alleged pursuit of 'economic development'. The foreign financing of the fiscal deficit frees the government from having to pursue an interest rate policy with realistic (that is, competitive and positive) rates. Third, as the distinction between interest payment and repayment of principal is, for foreign debt, much sharper than the same distinction for domestic debt (when there is inflation), the apparent fiscal deficit as conventionally measured (with interest payments above the line and amortization below the line) will appear smaller and thus more attractive.

*Determination of full employment level of output.* Fiscal policy for stabilization presupposes that the policy-makers can determine the full employment level of output (that is, the potential output) in order to determine the right dose of fiscal stimulus needed to move the economy close to that output level. An implicit assumption of traditional stabilization policy was that there were no supply bottlenecks up to the full employment level; at that point all the bottlenecks became operational at the same time. Furthermore, it was assumed that the policy-makers knew exactly when that point was reached.

Obviously, both of these assumptions are highly unrealistic for developing countries. First, on the way toward full employment, various constraints will become operational at different times thus strangling the growth of output and raising prices. Second, in these economies the concepts of capacity utilization and of full employment just do not have the same meaning as they might have in advanced industrial countries. The distinction between unemployment and underemployment is vague and the productive capacity of the unorganized sector cannot be determined. Therefore, policy-makers would have a hard time to determine the precise level of fiscal stimulus that would be necessary to bring the economy toward full employment. The fact that output and the rate of inflation may move in opposite directions raises the fundamental dilemma of whether stabilization policy should aim at price stability or full employment.

*Ability to make reliable forecast.*   Another requirement for an effective stabilizing fiscal policy is the availability of good forecasting. If the government is to play a stabilizing role in the economy, it must be able to anticipate the behaviour of the economy in the absence of policy changes. This is necessary because in most cases there is a substantial delay between the time when the government realizes the need to stabilize the economy and time when the effect of policy changes is felt by the economy. In developing countries the problem of good forecasting may be much more difficult than in large industrial countries mainly because the fluctuations in the economy are either weather-determined, and thus totally unpredictable, or foreign-determined, and thus difficult to predict. For example, for a country producing coffee, a frost in Brazil may be the determining destabilizing factor. The more difficult it is to make good forecast, the less likely it will be that counter-cyclical stabilizing fiscal policy will be successful.

*Control over fiscal instruments.*   Up to this point it has been argued that for fiscal policy to be successful as a policy tool for stabilization, it is necessary that the government anticipate the magnitude of the destabilizing forces as well as their timing. If the government can do that, the problem that remains to be solved is: what changes in the fiscal instruments will be necessary in order to bring about the necessary stabilizing changes in the level of aggregate demand? This question has received little attention in the literature but is fundamental to the pursuit of a successful fiscal policy for stabilization. It relates to the degree of control that the government has over the country's fiscal instruments. The basic point to be emphasized is that government control over some of the effective fiscal instruments in only indirect. What the government can hope to control directly are the statutory instruments as reflected by the various laws and regulations. If a given change in the statutory instrument (for example, in the legal rate of a given tax) always resulted in a given change in the effective tax rate (that is, in the revenue from that tax) fiscal policy would be far simpler. Unfortunately, this is not the case. Fiscal instruments are often similar to rifles without aims. The hunter can never be sure of where the bullet will hit.

Assume, for example, that on the basis of its forecast of economic conditions the government wishes to raise revenue by $x million over a quarter starting six months hence. Then the basic decisions to be made are which taxes should be changed and by how much should the statutory rates be changed so as to bring about the desired change in revenue, equal to $x million? If, as it is often assumed in macroeconomic textbooks, there were only one tax and this tax were paid without lags and without evasion, and the relationship between the change in the (legal) rate and the change in tax revenue had been established by econometric analysis or by previous experience, then the problem discussed here would be trivial. But this is not the case.

In most developing countries the tax system is characterized by a large number of taxes and rates. Unlike large industrial countries that can depend on two to three tax rates for an overwhelming share of their total revenues, developing countries' tax systems are very disperse and fragmented, depending on many measures and many rates. The technical problem of deciding which rates and which taxes to change is much more complex and the probability of error much greater. Once the technical decisions have been made, the legislative process has to be dealt with. Inevitably some of the technical decisions will be changed and again the determination of the effects of those changes on revenue will be more difficult than in industrial countries. Furthermore, the fragmentation of the public sector in various semi-autonomous entities as well as legal constraints (such as tax incentive legislation, earmarking) will reduce the scope even for legal actions. Finally, the net revenue effect of the legal change can only be assessed with a wide margin of error due to varying rates of evasion as well as varying collection lags.[3]

*Ability to reverse fiscal actions.* Short-run fiscal policy requires that certain instruments such as taxes and public expenditure at times are raised and at other times are reduced. The problem is that, for political reasons, it is often very difficult to reverse these actions. For example, taxes can be far more easily reduced than raised. The reverse is true for subsidies. In many cases legal commitments may limit or even eliminate the possibility of reversal of fiscal action. For example, a government may have committed itself not to tax some corporations for a given number of years. Or it may have promised pensions or subsidies to some groups. Or it may have committed itself to a certain price support or a given indexation scheme. In many cases stabilization policy would have to be carried out around a structural (long-run) fiscal disequilibrium which in itself is an indication that the government has lost full control over its fiscal instruments and which prevents the use of short-term stabilization policy. The net result is that stabilization policy is pursued either by simply postponing some payments (by building up arrears or by delaying inevitable wage increases) or by cutting down on capital spending.

*Absence of balance of payment constraint.* Traditional fiscal policy for stabilization paid little attention to the balance of payments constraint. However, because of the openness of the economy of most developing countries and because of the fact that fluctuations in the domestic economy inevitably spill over into the balance of payments, this constraint cannot be ignored. No policy of fiscal expansion can succeed if foreign exchange becomes unavailable; and foreign exchange will become scarcer whenever fiscal policy becomes expansionary. A sensible fiscal policy would be one that builds up foreign assets during good periods so that they can be run down during bad periods. In general, a country undergoing an export boom should sterilize at least part of that effect by building up foreign reserves (or by reducing its foreign debt) so that the level of imports and thus domestic activity can be maintained during periods of recession by running down the accumulated reserves (or increasing temporarily the foreign debt if that is possible). Under this policy the level of public expenditure would be set in relation to some long-term trend so that it would not be affected by fluctuations in national income (see Chapter 5). Taxes, on the other hand, would be associated with the current level of national income thus rising during the boom and falling during the recession. The surplus in the boom would be associated with the improvement in the foreign position of the country, while the deficit in the recession would be associated with a deterioration in the foreign position. But the surpluses and deficits would need to cancel each other out over time. This stabilization policy cannot be pursued along a deteriorating trend.

### Fiscal disequilibrium over the long run
The question of whether fiscal policy for stabilization should be pursued in less developed countries (LDCs) has become academic for many of them, as long-run structural disequilibrium has become endemic. To some extent, this structural disequilibrium is the inevitable result of specific policies that became fashionable in recent decades. Many of these could be explained in terms of the role that the Keynesian revolution and other theories which prevailed throughout the 1950s and 1960s gave to the government as well as in terms of objective factors. Some of the major tenets of the prevalent thinking can be summarized briefly. (See also Chapter 2.)

First and foremost was the evidence that became available in the late 1950s that incomes in many of these countries were only a small fraction of those of the advanced industrial countries. In a way, the statistical revolution of the late 1940s and 1950s brought about, in stark contrast, the difference between the wealth of the advanced countries and the poverty of the poor countries. This evidence provided the background for the popularity of some economic theories about the role that capital accumulation can play in economic development. Theories associated with the names of Harrod and Domar provided the impetus for policies that would be directed to capital accumulation and that would rapidly increase the per capita incomes of the developing countries. As the private sector was not supposed to be able to generate much saving for capital accumulation, it was left to the public sector to encourage activities that would accelerate economic growth. The role of the government was also promoted by two additional considerations. The first was the evidence that income distribution within these countries was at least as uneven as the income distribution across countries. The evidence that the per capita income of the richest 1 per cent of the population was often as high as 50 times that of the poorest 10 per cent gave impetus to policies that would try to redress the balance. Second, theoretical evidence about market failure provided further justification for governmental intervention.

The governments were urged to raise taxes while keeping current expenditure down, in order to bring about a higher rate of capital accumulation. However, because of their concern for income distribution and for employment, it was often difficult to hold down current expenditure. In some of these countries concern for capital accumulation, at the same time as the general tax burden was increasing, induced many countries to provide generous incentives to private investors; and concern about the low consumption of some groups induced them to enlarge the scope of subsidies. The net result was that in many countries public expenditure for both current and capital increased much faster than current revenue, thus creating a long-run fiscal disequilibrium that, depending on the countries, was either covered through money creation or through foreign borrowing. As discussed above, the scope for domestic non-inflationary financing of the deficit was generally limited.

The role of subsidies must be singled out for its importance as a major determinant of fiscal deterioration. Perhaps too much attention has been directed toward the subsidies given directly to consumers, mainly because these subsidies are most evident and can immediately be identified through the budget. However, although these particular subsidies have been important, there are others that are as important, but these are more difficult to quantify, as they are often indirect and not visible. These other subsidies may come in the form of concessionary credit, quantitative restrictions to imports, provision of foreign exchange at the official exchange rate, tax incentives, or exoneration from import duties. Of course, these 'subsidies' can be negative when they are associated with price controls, as is often the case with agricultural prices.

Intervention by the public sector in the economy has not come exclusively through taxation and expenditure, but it has come, to a large extent, through various regulations of economic activities and through various restrictions. It is one of the vicious circles of economic development that, by and large, underdevelopment increases the need for public sector intervention while at the same time it reduces the government's ability to intervene efficiently. Therefore, there is always the danger that intervention will do more damage than good (see Chapter 3). Fiscal disequilibrium is one of the indications of this possibility. The attempt to improve economic conditions has created a widening gap between revenues and expenditures and this gap has brought with it so many problems that it is fair to ask whether the economy would not have been better off if a more modest role for fiscal policy had been retained.

Perhaps as a conclusion to this chapter a few basic guidelines could be stated for the use of long-run fiscal policy:

(i)    avoid over-regulating the economy;

(ii)   try to make explicit all the subsidies that are given;

(iii)  limit the size of the public sector to the level where it can be efficient;

(iv)   do not replace market distortions with public sector distortions;

(v)    by and large do not make expenditure commitments which cannot be financed out of current resources;

(vi)   avoid inflationary finance at all costs, because over the longer run the benefits from it are just not worth all the costs that it will generate. In relation to this, try to balance the budget, or even run a small surplus, over the cycle, if not every year; and

(vii)  keep the tax system simple. A few broad taxes with moderate rates are far better that many taxes often levied on small bases with very high rates. Limit as much as possible the role of foreign trade taxes.

## Notes

1.  This can happen for a variety of reasons: monetary expansion increases demand while it sharply reduces the amount of foreign currency necessary to buy inputs for production; the costs of production increase faster than the price level; bottlenecks other than foreign exchange limit supply etc. Some of these points are discussed further below.
2.  They are all amortization when the interest rate is equal to or smaller than the rate of inflation.
3.  If evasion and collection lags were constant, policy-makers could correct for the biases that they create. Unfortunately, this is rarely the case.

## References

Buiter, Willem, 'The proper measurement of government budget deficits and its implications for policy evaluation and design', *IMF Staff Papers*, Volume 30, June 1983: 306–49.

Tanzi, Vito, 'Fiscal policy, Keynesian economics, and the mobilization of savings in developing countries', Chapter 2 of this book.

——'Inflation, real tax revenue, and the case for inflationary finance: theory with an application to Argentina', *IMF Staff Papers*, September 1978.

——'Fiscal disequilibrium in developing countries', *World Development*, December 1982.

# 5 Fiscal policy responses to exogenous shocks in developing countries

During the past decade, the developing countries have been subjected to various exogenous shocks that have made the pursuit of sound economic policy, and particularly that of sound fiscal policy, very difficult. In this chapter I discuss the factors associated with these exogenous shocks; the impact of these shocks on fiscal variables; and some of the policy responses by certain countries. 'Exogenous shocks' are defined as uncontrollable external events that have substantial effects on a country's income level.

**Factors associated with external shocks**
The most important exogenous shocks have been the following:

*Changes in export earnings*:   Many developing countries rely heavily on the export of one or few commodities (such as oil, coffee, copper) for their foreign exchange earnings. Shocks may originate from unexpected changes in the prices arising from changes in supply conditions or in the level of demand for these commodities. A frost in Brazil, that raises the international price of coffee, raises the foreign exchange earnings of other coffee exporters. An oil embargo by the major Middle Eastern oil-exporting countries had the same effect on the earnings of other oil-exporting countries. Major world booms and recessions, by affecting the level of commodity demand, have generated positive or negative shocks for less developed country (LDC) exports.

*Changes in major import prices*:   The most obvious example is provided by oil prices since 1973. In view of the great importance of oil in the imports of many countries, when oil prices rose sharply in the 1970s, the real incomes of many oil-importing countries were significantly reduced.

*Changes in the cost of foreign borrowing:*   As many developing countries are heavy borrowers, a change in the interest rate in international capital markets can be an important exogenous shock. The cost of international borrowing to a given country could also go up because of a changed perception of risk associated with lending to that country. Although the effects on borrowing costs may be the same, the latter is not a truly 'exogenous' shock. When the cost of borrowing rises, it affects the cost of new funds as well as the cost of servicing the existing stock of foreign debt. If the size of the debt is high and its maturity is short, the rise in interest expenditure can be substantial. If the foreign debt is mostly public, budgetary expenditures are directly affected.

*Changes in the availability of foreign credit*:   This type of shock is not the same as the previous one. Around 1982, the world witnessed a dramatic reduction in the willingness of commercial banks to lend to many developing countries. Mexico, for example, saw its foreign borrowing fall from $18 billion in 1981 to $5 billion in 1983. The debt crisis made new loans unavailable to many countries, thus reducing their ability to continue financing through this source their current expenditure levels.

*Changes in the level of foreign grants:* In many countries, and especially in the smaller ones, an important exogenous shock may come in the form of sudden changes in the availability of foreign grants or of concessionary loans. Countries that have relied on these sources for their domestic expenditure will be forced to reduce their spending when those grants are no longer available. Examples of these shocks abound, especially in Africa.

*Changes in other factors:*   Shocks may at times also be associated with factors such as changes in foreign workers' remittances, changes in direct foreign investment, changes in the level of capital outflow by nationals, and so on. In many cases these changes can be traced to the countries' own policies; therefore, they are not genuinely exogenous.

**Effects of exogenous shocks on fiscal variables**
The factors mentioned above affect not just the incomes of countries but also their fiscal variables. They may improve or worsen the fiscal situation and, by doing so, they may bring about policy responses. The automatic impact of external shocks on the fiscal variables is likely to be much more important in developing countries than in industrial countries. At the same time the ability of developing countries to neutralize these effects, if they wished to do so, is much more limited.

In industrial countries the external shocks affect incomes and economic activity much more than the fiscal variables themselves as the fiscal sector is not closely linked to the external sector. Therefore, the observed changes in the fiscal variables can be attributed to policy responses. For example, when the increase in the oil price of 1974 reduced the real incomes of industrial countries, the governments responded by increasing the level of public spending through transfers to families. This increase in public spending was not automatic but reflected a conscious, discretionary governmental reaction. Apart from the cyclical impact that affected tax revenues, the increase in fiscal deficits in OECD countries in 1975 were policy induced.

In the developing countries, the impact of external shocks on the fiscal variables is much more direct or automatic. Therefore, the observed change in the fiscal variables should not be attributed mainly to policy changes. For this reason, it is very difficult, when dealing with these countries, to isolate the changes in fiscal variables that reflect genuine policy responses from those that reflect automatic effects. Thus, studies that attempt to estimate from observed fiscal changes the fiscal policy response to exogenous shocks are likely to reach misleading conclusions.

The reason for the above conclusion is the close link that exists in LDCs between the budget and the foreign sector. This link depends on:

(i)    the high proportion of foreign trade taxes in total revenue;
(ii)   the high proportion of domestic sales taxes collected from imports;
(iii)  the heavy reliance of corporate income taxes on exports of mineral products;
(iv)   the reliance on the part of the public sector on foreign borrowing or foreign grants;
(v)    the high proportion of foreign debt that is public;
(vi)   the widespread attempts in these countries to insulate some domestic prices from movements in world prices; and so on.

Foreign trade taxes (import plus export duties) account for more than one-third of the total tax revenue of LDCs. This figure, however, does not convey the full importance of the external sector in public revenue as corporate income taxes, which are mostly collected from mineral exports, account for another 18 per cent and 'domestic' taxes on goods and services are often levied largely on imported goods. More than 50 per cent of the tax revenue of developing countries may be directly related to the foreign sector. Furthermore, in many of these countries some of the important export sectors (such as petroleum, phosphates, bauxite) are government owned (see Tanzi 1986a). When the price of those commodities changes, the effect on public revenue can be direct and immediate. Much of the foreign borrowing of LDCs is made by the public sector. When the availability or the cost of foreign loans changes, government resources are again immediately and directly affected.

To some extent the same close link between the fiscal sector and the foreign sector exists on the expenditure side. Some government expenditures are financed by earmarked taxes. When tax revenue falls, because of external shocks, the resources available for these expenditures also decline. The size of many subsidies depends on the difference between the international prices of some imported products and their domestic prices. When the international prices increase or the exchange rate appreciates, the amount of the subsidy and thus the budget deficit also increase. Some external shocks have an immediate impact on the financing of investment expenditure as concessional loans or grants are often tied to specific projects, so that when these loans or grants change, the resources available for these investments also change.

In conclusion, while shocks affect the levels of real incomes in both industrial and developing countries, they have far more pronounced and direct effects on the fiscal sectors of the LDCs.

### Policy response

There is some literature that is relevant for assessing what the 'optimal' fiscal reaction of developing countries to exogenous shocks should be (see Tabellini, 1985). However, much of this literature is highly theoretical and it assumes that over the short run, policy-makers can control the policy instruments; it also assumes that they have the interest and the knowledge to pursue optimal policies. Unfortunately the real world is much more complex. Some obstacles that exist in *all* countries are far more important in LDCs.

First, there are the contrasting views on how these economies operate and how they respond to various policy tools. Under the best of circumstances policy-makers would receive conflicting advice. The ongoing controversy about International Monetary Fund (IMF) programmes is an indication of this aspect. Second, some of the civil servants entrusted with implementing the policies decided upon by the policy-makers may not respond in the required fashion. For example, it is easy to change a tax law; it is much more difficult to make the tax administrators fully implement the change. Third, statistics that are essential for good policy-making are often not available or are available with considerable delays or with sizable errors. Fourth, changes in policy instruments are often neutralized by the reaction of forces outside the control of the policy-makers or even of the civil servants. For example, an increase in import duties or in income tax rates may have little effect on revenue if smuggling is easy and tax evasion is rampant. Fifth, authorities often find unacceptable, for various reasons, policies that may be seen as desirable by economists. Considering all these reasons, one should expect different fiscal responses to exogenous shocks in LDCs as compared to industrial countries. There is also the complication that exogenous shocks generate not just fiscal imbalances but also external imbalances, which may not be easily financeable. The policy-makers often find themselves in situations where they have to co-ordinate conflicting objectives concerning internal and external imbalances.

The countries that, in the 1970s, were faced with rising public revenues due to higher export prices generally reacted in three different ways. A first (and very small) group considered the increase as a temporary windfall which would affect only marginally the permanent income of the country and of the government.

These countries used the additional revenue to pay off foreign debt or to accumulate foreign assets (in the form of foreign exchange or in real assets). These assets could be liquidated in future years when foreign earnings declined in order to maintain the level of domestic spending on some, hopefully permanent, trend. This behaviour is an application of the permanent income hypothesis of consumption to the government.

A second, and larger, group engaged in capital accumulation at home by expanding the level of public investment. Provided that the investment has as high a rate of return as what the country could have received from foreign assets, that the 'additional' investment spending is limited to the windfall income, and that this spending can be phased out when the windfall income begins to disappear, this policy response can also be considered as a good one. However, experience indicates that often the requirements mentioned above were not met. Investment was often not as productive as it could have been having been distorted by poor management and by political considerations; it was often too large; and it was too rigid to be phased out when needed. These countries faced difficulties when the windfall disappeared and foreign financing dried up. These changes would have required a quick reduction of the investment expenditure.

A third and largest group increased public spending by increasing public employment, increasing the size of transfers, increasing investment, and so on. In this particular situation, when the decline in foreign earnings inevitably came, the countries were tied to patterns and levels of spending that were very difficult to change. As long as foreign loans were available, the countries used this source to maintain the level of spending that could no longer be maintained with ordinary revenue. This reaction postponed the problem and in many cases made it worse by leaving the countries with huge foreign debts. When the crisis came, and the countries found that they had to adjust, as financing was no longer available, the consequences were very serious.

Shocks that reduce public sector revenue are even more difficult to deal with. In this case, the countries are often unable to make up the revenue losses in the short run. The losses of foreign trade taxes could in theory be compensated by increasing income taxes or taxing domestically produced products. But income taxes take a very long time to introduce and collect, and their scope in LDCs is limited. For this reason, countries have often been forced to rely on inferior revenue sources such as inflationary finance, regressive excises, or the building up of arrears.

## Conclusions

Unlike the industrial countries, where the government has much greater control over revenue sources, where revenues are rarely tied to the foreign sector, and where there is always the option of selling bonds domestically to generate additional domestic revenue for the public sector in a non-inflationary way, in the developing countries the degree of freedom in the policy areas is much more restricted for some of the reasons indicated. Another reason is that the generation of domestic non-inflationary and non-tax sources of revenues is extremely limited. Therefore, in the absence of foreign borrowing, and once the possibility of financing spending through the building up of arrears has been exhausted, there is a limit to the amount of public spending (expressed in real terms or as a share of gross national product) that the government will be able to maintain. This limit is not a rigid one but it exists all the same (see Tanzi, 1986b). Attempting to exceed that limit will bring inflation as the government will have to finance the additional spending through money creation. This channel itself has a limit and inflationary finance may reduce the real value of tax revenue (see Tanzi, 1978). That absolute limit on real government spending falls when an exogenous shock reduces tax revenue; it falls even more when foreign borrowing is constrained by the unwillingness of the commercial banks to lend to the country. Of course, within the budget itself, to the extent that the servicing of the foreign public debt increases, other expenditures have to be limited even more.

Thus, often the only realistic alternative that these countries have is to reduce public spending. As it is often politically difficult to reduce current spending in the short run, the adjustment pressure is often shifted to capital spending. This is normally seen as an undesirable type of adjustment, although if what is eliminated is unproductive investment projects, it may not be as undesirable as it is often believed.

### References

Tabellini, Guido, 'The reaction of fiscal policies to the 1979 shock in selected developing countries: theory and facts;, mimeo 1985.

Tanzi, Vito, 'Inflation, real tax revenue, and the case for inflationary finance: theory with an application to Argentina', *IMF Staff Papers* 25 September 1978: 417–51.

——(1986a) 'Quantitative characteristics of the tax systems of developing countries', in *Modern Tax Theory for Developing Countries*, David Newbery and Nicholas Stern (eds), Washington, International Bank for Reconstruction and Development, 1986.

——(1986b) 'External versus internal debt as a means of financing fiscal deficits in developing countries' in *Public Finance and Public Debt*, Bernard Herber (ed.), Proceedings of the 40th Congress of the International Institute of Public Finance, 1986.

# 6 Is there a limit to the size of fiscal deficits in developing countries?

## Introduction

The questions that I wish to raise in this chapter are the following: are there limits to the level of public expenditure of a country at a given moment of time? And, if there are limits, what are the factors that determine them? Perhaps another way of raising the same issue is by asking the related question about what is the maximum level of fiscal deficit that a country can have over a given fiscal year.

The basic conclusion of this paper is the following: in nominal values, a country can plan to have, and can, have any level of fiscal deficit (and any level of public expenditure) that it wishes. However, in real terms, or as a proportion of its national income, the country will find that there is a concrete limit to that deficit (and to that expenditure). This limit is not rigid and varies among countries or, in a given country over time, but it exists all the same. An attempt on the part of a country's policy-makers to exceed that limit will often prove counterproductive and frustrating. Should the policy-makers, at the beginning of the fiscal year, plan to exceed that limit – say, by legislating a higher level of public expenditure in real terms – they will find their plans frustrated. *Ex post*, at the end of the fiscal year, they will find that the ratio of the deficit (and of public expenditure) to national income is lower than they had planned or budgeted. These limits are imposed by the limitation that a country has on the sources of finance of its deficit.[1]

The literature on the financing of fiscal deficits is limited. Economic writing has concentrated on the consequences rather than the sources of deficit financing. Furthermore, having originated mostly in the United States and other industrial countries, it has emphasized the bond-versus-money creation distinction. More recently, some writing on developing countries has paid attention to foreign borrowing. Reality, however, is much more complicated than that and one never ceases to be amazed at the variety of ways in which fiscal deficits get financed. The fiscal deficit can be financed in a variety of ways, some more orthodox than others. A brief description of these ways will be useful for our discussion of limits to financing. In order to account for all major sources of financing, the deficit is defined on an accrual basis. I shall distinguish domestic from foreign sources. Within each of these categories further important distinctions will also prove useful. Some statistics about the relative importance of these sources in developing countries will be provided.

### Foreign financing

Foreign financing of the fiscal deficit can come in at least four categories, namely, grants, concessionary loans, commercial borrowing, and building up of arrears.

*Grants*. Grants can be of at least three types. First, they can come in the form of cash. A donor country (for example, United States, Canada, France, Sweden, Saudi Arabia) may make available a certain amount of foreign currency to the deficit country to finance the deficit. Clearly, the domestic currency counterpart of the grant depends on the exchange rate. If the government has expenditures abroad (on imports by the public sector or for servicing external debt obligations), the grant can be utilized directly to meet these needs. Second, grants can come in the form of commodity aid. For example, the government may receive wheat, rice, or some other commodity from a donor country. This commodity may be sold domestically and the funds thus raised may be used to finance the deficit. Or, it may be used directly by making 'payments' in kind. A third form of grant is project aid: a donor country agrees to cover all the costs associated with the construction of a given project (for example, building, road). In this case, the additional spending and at least part of the needed financing increase *pari passu*.

*Concessionary loans*. These are loans that come with a lower-than-market rate of interest, have a substantial grace period, and have a long maturity. They may be given by governments or by international institutions (such as the International Bank for Reconstruction and Development (IBRD), the International Development Bank (IDB) and the Asian Development Bank (ADB)). Often, they are tied to projects and thus require domestic counterpart expenditure. They all contain a grant element in the sense that the present value of the (discounted) servicing cost is less than the loan.

*Commercial loans*. These can come from foreign commercial banks or from foreign suppliers. Those coming from commercial banks may have maturities ranging from a few months to over a decade. These loans can be very large as the experience of Mexico, Brazil, Argentina, Venezuela, the Philippines, and other countries in recent years shows. If commercial banks are highly liquid, if they assess optimistically the future economic prospects of the borrowing country, and if the country is willing to pay a premium for getting these loans, this source of financing can become very large in the short run.[2] But, as the painful experience of recent years indicates, there may come a time when a country finds itself cut out from this source and this is likely to occur when its need for these loans is greatest. In these circumstances, the control that countries have over this source becomes very limited indeed.[3] Some influence over this source can be exercised by pursuing adjustment policies aimed at convincing the banks that the country will be able to service these loans. For example, an agreement with the International Monetary Fund (IMF) on a programme is likely to influence the commercial banks' willingness to increase the financing that they make available.

*External arrears.* When interest payments to foreign lenders are due and are not made on time, the accrued interest swells the deficit, but this part of the deficit is automatically financed by the non-payment of interest. Or, if the payment to foreign suppliers of goods and services is due and that payment is not made, part of the fiscal deficit is again automatically financed by the non-payment. These forms of financing represent 'lending' which often is not voluntary.[4] These arrears toward foreign lenders can become large and can play a significant role in explaining how a country can finance such a large deficit in a given year.

The size of foreign grants or concessionary loans available to a country at some moment of time is not a variable that the country can easily influence. Obviously, better economic policies or particular political behaviour may influence the behaviour of the donors and may have some effect on the timing or even the size of a grant. However, the leverage that the recipient country is likely to have over this variable is small. If foreign grants and concessionary loans are large, and if there are no supply bottlenecks that limit imports that can be financed with them (say, limited harbour or storage facilities), then large deficits could be financed by this source. But, again, as far as the country is concerned, there are clear limits to the size of this financing source.

**Domestic financing**
If countries did not have access to foreign sources, a fiscal deficit would exist only if it could be financed domestically. Domestic financing can come in various forms. A basic distinction that can be made is between borrowing from the non-bank public and borrowing from the banking system. Further distinctions within each of these categories are also useful.

*Borrowing from the public*
*Free sales of bonds.* In a country such as the United States, borrowing from the public means selling bonds to individuals or institutions who have the option of buying or not buying them. In this case, if the government chooses to finance its deficit in this way, it must make these bonds attractive enough to induce buyers to buy them. This requires that bond prices must come down (interest rates must go up) which, in turn, attracts foreign capital and leads to an appreciation of the exchange rate. In developing countries, and in some industrial countries as well, this option is very limited. One reason is the limitation of the size of the capital market that, by itself, sets a limit at a relatively small level to the size of the deficit

that could be financed in this way regardless of the level of interest rates. Another is that many governments are reluctant to let real interest rates become positive and competitive. In reality one finds that in most developing countries this source of financing is small and often insignificant.

*Sale of bonds to captive markets.* While the scope for financing a fiscal deficit through the voluntary placing of bonds in the market is limited, there is an alternative that is of far greater significance. This is the sale of bonds to captive buyers. In a large number of developing countries, and in quite a few industrial countries, many institutions and occasionally even some individuals, such as public sector employees, are required to invest in public bonds. Social security institutions, pension funds, public as well as private enterprises, among others, are required by law to buy government bonds. In some cases, the placing of these bonds can be quite unorthodox. In one African country, for example, in 1982 the government suddenly announced that currency bills of a certain denomination were no longer legal tender. These bills could only be converted into government bonds. In other cases, individuals may buy government bonds at a discount and use them to pay taxes at a later time. In other cases, the government payments, say for tax refunds or for the purchase of property, are made in bonds. As these bonds often pay low interest rates, there is an element of taxation in this transaction. This captive market for government bonds accounts for much of the non-banking domestic source of financing.

*Building up of domestic arrears.* Borrowing from the public is not limited to the sale of bonds. Another important source is the building up of arrears *vis-à-vis* domestic suppliers of goods and services. Theoretically, arrears are equivalent to interest-free loans. They can accumulate *vis-à-vis* domestic suppliers of goods and services, those who carry out capital projects, public employees in the form of delayed payment of wages, tax-payers in the form of delays in the payment of tax rebates or refunds and in other ways.

All of these sources have clear, if not inflexible, limits. The sale of bonds to institutions is limited by the revenue of those institutions. The building up of arrears is possible and, at given times, can be important; but again there is a limit. When arrears become high, suppliers either refuse to continue providing the supplies or services to the government or they inflate the prices at which they will continue supplying those goods and services, thus pushing up the level of the deficit. The sale of bonds to individuals can be influenced by the interest rate policy, but the size of the domestic capital market will in any case limit this possibility regardless of the level of interest rates. Higher expected inflation is likely to reduce the willingness of individuals to buy bonds or to allow the building up of arrears.[5]

*Borrowing from the banking system.* All the sources of financing discussed so far have clear, if not inflexible, limits in real terms. If they were the only ones available, one could make an easy case that the fiscal deficit of a country could not exceed some proportion of national income over the fiscal year. However, when the possibility of going to the banking system is available, is there still a limit? Borrowing from the work on inflationary finance, I shall show, however, that even when the Treasury has access to the printing press, there is still a limit to how much fiscal deficit is possible in a country.[6]

Although borrowing from the banking system may not necessarily mean borrowing from the central bank (as the government can borrow from domestic commercial banks), in practice this distinction is not important if, as often happens, the monetary authorities accommodate that borrowing by increasing the reserves of the commercial banks. Thus, whether the government borrows directly from the central bank or (perhaps because of legal constraints) indirectly by going to the commercial banks and, at the same time, influencing or inducing the central bank to increase the lending capacity of the commercial banks, the net result is similar. In both cases, there is an increase in the money supply.[7] Now the relevant question is: how much fiscal deficit can be financed by monetary expansion?

Monetary expansion increases the general price level and thus reduces the real value of the monetary unit. As Friedman (1942) and Bailey (1956) showed many years ago, this reduction in real value can be considered a tax on those who hold money. If the real growth of an economy is zero or is ignored, and if inflation is fully anticipated, and equal to actual real balances. Then, the rate of inflation $\pi$ is equivalent to the rate of change of the money supply and is also equivalent to the inflation tax rate.[8] The tax base, on the other hand, is equivalent to the real cash balances held $(\frac{M}{P})_t$. Therefore, the revenue from the inflation tax, $R_t^\pi$, is

$$R_t^\pi = \pi_t \left( \frac{M}{P} \right)t \tag{1}$$

Equation (1) indicates that the inflation tax is an excise tax levied at the rate of $\pi_t$ on the tax base, that is, $(\frac{M}{P})_t$. Given the real cash balances, an increase in money creation to finance a fiscal deficit will generate higher revenue. Alternatively, given the inflationary expectations, the higher the real balances, the higher the revenue from inflationary finance. However, and this is a point of fundamental importance, the real balances are affected by inflationary expectations. The higher the latter, the lower the former.

Just how sensitive real balances can be to inflation can perhaps best be seen by a couple of concrete examples. Table 6.1 shows this relationship for Argentina and Israel in recent years. In Argentina, when the rate of inflation was relatively low, in 1970 and 1974, the ratio of currency and M1 to gross domestic product (GDP) rose dramatically. When the rate of inflation became very high in 1976 and 1983, the ratio fell equally dramatically. In Israel, as the rate of inflation rose from 12 per cent in the early 1970s to over 100 per cent in the early 1980s, the ratio of currency to GDP fell from around 7 per cent to around 2 per cent of GDP and the ratio of M1 to GDP fell from over 18 per cent to around 5 per cent. As the rate of inflation rises, the cost of holding money increases. As a consequence, individuals try to economize on real balances.[9] We thus have the relationship shown in Figure 6.1 where LL represents a demand schedule for real balances. Real balances can be measured as proportions of national income (M/Y). Figure 6.1 allows us to assess graphically the revenue from inflationary finance. When the rate of inflation is zero, no money is being created to finance the deficit. In such case, real balances are equal to OA. As the government begins to finance the deficit through monetary expansion, the rate of inflation increases while the holding of real balances falls. For a while the positive effect on $R^{\pi}$ coming from higher values of $\pi$ more than compensates for the negative effects coming from the fall in M/Y. At some combination of M/Y and $\pi$, the product of these two variables is maximized and the inflation tax generates the maximum

Table 6.1    Inflation and real money balances in Argentina and Israel (in per cent)

| Year | Argentina | | | Israel | | |
|------|-----------|-------------|--------|--------|-------------|--------|
|      | $\pi$ | Currency/GDP | M1/GDP | $\pi$ | Currency/GDP | M1/GDP |
| 1970 | 14  | 7.2 | 14.7 | 12  | 6.9 | 18.3 |
| 1971 | 39  | 6.0 | 12.7 | 12  | 6.7 | 18.4 |
| 1972 | 77  | 4.3 | 10.0 | 13  | 6.5 | 18.4 |
| 1973 | 50  | 4.6 | 11.0 | 20  | 7.0 | 19.2 |
| 1974 | 20  | 6.4 | 15.0 | 39  | 5.8 | 16.0 |
| 1975 | 192 | 4.9 | 11.2 | 39  | 5.1 | 13.7 |
| 1976 | 499 | 2.7 | 7.0  | 32  | 4.8 | 13.5 |
| 1977 | 149 | 2.8 | 6.8  | 35  | 4.4 | 13.0 |
| 1978 | 146 | 3.2 | 6.6  | 51  | 3.7 | 11.4 |
| 1979 | 149 | 3.2 | 6.2  | 78  | 2.7 | 8.0  |
| 1980 | 75  | 4.2 | 6.3  | 131 | 2.0 | 6.7  |
| 1981 | 110 | 3.8 | 6.3  | 117 | 1.8 | 5.1  |
| 1982 | 256 | 3.9 | 4.9  | 120 | 1.9 | 4.7  |
| 1983 | 430 | 2.2 | 3.8  | 191 | 2.2 | 4.1  |

Sources: Central Banks of Argentina and Israel and IMF, *International Financial Statistics*.
Note: $\pi$ for Argentina refers to Wholesale Prices Index; for Israel it refers to Consumer Price Index.

revenue. This sets the limit to the size of (real) fiscal deficit that can be financed by the printing press. In Figure 6.1, this takes place at point C where the area of the quadrangle OBCD is maximized. Should the government attempt to raise more revenue by increasing the money supply at a rate faster than OD, it would fail as the area of the quadrangle would become smaller. At point C, the elasticity of the LL curve is obviously equal to –1.

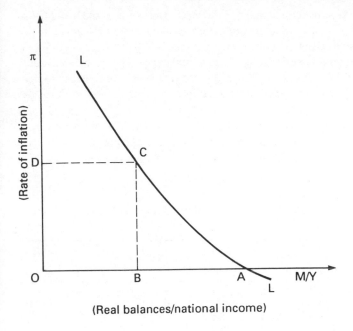

*Figure 6.1*

Following Cagan (1956), the equation for the LL curve can be described as follows:

$$(M/Y)^d = ae^{-b\pi} \qquad (2)$$

where $(M/Y)^d$ is the ratio of money demanded to income at time t; a is the ratio of money to income when the expected rate of inflation is zero (OA in Figure 6.1); $\pi$ represents inflationary expectation which is equal to the percentage change in money supply; e is the base for natural logarithms; and b is a measure of sensitivity of the demand for real balances to the anticipated rate of inflation. The absolute value of the exponent of e – that is $|b\pi|$ – is the elasticity Em of the demand for money.

Combining equations (1) and (2), expressing the macrovariables, R and M, as ratios of national income, and continuing to assume that actual price changes are equal to inflationary expectations, the equation for revenue from inflationary finance, $R^\pi$, can be written as

$$R^\pi = \pi ae^{-b\pi} \qquad (3)$$

Equation (3) can be solved for actual or simulated values of π, a, and b. Table 6.2 shows the results of a computer simulation in which: a is assumed to be alternatively 10 and 20 per cent of national income; b is given values of 0.5, 1.0, 2.0, and 3.0; and π is allowed to range from 5–500 per cent per year. The values used for b represent the range found for developing countries in empirical studies; the lower value for a (10 per cent of national income) is more realistic than the higher value.

Table 6.2 shows that a country with a = 0.10 and b = 0.5 could finance a maximum of 7.4 per cent of national income from central bank financing. That maximum would require a rate of inflation of 200 per cent per year.

*Table 6.2*   *Revenue from inflationary finance[1] (ratios of revenue to gross domestic product)*

| π | a = 0.10 | | | | a = 0.20 | | | |
|---|---|---|---|---|---|---|---|---|
| | *b = 0.5* | *b = 1.0* | *b = 2.0* | *b = 3.0* | *b = 0.5* | *b = 1.0* | *b = 2.0* | *b = 3.0* |
| 0.0500 | 0.0049 | 0.0048 | 0.0045 | 0.0043 | 0.0098 | 0.0095 | 0.0090 | 0.0086 |
| 0.1000 | 0.0095 | 0.0090 | 0.0082 | 0.0074 | 0.0190 | 0.0181 | 0.0164 | 0.0148 |
| 0.1500 | 0.0139 | 0.0129 | 0.0111 | 0.0096 | 0.0278 | 0.0258 | 0.0222 | 0.0191 |
| 0.2000 | 0.0181 | 0.0164 | 0.0134 | 0.0110 | 0.0110 | 0.0327 | 0.0268 | 0.0220 |
| 0.2500 | 0.0221 | 0.0195 | 0.0152 | 0.0118 | 0.0441 | 0.0389 | 0.0303 | 0.0236 |
| 0.3000 | 0.0258 | 0.0222 | 0.0165 | 0.0122 | 0.0516 | 0.0444 | 0.0329 | 0.0244 |
| 0.3500 | 0.0294 | 0.0247 | 0.0174 | 0.0122 | 0.0588 | 0.0493 | 0.0348 | 0.0245 |
| 0.4000 | 0.0327 | 0.0268 | 0.0180 | 0.0120 | 0.0655 | 0.0536 | 0.0359 | 0.0241 |
| 0.4500 | 0.0359 | 0.0287 | 0.0183 | 0.0177 | 0.0719 | 0.0574 | 0.0366 | 0.0233 |
| 0.5000 | 0.0389 | 0.3030 | 0.0184 | 0.0112 | 0.0779 | 0.0607 | 0.0368 | 0.0223 |
| 0.6000 | 0.0444 | 0.0329 | 0.0181 | 0.0099 | 0.0889 | 0.0659 | 0.0361 | 0.0198 |
| 0.7000 | 0.0493 | 0.0348 | 0.0173 | 0.0086 | 0.0987 | 0.0695 | 0.0345 | 0.0171 |
| 0.8000 | 0.0536 | 0.0359 | 0.0162 | 0.0073 | 0.1073 | 0.0719 | 0.0323 | 0.0145 |
| 0.9000 | 0.0574 | 0.0366 | 0.0149 | 0.0060 | 0.1148 | 0.0732 | 0.0298 | 0.0121 |
| 1.0000 | 0.0607 | 0.0368 | 0.0135 | 0.0050 | 0.1213 | 0.0736 | 0.0271 | 0.0100 |
| 1.2000 | 0.0659 | 0.0361 | 0.0109 | 0.0033 | 0.1317 | 0.0723 | 0.0218 | 0.0066 |
| 1.4000 | 0.0695 | 0.0361 | 0.0085 | 0.0021 | 0.1390 | 0.0690 | 0.0170 | 0.0042 |
| 1.6000 | 0.0719 | 0.0323 | 0.0065 | 0.0013 | 0.1438 | 0.0646 | 0.0130 | 0.0026 |
| 1.8000 | 0.0732 | 0.0298 | 0.0049 | 0.0008 | 0.1464 | 0.0595 | 0.0098 | 0.0016 |
| 2.0000 | 0.0736 | 0.0271 | 0.0037 | 0.0005 | 0.1472 | 0.0541 | 0.0073 | 0.0010 |
| 2.5000 | 0.0716 | 0.0205 | 0.0017 | 0.0001 | 0.1433 | 0.0410 | 0.0034 | 0.0003 |
| 3.0000 | 0.0669 | 0.0149 | 0.0007 | 0.0000 | 0.1339 | 0.0299 | 0.0015 | 0.0001 |
| 3.5000 | 0.0608 | 0.0106 | 0.0003 | 0.0000 | 0.1216 | 0.0211 | 0.0006 | 0.0000 |
| 4.0000 | 0.0541 | 0.0073 | 0.0001 | 0.0000 | 0.1083 | 0.0147 | 0.0003 | 0.0000 |
| 4.5000 | 0.0474 | 0.0050 | 0.0001 | 0.0000 | 0.0949 | 0.0100 | 0.0001 | 0.0000 |
| 5.0000 | 0.0410 | 0.0034 | 0.0000 | 0.0000 | 0.0821 | 0.0067 | 0.0000 | 0.0000 |

π denotes the inflation rate.
b denotes the sensitivity of the demand for money with respect to the rate of inflation.
1 denotes the ratio of money to income at zero inflation.

*Ceteris paribus,* if b = 1, the maximum would be 3.7 per cent and would be reached at a rate of inflation of 100 per cent. Should the rate of monetary expansion be pushed beyond those levels, real revenue from inflationary finance would fall. For example, with a = 0.10 and b = 0.5, a rate of monetary expansion of 400 per cent would generate only 5.4 per cent of national income in revenue. Obviously, a and b diverge among countries, but the basic message is the same: there is a maximum level of fiscal deficit that can be financed by central bank financing.

### Statistical evidence on financing sources

Up to this point, the discussion about limits to the sources of deficit financing has been either impressionistic or theoretical. It should have established that there are limits to the real size of the fiscal deficit and thus to the level of public expenditure at a given moment in time. However, except for borrowing from the central bank, little empirical evidence was provided about the relative importance of those financing sources. In this section, an attempt is made to remedy this shortcoming by providing, for 64 developing countries, data on fiscal deficits and on the main sources of financing. Unfortunately, except for a few countries, the breakdown available is not as detailed as would have been desirable. The statistical information is shown in Table 6.3. The table refers mainly to 1981 or 1982, and shows the overall fiscal deficit, foreign financing – broken down by grants and others – and domestic financing – broken down by bank financing and others.

The data assembled in Table 6.3 require some strong words of caution. As there is no single place where one can obtain the information shown in this table, it had to be assembled from different and often not strictly comparable sources. Therefore, precise cross-country comparisons should not be made. For example, the definition of central government is not the same for all countries and, in a few cases, broader concepts such as public sector or general government are used. Also, as the statistics are shown as proportions of GDPs, and as national accounts are notoriously unreliable for some countries, the possibility exists that overestimation or underestimation of GDP may have resulted in distorted figures. The allocation of financing by source was not always clearcut; for example, in some cases concessionary loans may have been classified as grants. Finally, it was not always possible to show overall deficits gross of arrears, as this information is not available for many countries.

Out of 64 countries, three have overall deficits exceeding 20 per cent of GDP – Jordan, Syria, and Western Samoa. This seems to be just about the upper limit for fiscal deficits. Eleven had deficits exceeding 15 per cent of GDP. Many of these countries – Israel, Jordan, Sri Lanka, Syria, Tanzania, Western Samoa – had substantial foreign assistance, either in the form of grants or concessionary loans. Without this assistance, it is unlikely that they would have been able to

Table 6.3 Central government's fiscal deficits and financing sources: selected countries and years (percentage of GDP)

| Country and Year | Overall Deficit or Financing | External Financing | | | Domestic Financing | | |
|---|---|---|---|---|---|---|---|
| | | Total | Grants** | Other | Total | Banking system | Other |
| Barbados (1981/82) | 6.6 | 4.8 | – | 1.7 | 1.7 | 1.7 | 0.0 |
| Argentina (1981) | 8.0 | 1.7 | 0.0 | 0.0 | 6.3 | 5.1 | 1.2 |
| Bangladesh (1981/82) | 10.0 | 9.5 | 9.5 | 0.0 | 0.5 | 0.1 | 0.4 |
| Belize (1982/83) | 14.2 | 10.4 | 5.0 | 5.4 | 3.7 | 3.7 | 0.0 |
| Bolivia (1981) | 6.5 | 3.6 | – | – | 2.9 | 2.8 | 0.1 |
| Brazil (1982)* | 15.8 | 2.4 | 0.0 | 2.4 | 13.4 | 9.5 | 3.9 |
| Burma (1980/81)* | 8.8 | 4.2 | 1.7 | 2.5 | 4.6 | 4.6 | 0.0 |
| Central African Republic (1981) | 6.8 | 4.7 | 3.0 | 1.7 | 2.0 | 2.0 | 0.0 |
| Chile (1982)* | 3.4 | 1.1 | 0.0 | 1.1 | 2.3 | 1.9 | 0.4 |
| Colombia (1982) | 3.5 | 0.6 | 0.0 | 0.6 | 2.9 | 2.9 | 0.0 |
| Costa Rica (1982) | 3.4 | 2.4 | – | 2.4 | 1.0 | – | – |
| Cyprus (1980) | 8.6 | 5.8 | 2.5 | 3.3 | 2.8 | 2.5 | 0.3 |
| Dominican Republic (1982) | 2.8 | 0.6 | 0.0 | 0.6 | 2.2 | 1.9 | 0.3 |
| Ecuador (1982) | 4.8 | 2.5 | – | – | 2.3 | – | – |
| El Salvador (1980) | 6.2 | 0.3 | 0.3 | 0.0 | 5.9 | 3.1 | 2.8 |
| Ethiopia (1981/82) | 6.3 | 5.3 | 1.1 | 4.2 | 1.0 | 0.7 | 0.3 |
| Fiji (1982) | 7.1 | 2.7 | 1.0 | 1.7 | 4.4 | 1.7 | 2.7 |
| Gambia (1982/83) | 12.6 | 8.9 | 3.2 | 5.7 | 3.7 | 3.7 | 0.0 |
| Ghana (1982) | 4.7 | 0.5 | 0.1 | 0.4 | 4.2 | 0.5 | 3.8 |
| Greece (1981) | 12.6 | 2.1 | – | – | 10.4 | 8.1 | 2.3 |
| Guatemala (1980) | 4.4 | 1.4 | 1.4 | 0.0 | 2.9 | 2.8 | 0.1 |
| Haiti (1982) | 8.6 | 5.6 | 3.2 | 2.4 | 3.0 | 2.2 | 0.8 |
| Honduras (1982) | 10.2 | 4.9 | 5.3 | 0.3 | 4.6 | 4.3 | 1.0 |
| India (1981/82) | 6.0 | 0.9 | 0.2 | 0.7 | 5.1 | 2.6 | 2.5 |
| Indonesia (1982/83) | 5.1 | 3.6 | 0.1 | 3.5 | 1.4 | 1.4 | 0.0 |
| Israel (1982) | 18.6 | 10.5 | 5.2 | 5.3 | 8.1 | 5.5 | 2.6 |
| Ivory Coast (1982)* | 12.3 | 10.7 | 0.3 | 10.4 | 1.6 | 0.9 | 0.7 |
| Jamaica (1981/82) | 16.4 | 9.4 | – | – | 7.0 | 3.5 | 3.5 |
| Jordan (1982) | 21.7 | 16.8 | 13.7 | 3.1 | 4.9 | 4.5 | 0.4 |
| Kenya (1981/82) | 7.6 | 2.9 | 1.3 | 1.6 | 4.7 | 2.5 | 2.2 |
| Korea (1982)* | 4.3 | 1.3 | 0.0 | 1.3 | 3.0 | 0.6 | 2.4 |
| Liberia (1981/82) | 14.3 | 7.3 | 3.7 | 3.6 | 7.0 | 4.0 | 3.1 |

Table 6.3 Central government's fiscal deficits and financing sources: selected countries and years (percentage of GDP)

| Country and Year | Overall Deficit or Financing | External Financing | | | Domestic Financing | | |
|---|---|---|---|---|---|---|---|
| | | Total | Grants** | Other | Total | Banking system | Other |
| Barbados (1981/82) | 6.6 | 4.8 | – | 1.7 | 1.7 | 1.7 | 0.0 |
| Argentina (1981) | 8.0 | 1.7 | 0.0 | 0.0 | 6.3 | 5.1 | 1.2 |
| Bangladesh (1981/82) | 10.0 | 9.5 | 9.5 | 0.0 | 0.5 | 0.1 | 0.4 |
| Belize (1982/83) | 14.2 | 10.4 | 5.0 | 5.4 | 3.7 | 3.7 | 0.0 |
| Bolivia (1981) | 6.5 | 3.6 | – | – | 2.9 | 2.8 | 0.1 |
| Brazil (1982)* | 15.8 | 2.4 | 0.0 | 2.4 | 13.4 | 9.5 | 3.9 |
| Burma (1980/81)* | 8.8 | 4.2 | 1.7 | 2.5 | 4.6 | 4.6 | 0.0 |
| Central African Republic (1981) | 6.8 | 4.7 | 3.0 | 1.7 | 2.0 | 2.0 | 0.0 |
| Chile (1982)* | 3.4 | 1.1 | 0.0 | 1.1 | 2.3 | 1.9 | 0.4 |
| Colombia (1982) | 3.5 | 0.6 | 0.0 | 0.6 | 2.9 | 2.9 | 0.0 |
| Costa Rica (1982) | 3.4 | 2.4 | – | 2.4 | 1.0 | – | – |
| Cyprus (1980) | 8.6 | 5.8 | 2.5 | 3.3 | 2.8 | 2.5 | 0.3 |
| Dominican Republic (1982) | 2.8 | 0.6 | 0.0 | 0.6 | 2.2 | 1.9 | 0.3 |
| Ecuador (1982) | 4.8 | 2.5 | – | – | 2.3 | – | – |
| El Salvador (1980) | 6.2 | 0.3 | 0.3 | 0.0 | 5.9 | 3.1 | 2.8 |
| Ethiopia (1981/82) | 6.3 | 5.3 | 1.1 | 4.2 | 1.0 | 0.7 | 0.3 |
| Fiji (1982) | 7.1 | 2.7 | 1.0 | 1.7 | 4.4 | 1.7 | 2.7 |
| Gambia (1982/83) | 12.6 | 8.9 | 3.2 | 5.7 | 3.7 | 3.7 | 0.0 |
| Ghana (1982) | 4.7 | 0.5 | 0.1 | 0.4 | 4.2 | 0.5 | 3.8 |
| Greece (1981) | 12.6 | 2.1 | – | – | 10.4 | 8.1 | 2.3 |
| Guatemala (1980) | 4.4 | 1.4 | 1.4 | 0.0 | 2.9 | 2.8 | 0.1 |
| Haiti (1982) | 8.6 | 5.6 | 3.2 | 2.4 | 3.0 | 2.2 | 0.8 |
| Honduras (1982) | 10.2 | 5.6 | 5.3 | 0.3 | 4.6 | 4.3 | 0.3 |
| India (1981/82) | 6.0 | 0.9 | 0.2 | 0.7 | 5.1 | 2.6 | 2.5 |
| Indonesia (1982/83) | 5.1 | 3.6 | 0.1 | 3.5 | 1.4 | 1.4 | 0.0 |
| Israel (1982) | 18.6 | 10.5 | 5.2 | 5.3 | 8.1 | 5.5 | 2.6 |
| Ivory Coast (1982)* | 12.3 | 10.7 | 0.3 | 10.4 | 1.6 | 0.9 | 0.7 |
| Jamaica (1981/82) | 16.4 | 9.4 | – | – | 7.0 | 3.5 | 3.5 |
| Jordan (1982) | 21.7 | 16.8 | 13.7 | 3.1 | 4.9 | 4.5 | 0.4 |
| Kenya (1981/82) | 7.6 | 2.9 | 1.3 | 1.6 | 4.7 | 2.5 | 2.2 |
| Korea (1982)* | 4.3 | 1.3 | 0.0 | 1.3 | 3.0 | 0.6 | 2.4 |
| Liberia (1981/82) | 14.3 | 7.3 | 3.7 | 3.6 | 7.0 | 4.0 | 3.1 |

finance the level of deficits that they did. Only seven countries – Brazil, Greece, Portugal, Sierra Leone, Trinidad and Tobago, Zaire and Zambia – were able to finance more than 10 per cent of GDP from domestic sources. At least four of these countries fall within the category of semi-industrial countries. If the domestic banking system had been the only source of financing, only five countries would have financed deficits of more than 10 per cent of GDP. The table shows also the relative unimportance of non-banking domestic sources of financing. Where these were important, they were often associated with captive markets for government bonds.

## Concluding remarks

This chapter has attempted to make a point that seems obvious but that, unfortunately, is often not appreciated. *Ex ante,* a country can plan to have, for a given fiscal year, any level of public expenditure and fiscal deficit. However, *ex post,* the maximum deficit that it can have (expressed as a proportion of GDP) will be limited by the sources of financing. Some of these sources are likely to be inflexible. Others can be increased, up to a point, if the country is willing to pay a price in terms of higher real interest rates for domestic bond finance, or a higher rate of inflation for inflationary finance.

It is often thought that recourse to central bank financing frees a country from these constraints. However, this is not correct. First, as the country pursues inflationary finance and thus experiences higher rates of inflation, some of the other sources of financing will be reduced. For example, it will be more difficult for the country to get foreign commercial loans and to sell bonds domestically. Second, inflation is likely to reduce public sector revenues from taxes and from the sale of public services.[10] Third, even if inflation did not affect the other sources, a higher rate of central bank financing will increase real revenue (from inflationary finance) only up to a given rate of inflation. Beyond that rate, more inflation will be associated with lower real revenue as real money balances, that form the base for the inflation tax, shrink relative to their pre-inflation levels.

## Notes

1. It should be made clear that maximum deficit for one year does not mean optimal deficit for longer periods. Maximizing the deficit this year may reduce the size of future financeable deficits and, perhaps, the size of future real public expenditure. Thus, the dynamic aspects of the problem are ignored.
2. For a review of the literature on the supply of external finance, see McDonald (1982); Katz (1982).
3. A striking example is provided by Mexico. External commercial loans to the public sector that were $17.8 billion in 1981 fell to $6.8 billion in 1982. In 1983, these loans amounted to $5 billion.
4. In effect, the foreign bank or supplier has little choice but to extend a loan equal to the interest or to the payment.
5. If there is high inflation and the government decides to issue indexed bonds, these may become close substitutes for money, especially if they are of short maturity. They may thus imply a direct monetization of the deficit.

6. This section draws from Tanzi (1978).
7. It is possible that commercial banks divert toward the government loans that they would have provided to the private sector out of a given total credit expansion. In such case, the deficit would be financed by the direct crowing out of the private sector.
8. When inflation is a new phenomenon, individuals may not fully anticipate the rate of monetary expansion or may not see the connection between that rate and the rate of inflation. In that case, the revenue from monetary finance may be temporarily higher than assumed by our analysis. See Khan and Knight (1982).
9. They will also engage in currency substitution. In other words, they will replace domestic currency with foreign currency (especially dollars).
10. See Tanzi, Chapter 7.

# References

Bailey, Martin J., 'The welfare cost of inflationary finance', *Journal of Political Economy* 64, April 1956: 98–110.

Barro, Robert J., 'Are government bonds net wealth?', *Journal of Political Economy* 82, November–December 1974: 1095–1117.

Cagan, Phillip, 'The monetary dynamics of hyperinflation', in *Studies in the Quantity Theory of Money,* Milton Friedman (ed.), University of Chicago Press, 1956: 25–117.

Friedman, Milton, 'Discussion of the inflationary gap', *American Economic Review* 32, June 1942: 308–14.

Katz, Menachem, 'Government policy, external public indebtedness, and debt service', mimeo 26 March 1982.

Khan, Mohsin S. and Knight, Malcolm D., 'Unanticipated monetary growth and inflationary finance', *Journal of Money, Credit, and Banking* August 1982: 347–64.

McDonald, Donogh C., 'Debt capacity and developing country borrowing: a survey of the literature', *IMF Staff Papers* 29, December 1982: 603–46.

Tanzi, Vito and Blejer, Mario I., 'Inflation, interest rate policy, and currency substitution in developing economics: a discussion of some major issues', *World Development* 10, September 1982: 781–9.

——'Fiscal deficits and balance of payments disequilibrium in IMF adjustment programs', pp. 117–36 in *Adjustment, Conditionality, and International Financing,* Joaquin Muns (ed.), Washington, DC: International Monetary Fund 1984.

Tanzi, Vito, 'Inflation, lags in collection, and the real value of tax revenue', *IMF Staff Papers* 24, March 1977: pp. 154–67.

——'Inflation, real tax revenue and the case for inflationary finance: theory with an application to Argentina', *IMF Staff Papers* September 1978: 417–51.

# 7 Inflation, lags in collection, and the real value of tax revenue

The literature dealing with the impact of inflation on taxation is so extensive that it may suggest that it would be difficult to write anything novel on this subject. Yet a close perusal of this literature shows that it has been biased by the recent experiences of the industrialized countries. For these countries, inflation has generally been associated with increases in the real value of tax revenues, so that many authors have been led to believe that the main inflation-induced problems are the prevention of this supposedly unwanted, or at least unlegislated, increase in revenue and the neutralization of the inevitable effects on the redistribution of the tax burden among income groups. The increase in real revenue is likely to occur mainly when the lags in the collection of taxes are short, and the tax systems are elastic. However, while these conditions seem to characterize many industrialized countries, they are not common to all countries.

When one deals with countries having somewhat longer lags in the collection of taxes, and tax systems with money–income elasticities not much greater, or even less, than unity, the consequences of inflation can be very different, especially when the rate of inflation becomes high. Unfortunately, these alternative situations are not products of an economist's imagination but, on the contrary, have either existed or continue to exist in many developing countries, and perhaps even in some industrialized countries. For these countries, the problem has not been an increase, but rather an inflation-induced fall in real revenue. In many cases, this fall has, in itself, become a contributing factor in the inflationary process when the affected governments have financed the fiscal deficits through the printing of new money.

There has been hardly any analysis of what happens to real tax revenue when the tax systems are not elastic, the lags in tax collection are not short, and the rate of inflation becomes high. The main objective of this chapter is to show that when the rate of inflation becomes high, the inevitable lags in the collection of taxes become very important and, unless compensated for by high elasticities, may often lead to a decrease in real revenue. The impact of lags has generally been ignored.[1] After a theoretical discussion of the issues, the chapter will use Argentina as a concrete example of a country in which the combination of high inflation, a relatively long average lag in tax collection, and a low elasticity of the tax system has recently brought about a drastic fall in real revenue. The chapter will focus on the effects of the lags, and will thus ignore the inflation-induced distortions in taxable bases that may also affect real revenues.

## Theoretical analysis
### Taxable events and de jure elasticity
This chapter defines a *taxable event* as one that creates a legal financial liability on the part of a tax-payer (individual, retailer, corporation) toward the state. For example, the earning of income may create an obligation on the part of the income earner to pay an income tax; the spending of income may create a legal obligation on the part of the buyer or seller to pay a sales tax on that expenditure;[2] or the ownership of a real asset may create an obligation to pay a property tax. This chapter will assume that a seller sells X dollars worth of commodities that are subject to a sales tax at an *ad valorem* rate of $\alpha$. Or, alternatively, it will assume that an individual earns Y dollars and that this income is subject to a proportional income tax levied at the rate of ß. In the first case, the taxable event (that is, the sale) has created a liability of $\alpha X$; in the second, it has created a liability of ßY. However, while these liabilities have been created at the moment the taxable event has occurred (that is, at the moment when income has been earned or spent), the government will receive the payment only at a later time. In the first case, the seller may not transfer the tax to the government until some later period. In the second case, the taxpayer himself, or, alternatively, the employer who may have withheld the tax will transfer the tax money after some delay.

These lags introduce complications in the proper definition of tax elasticity, and even that of the average tax rate. In a theoretical world in which payments were made at the same time that taxable events occurred, there would be a clearly definable elasticity of the tax payment with respect to income, or some other taxable base, that would not be affected by any lag in the payments. As national income changed, depending on the legal characteristics of the tax, the percentage change in the tax collection would be equal to, or more or less than, the percentage change in national income. This theoretical, or *de jure* elasticity would consequently be equal to, or more or less than, unity. In this lagless world, if the elasticity of the tax system were greater than unity, inflation would, *ceteris paribus*, bring about a real increase in tax payments, so that the ratio of taxes to national income would, in fact, rise.[3]

An alternative way of looking at this theoretical or *de jure* elasticity is to relate the tax collection *at a given time* to the income (or, perhaps, the expenditure) at the time when the event that created the legal liability occurred (in other words, to its legal base). In this case, if the earning of an income $Y_0$ – where 0 indicates the period when the taxable event occurred – creates a tax liability equal to $ßY_0$, which, because of a lag in collection, is paid, say, two periods later when nominal income has risen to $Y_2$, one could calculate the elasticity (or even the average tax rate) by relating the tax payment ßY$_0$ to the original income Y$_0$, rather than to the present higher income Y$_2$, as is generally done. However, the elasticity – or even the average tax rate – calculated on this basis would be different from the effective one normally estimated statistically, which relates revenue received in a given period to income received in the same period, and thus ignores the legal connection defined above.[4] In conclusion, whenever nominal income is growing and there are lags in tax collection, both the elasticity of the tax and the average tax rate will be different, if they are estimated with respect to current income rather than with respect to the income prevailing at the time of the taxable event. This difference can become substantial whenever there is considerable inflation associated with sizable lags. The nature of these lags will be discussed later. For the time being, it is sufficient to assume that these lags exist and that somehow they can be measured.

*Inflation, lags, and real tax revenue*
The impact of different lags and rates of inflation on the real value of one dollar of tax revenue can be estimated by solving the equation

$$R = \frac{1}{(1+p)^n} \tag{1}$$

where R is the real value of a dollar of tax revenue collected today but measured in prices of the period when the taxable event occurred; p is the monthly rate of inflation; and n is the size of the lag, expressed in months.

Table 7.1 has been calculated by solving the equation (1) in relation to various rates of inflation and lags. The table assumes that taxes are collected successively, with lags that may be zero, 1 month, 2 months, 3 months...up to 12 months. Surely, these alternatives embrace the realities of the tax systems of most countries, although particular taxes may be, and are at times, collected with even longer lags. These lags are shown horizontally at the top of the table. Vertically, on the left, the table indicates selected monthly rates of inflation. It starts with the assumption of a zero inflation rate per month, then it considers 1 per cent per month, 2 per cent, 3 per cent, and selective rates all the way up to 50 per cent per month.[5] All of these rates have been experienced by some countries, at least for some months, in recent years. The alternative lags and rates of inflation provide a matrix that is likely to include the experience of most countries.

If the price elasticity of a country's tax system were one, Table 7.1 could also be used to raise questions about the effect of inflation on total tax revenue. In other words, it would allow one to answer the following question: Assuming that taxes in a given country are collected with an average lag of x months, and that the country is experiencing a monthly rate of inflation of y, what will be the impact on the real value of its tax revenue?[6] Each row in the table will then tell us what happens to the real value of the tax revenue when, given a certain rate of

*Table 7.1 Impact of lags in tax payments and of rates of inflation on the real value of tax payment*

| Monthly Rates of Inflation | Monthly Lags in Payment of Taxes | | | | | | | | | | | | |
|---|---|---|---|---|---|---|---|---|---|---|---|---|
| | 0 | 1 | 2 | 3 | 4 | 5 | 6 | 7 | 8 | 9 | 10 | 11 | 12 |
| 0 | 1.00 | 1.00 | 1.00 | 1.00 | 1.00 | 1.00 | 1.00 | 1.00 | 1.00 | 1.00 | 1.00 | 1.00 | 1.00 |
| 1 | 1.00 | 0.99 | 0.98 | 0.97 | 0.96 | 0.95 | 0.94 | 0.93 | 0.92 | 0.91 | 0.90 | 0.90 | 0.89 |
| 1.5 | 1.00 | 0.99 | 0.97 | 0.96 | 0.94 | 0.93 | 0.91 | 0.90 | 0.89 | 0.87 | 0.86 | 0.85 | 0.84 |
| 2 | 1.00 | 0.98 | 0.96 | 0.94 | 0.92 | 0.91 | 0.89 | 0.87 | 0.85 | 0.84 | 0.82 | 0.80 | 0.79 |
| 3 | 1.00 | 0.97 | 0.94 | 0.91 | 0.89 | 0.86 | 0.84 | 0.81 | 0.79 | 0.77 | 0.74 | 0.72 | 0.70 |
| 4 | 1.00 | 0.96 | 0.92 | 0.89 | 0.85 | 0.82 | 0.79 | 0.76 | 0.73 | 0.70 | 0.68 | 0.65 | 0.63 |
| 5 | 1.00 | 0.95 | 0.91 | 0.86 | 0.82 | 0.78 | 0.75 | 0.71 | 0.68 | 0.65 | 0.61 | 0.58 | 0.56 |
| 6 | 1.00 | 0.94 | 0.89 | 0.84 | 0.79 | 0.75 | 0.70 | 0.67 | 0.63 | 0.59 | 0.56 | 0.53 | 0.50 |
| 7 | 1.00 | 0.93 | 0.87 | 0.82 | 0.76 | 0.71 | 0.67 | 0.62 | 0.58 | 0.54 | 0.51 | 0.48 | 0.44 |
| 8 | 1.00 | 0.93 | 0.86 | 0.79 | 0.74 | 0.68 | 0.63 | 0.58 | 0.54 | 0.50 | 0.46 | 0.43 | 0.40 |
| 9 | 1.00 | 0.92 | 0.84 | 0.77 | 0.71 | 0.65 | 0.60 | 0.55 | 0.50 | 0.46 | 0.42 | 0.39 | 0.36 |
| 9.4 | 1.00 | 0.91 | 0.84 | 0.76 | 0.70 | 0.64 | 0.58 | 0.53 | 0.49 | 0.45 | 0.41 | 0.37 | 0.34 |
| 10 | 1.00 | 0.91 | 0.83 | 0.75 | 0.68 | 0.62 | 0.56 | 0.51 | 0.47 | 0.42 | 0.39 | 0.35 | 0.32 |
| 20 | 1.00 | 0.83 | 0.69 | 0.58 | 0.48 | 0.40 | 0.33 | 0.28 | 0.23 | 0.19 | 0.16 | 0.13 | 0.11 |
| 30 | 1.00 | 0.77 | 0.59 | 0.46 | 0.35 | 0.27 | 0.21 | 0.16 | 0.12 | 0.09 | 0.07 | 0.06 | 0.04 |
| 40 | 1.00 | 0.71 | 0.51 | 0.36 | 0.26 | 0.19 | 0.13 | 0.09 | 0.07 | 0.05 | 0.03 | 0.02 | 0.02 |
| 50 | 1.00 | 0.67 | 0.44 | 0.30 | 0.20 | 0.13 | 0.09 | 0.06 | 0.04 | 0.03 | 0.02 | 0.01 | 0.01 |

inflation, the length of the lag changes from zero to 12 months. Thus, for example, if the monthly rate of inflation were 10 per cent, and the country collected its taxes with a zero lag, it would not experience any fall in the real value of its revenue; however, if it collected its taxes with a 1-month lag, it would experience a 9 per cent fall; if it collected its taxes with a lag of 5 months, it would experience a 38 per cent fall, and so on. The higher the monthly rate of inflation and the longer the lag in payment, the greater will be the reduction in the real value of tax revenue that a country will experience. This is seen clearly in the table by reading down the columns and across the rows.

Alternatively, the columns in the table show what happens when, given a certain average lag in collection, the rate of inflation is assumed to become progressively higher. Thus, for example, a country that had an average lag of four months would lose 4 per cent of the real value of its tax revenue if, after a period of price stability, it entered an inflationary period in which prices increased at the rate of 1 per cent per month; it would lose 18 per cent if the rate of inflation rose to 5 per cent per month, and 32 per cent if it rose to 10 per cent. If the rate of inflation should become extremely high, say 50 per cent per month, the real value of taxes would be reduced to 20 per cent of what they would be in the absence of inflation. If the rate of inflation is zero, there is no fall in the real value of taxes, since the value of the dollar collected would remain unchanged over time.[7] Alternatively, if the lag should be zero, then there would be no decrease in the real value of tax revenue regardless of the rate of inflation.[8]

In summary, the main conclusions so far are as follows: first, given the rate of inflation, and assuming that the price elasticity of the tax system is one, the longer the lag in the collection of taxes, the greater will be, *ceteris paribus*, the net inflation-induced real reduction in the tax revenues that the government receives. Second, given the lag in the collection of taxes, the higher the rate of inflation, the lower, *ceteris paribus*, will be the real value of the tax revenue. Finally, the table also shows the gains that are possible to a country from the reduction of the lags in payments. For example, a country experiencing an inflationary period could replace an income tax with a value-added tax collected with a much shorter lag, and would benefit from the change even if, in the absence of inflation, that change would have been associated with a zero net change in revenue.

### Inflation, lags, and revenue when the elasticity is not one

An assumption used above was that of a unitary *de jure* elasticity of the tax system. This implies that inflation *per se*, in the absence of any other factors, would not generate any real increase or fall in revenues. The assumption of unitary elasticity for the tax system *in toto* is a realistic one for most developing countries (as well as for some developed countries), as their personal income tax is not of overwhelming importance and often is not particularly progressive.

However, if a country were highly dependent on personal income taxes, and if these taxes were collected with a short lag,[9] then, as the current literature on the impact of inflation on taxes has emphasized, the inflationary conditions would bring about, *ceteris paribus,* an increase in the real value of revenues by shrinking the real size of the exemptions and the brackets. Thus, if taxes are collected with a lag, the gain coming from the above-mentioned progressivity (and possibly from distortions in components of income other than wages) would have to be balanced against the losses emphasized in the table. Whether revenues in real terms would increase or decrease over a given period would depend on the interrelationship among the elasticity, the rate of inflation, and the lag in collection.

Given the existence of a lag, and given an elasticity that exceeds unity, a steady increase in the general price level (following a period of price stability) will, at first, lead to the same fall in real revenue shown in the table; then, as the average price level becomes progressively higher, and as the increase in the price level is accompanied by a greater than proportional increase in nominal tax revenue, real tax revenue (and thus the share of revenue in the income of the current period) will start increasing and will continue increasing as long as the price level keeps rising. In time, the initial loss in revenue will be made up and, if inflation continues, real revenue will rise. The shorter the lag in collection, and the higher the elasticity, the more quickly will the real level of tax revenue regain and exceed the preinflationary level. The relationships between real revenue and the rate of inflation, the level of prices, the elasticity of the tax system, and the size of the lag are analysed mathematically in the Appendix.

Once the issue of elasticity is introduced (in other words, once one assumes that the *de jure* elasticity of the tax system is different from one), the arithmetic computations needed to recalculate the results given in the table become more complex; furthermore – and this is more important – the results in the table can no longer be used as estimates of what happens to the total real tax revenue of a country as a result of changes in the rate of inflation.[10] It must, however, be emphasized that the issue of elasticity is important mainly for the personal income tax, and may be compensated for in part by the existence of other taxes (such as those on property and on sales that are levied with specific rates) that are likely to have an elasticity of less than one. Therefore, as a working hypothesis for developing countries, a unitary elasticity for the whole tax system would often be a defensible one. This is the hypothesis used in connection with Argentina (pp. 10–12).

**The measurement of the average lag**
The lag in the collection of a given tax – that is, the lapse of time between the taxable event and the tax collection connected with that event – is made up of two parts, which could be called, respectively, the legal lag and the delinquency lag.

The first is the government-sanctioned delay in payment, which carries no penalty. For example, a self-employed individual is normally required to pay his income tax some time after the earning of the income; similarly, a retailer transfers the receipts from sales taxes to the authorities some time after the sales have taken place. The delinquency lag exists when the payment is made after the time it falls due. In most cases the legal lag is the most important, although under particular circumstances the delinquency lag can become very significant.

In order to deal with the whole tax system of a specific country, one needs to determine the size of the lag for that tax system. This lag, of course, is likely to differ among countries; it will be affected by the lag of each tax used and by the particular tax structure of the country. If the size of the lag for each tax is known, then the lag for the whole system can be determined by taking a weighted average of all the lags related to the specific taxes. The weights in this calculation are determined by the relative importance of each tax in the total tax revenue. It follows that the fewer the tax sources on which the country depends, the easier will be the estimation of the overall lag. The lag that applies to each tax can often be determined only by having discussions with the authorities in charge of tax collection, as the tax laws are often not very helpful on this matter. These discussions should cover items such as the method of payment, the time when payment is made, the variability of the lag.

Let us assume that $T_i$ refers to the proportion of the total tax revenue generated by a particular tax, and that $L_i$ is the lag between the time when the liability for that tax payment is created (that is, the time of the taxable event) and the time when the tax payment is actually made.[11] The $i...., n$ refer to the specific taxes (on income, wealth, etc.) that are being used in the country to collect revenue. The tax system's total lag $L^t$ is

$$L^t = \sum_{i=1}^{n} T_i L_i \qquad (2)$$

This is the lag used in Table 7.1.

### An application to Argentina

In Argentina, the number of taxes being collected at any particular moment is truly very large. For example, in June 1976 the Tax Bureau (*Dirección General Impositiva*) was collecting revenue in connection with 34 existing taxes and 48 defunct taxes; furthermore, the Tax Bureau was not the only agency responsible for tax collection, since part of total tax revenue was collected by the customs administration, by the local governments, and by the social security administration. However, the specific taxes can be grouped by main categories, and the average lag for each one of these categories can be estimated. Discussions with the authorities responsible for tax collection indicated that in 1975 and for the first half of 1976, the sales or value-added tax was collected with a lag of 90 days, stamp taxes with a lag of 30 days, fuel taxes with a lag of 45 days, import and export taxes with lags of 45 days, excise taxes with a lag of 120–50 days, social security taxes with a lag of 30 days, and income and property taxes with lags of at least a year.[12]

The basic information for estimating the average lag for the tax system of Argentina has been summarized in Table 7.2.[13] By using this information to solve equation (2), one obtains, alternatively, a lag of 4.3 months when social security taxes are included (column 2), and a lag of 5.7 months when social security taxes are excluded (column 3).

*Table 7.2    Argentina: tax revenue by type of tax (1974) and lags in collection (1975)*

| Taxes | Revenue, 1974 | | | |
|---|---|---|---|---|
| | Amount | Ti[2] | | Li[1] |
| | (1) | (2)[3] | (3)[4] | (4) |
| | *(billion pesos)* | *(per cent)* | | *(months)* |
| Income | 6.44 | 11.9 | 16.9 | 12 |
| Property | 2.38 | 4.4 | 6.3 | 12 |
| Sales (value-added tax) | 4.26 | 7.9 | 11.2 | 3 |
| Excises | 3.25 | 6.0 | 8.6 | 4 |
| Fuel | 4.32 | 8.0 | 11.4 | 1.5 |
| Import | 1.72 | 3.2 | 4.5 | 1.5 |
| Export | 4.27 | 7.9 | 11.2 | 1.5 |
| Others[5] | 11.37 | 21.0 | 29.9 | 6 |
| Social Security | 16.09 | 29.7 | — | 1 |
| Total | 54.10 | 100.0 | 100.0 | |

Sources: The revenue data were provided by the Argentine Ministry of Economics, and the information on lags by officials from the different collecting agencies.
Notes:
[1] Lag between the creation of the liability for payment and the actual payment.
[2] Proportion of total revenue generated by a particular tax.
[3] Including social security taxes.
[4] Excluding social security taxes.
[5] These are partly stamp taxes collected with a 30-day lag and partly local property taxes collected with at least a 12-month lag. The specific breakdown is not available.

In 1974 the ratio of total taxes, including social security, to gross domestic product (GDP) for Argentina was 17.74. By 1975 this ratio had fallen to 12.24, or by 31 per cent. If social security taxes were excluded, then the ratio fell from 12.60 to 7.75, or by 38 per cent. It would be interesting to see to what extent one can approximate this reduction in taxes by looking at the behaviour of prices between 1974 and 1975. In 1974 the wholesale price index (WPI), which is the most reliable one in the case of Argentina, rose at an average monthly rate of 1.5 per cent. In 1975 the monthly increase in the WPI was 9.4 per cent. Using the above-determined lags in connection with Table 7.1, it can be calculated that an increase in the monthly rate of inflation from 1.5 per cent to 9.4 per cent would have been associated with a fall in real revenues of 26 per cent if the lag were 4.0 months, 31 per cent if the lag were 5.0 months, and 36 per cent if the lag were 6.0 months. Since, as indicated above, the estimated lag for the tax system was at least 4.3 months with social security and 5.7 months without social security, it can be concluded that in 1975 the actual behaviour of tax revenues followed very closely the behaviour that would be expected from the theoretical analysis. In fact, if lags of 5.0 months (including social security) and 6.0 months (excluding social security) are taken, the expected fall in real revenues turns out to be almost exactly equal to the actual fall.[14]

In the early part of 1976, the rate of inflation accelerated and for some months became very high. For example, it was 19.1 per cent in January, 28.5 per cent in February, 53.8 per cent in March, and 26.3 per cent in April. At this rate of inflation, lags of 5.0 months would have reduced the real revenues by about 75 per cent. The preliminary information available indicates, in fact, that revenues fell by at least this percentage. By the end of 1975 and early 1976, other factors came into play, resulting in the distortion of the theoretically estimated relationship between the behaviour of taxes and the behaviour of prices. These other factors, a discussion of which is beyond the scope of this paper, concern the increasing rate of tax evasion and particularly the increasing lag in payment owing to the fact that many tax-payers faced with very low penalties for tax delay often resorted to a postponement of their taxes as the cheapest form of available credit. Therefore, by 1976 one would expect a fall in revenues that exceeds the theoretically estimated fall. At least for the first few months of 1976 this, in fact, happened.

**Concluding remarks**

The foregoing analysis indicates that countries that face highly inflationary pressures, or that are likely to face them at some stage, should pay much more attention to the impact that lags in the payment of taxes may have on real revenue. No country, of course, can collect taxes without any delay, and some taxes require longer lags than others. However, for most countries the necessary delay – that is, the legal lag – in tax collection can be substantially reduced while still recognising that tax-payers require time to gather all the information needed to calculate their tax payments and to make them.

Policy should be aimed at trying to reduce the legal lag to some 'optimal' level, and the delinquency lag to zero. This delinquency lag can be eliminated by stiff penalties, applied on top of tax payments, that have been adjusted for the change in the price level that has occurred during the delay. Stiff penalties alone are not sufficient, as a number of countries have learned, since what appears to be a stiff penalty when the rate of inflation is low may become insignificant when the rate of inflation becomes very high.

Argentina has recently passed a law that will require the indexation of payments due to the government, in addition to the penalties. As to the legal lag – that is, the one between the taxable event and the time when the tax is due – governments should attempt to reduce it without creating difficulties of an accounting nature for the tax-payer. Citing again the case of Argentina, the lag in the value-added tax, which was 90 days, is being reduced to 60 days, which still appears to be relatively long. It is reported that in Chile the value-added tax is now being paid twice a month in order to reduce to a minimum the erosion in real value associated with inflation. Other taxes on production, transactions, imports, and exports can also be collected with lags that can be reduced to perhaps not much more than one month.

For property and income taxes, however, the question will remain much more complex, as long as these taxes are paid on the annual, rather than on a monthly, basis, as is the case with income taxes collected at the source on wages and salaries. For these taxes there is the problem of estimating the base on which they are calculated. For example, in Argentina the advance payments of taxes on the income of enterprises were estimated on the basis of the previous year's income. In a situation where prices have increased significantly between one year and the next, an advance payment based on the previous year's nominal income becomes much too low in relation to present income. A solution that is being considered in Argentina, and that seems to be a reasonable one, would be to base the advance payment of the previous year's income adjusted for the change in prices over the year. An alternative solution could be to make the taxpayer estimate the income that he expects to receive in the current year, and make him pay monthly or quarterly instalments based on it. At the time when he settled the final payment, he would have to escalate the payment for the price change since the middle of the taxable year if such a payment was due to the government. For property taxes, the same problem occurs. With high rates of inflation, it would be necessary to escalate the previous year's assessment by the rate of inflation before the tax was calculated for the current year.

## Appendix[15]

Define:

R    =    real value of tax revenue accruing in period 0 but paid n periods later, in terms of resources in period 0 (i.e., the period the taxable event took place)

T    =    nominal value of accruals in period 0

P0    =    price level at time 0

$$\dot{p} = \frac{1}{P0} \frac{dP0}{dt} = \text{instantaneous rate of inflation at time 0}$$

$$R = \frac{T}{P0(1 + \dot{p})^n} \tag{3}$$

To give an economic interpretation to equation (3), one needs to take small discrete values of n and p.

E = elasticity of tax accrual with respect to changes in the price level (*de jure* elasticity)

$$E = \frac{dT}{dP0} \cdot \frac{P0}{T} \tag{4}$$

Equation (4) can be rewritten as

$$\frac{dT}{dP0} = \frac{ET}{P0} \text{ and} \tag{5}$$

$$P0dT - ETdP0 = 0 \tag{6}$$

Dividing by POT, we get

$$\frac{dT}{T} - E\frac{dP0}{P0} = 0 \text{ from which, taking the integral, we get} \tag{7}$$

$$\int \frac{1}{T}dT - \int \frac{E}{P0} dP0 = C \tag{8}$$

where C is the constant of integration. From (8) we get

$$LnT - ELnP0 = C \text{ or,} \tag{9}$$
$$TP0^{-E} = e^c = K \text{ and } T = KP0^E \tag{10}$$

Substituting in equation (3), we get

$$R = \frac{KP0^E}{P0(1 + \dot{p})^n} = \frac{KP0^{E-1}}{(1 + \dot{p})^n} \tag{11}$$

Equation (11) can be differentiated partially with respect to the rate of inflation $\dot{p}$, the absolute price level P, the elasticity E, and the lag n. The equations so derived are as follows:

$$\frac{\delta R}{\delta \dot{p}} = \frac{-nKP0^{E-1}}{(1 + \dot{p})^{n+1}} \tag{12}$$

$$\frac{\delta R}{\delta P} = \frac{(E - 1)KP0^{E-2}}{(1 + \dot{p})^n} \tag{13}$$

$$\frac{\delta R}{\delta E} = \frac{KP0^{E-1}LnP0}{(1 + \dot{p})^n} \tag{14}$$

$$\frac{\delta R}{\delta n} = \frac{-KP0^{E-1} Ln(1 + \dot{p})}{(1 + \dot{p})^n} \tag{15}$$

Equation (12) indicates that the real value of tax revenue R will fall with an increase in the rate of inflation as long as the lag n is greater than zero. If n = 0, R will not change with p regardless of the size of elasticity E.

Equation (13) indicates that $\frac{\delta R}{\delta P} \gtrless 0$ as E $\gtrless$ 1.

If the elasticity E is equal to unity, the real value of revenue R will not depend on the absolute price level, but only on the rate of inflation and the length of the lag.

Equation (14) indicates that, given the initial price level P0 and the rate of inflation $\dot{p}$, then the higher elasticity E is, the higher real revenue R will be.

From equation (15) it can be seen that, given a positive rate of inflation, the longer the lag, the smaller real revenue will be.

# Notes

1.  One important exception is the paper by Teruo Hirao and Carlos A. Aguirre, 'Maintaining the level of income tax collections under inflationary conditions', *Staff Papers* 17, July 1970: 277-325. Hirao and Aguirre limit the discussion to the income tax, while the discussion in this chapter refers to all taxes. Of interest also is the paper by Pedro Rado, 'Income payment systems and inflation', mimeo 2 July 1975.

2.  Legally the tax may be levied either on the seller or on the buyer although, except for an expenditure tax, it is the seller who generally transfers the tax payment to the authorities.

3.  By the same token, the real value of revenues would not be affected by inflation if the elasticity were one. Thus, if indexation of the tax system succeeded in making the elasticity equal to one, there would not be, in this lagless world, any inflation-induced increases in the ratio of taxes to national income. But, of course, this theoretical situation is not practically possible.

4.  During this whole discussion the underlying legal structure is assumed to remain unchanged. This chapter is, therefore, talking about automatic, or built-in, elasticity that excludes the effects of discretionary changes.

5.  In order to use Table 7.1 in connection with the Argentine situation, the results associated with monthly inflation rates of 1.5 per cent and 9.4 per cent are also shown.

6.  To simplify the analysis and emphasize the impact of price changes, real growth during the inflationary period is assumed to be either zero or insignificant.

7.  Even with zero inflation the tax-payer gets some advantage owing to the postponement of taxes. The higher the rate of discount, the greater the advantage related to a given lag.

8.  Even in this case, real revenue would be affected to the extent that inflation distorted the taxable bases (capital gains, interest, profits, property values, etc.). However, the change in real revenue would not be induced by the lag. It should be recalled that this chapter has assumed a unitary price elasticity of the tax system. For an analysis of the inflation-induced distortions of interest income, see Vito Tanzi, 'Inflation, indexation and interest income taxation', Banca Nazionale del Lavoro, *Quarterly Review* 29, March 1976: 64–76.

9.  In most countries, income taxes, except for those withheld at the source, are collected with considerable lags.

10. But they still indicate how lags reduce the real value of each revenue dollar collected compared with the real value of a tax liability of a dollar at the time when it accrues – in other words, in relation to what real revenue would be in a lagless world.

11. It will be necessary to assume that the variance for these specific lags is so small that it can be ignored. If the variance is not small, the whole issue becomes much more complex and the method suggested in this section may give results that are no longer reliable.

12. The government is, at the present time, contemplating the possibility of reducing some of these lags.

13. The revenue figures relate to 1974, which, by Argentine standards, can be considered a good year.

14. Since the change in real GDP was overwhelmed by the price change, the ratio of taxes to GDP is a close indicator of the behaviour of real revenue.

15. The author wishes to thank William J. Byrne for his help with this mathematical appendix.

# 8 The impact of macroeconomic policies on the level of taxation (and on the fiscal balance) in developing countries

## Introduction

In recent years the level of taxation of many developing countries has experienced considerable fluctuations over relatively short periods. These fluctuations cannot, in many cases, be attributed to deteriorating tax administrations or to changes in the traditional determinants of tax levels, such as openness, exports of minerals, and per capita income. Other factors must consequently have played a significant role. This paper identifies these other factors as the countries' macroeconomic policies.

This chapter first discusses the extent to which tax revenue is related to the level of the exchange rate and to the degree of import restrictiveness. The level of the official exchange rate is shown to have important effects on import duties, export taxes, sales taxes, and excise taxes. Import substitution policies are also shown to reduce tax revenue in the typical developing country.

The chapter then discusses the connection between trade liberalization and tax revenue. It argues that a policy of trade liberalization, consisting of reduction in high import duties, imposition of (low) import duties on previously exempt imports, removal of quantitative restrictions, and devaluations will often be accompanied by important increases in revenue. Their effect on the fiscal balance will, however, depend on other considerations.

The issue of the impact of devaluation on the fiscal balance in the presence of a large external public debt, is then considered. It challenges the conclusion of several economists that in this case devaluation inevitably worsens the fiscal balance.

A summary is presented of some earlier work by the author on the effect of an acceleration in the rate of inflation on the tax-to-gross domestic product (GDP) ratio. The absolute size of the fall in this ratio is shown to depend on the increase in the rate of inflation, the size of the collection lag, and the initial level of taxation.

Finally, the effects on tax revenue of financial policies are discussed. Low or negative real interest rates on domestic lending are likely to reduce the tax level by promoting the expansion of a curb market, the stimulation of capital flight, the dollarization of the economy, and the purchase of real assets.

*116*

The chapter concludes that when macroeconomic policies are changing rapidly and significantly, it will be much more difficult for tax reforms to have important and identifiable revenue effects. In these circumstances, tax reform should insulate, to the extent possible, tax revenue from damaging macroeconomic developments.

## The determinants of tax levels

The level of taxation, expressed as a percentage of gross domestic product (T/GDP), varies considerably among the world's developing countries. In a few of them, it is below 10 per cent. In a few others it is above 30 per cent. For the majority of countries, however, that level ranges between these two limits with an overall average of about 18 per cent and a substantial proportion of developing countries in the 15–25 per cent range (see Tanzi, 1987).[1] Over the past two to three decades these levels have attracted the attention of many economists who have tried to determine the factors that bring about these variations.[2] They have identified many such factors reflecting either characteristics of the developing countries' economies, socio-political features of societies, or aspects of the tax systems themselves. Some of these factors are briefly discussed here under the heading of statistical determinants, institutional or social determinants, and tax policy determinants.

*Statistical determinants*
Many of the quantitatively-oriented studies on the level of taxation have regressed T/GDP against some of the following factors:

(a)    the level of per capita income, often taken as a proxy for the level of economic development;
(b)    the degree of urbanization;
(c)    the literacy rate;
(d)    the degree of monetization of the economy;
(e)    the ratio of exports and imports to GDP (the so-called openness factor);
(f)    the share of mining or agriculture in GDP;
(g)    and the size of the country and so forth.

As Richard Musgrave and others have argued, some of these factors play an important role in determining the tax bases or the 'tax handles' that can be used by governments to raise the desired level of revenue (Musgrave, 1969).

Recognizing that the extent to which developing countries fully exploit their 'taxable capacities' is likely to depend on their revenue needs, a recent study has included the level of public expenditure among the independent  variables (Tabellini, 1985).[3] The impact of the public debt (domestic and foreign) on the level of taxation should also be mentioned. The existence of a large public debt has important implications for the tax level since in the presence of such a debt the government needs to raise the revenues necessary to service it unless non-interest expenditures can be reduced or unless the government can get access to increasing amounts of loans. When interest on the debt exceeds net borrowing plus the possible reduction in non-interest expenditure, the level of taxation must go up unless the rate of growth of the economy is high enough to neutralize this increase. Therefore, the size of the public debt becomes a positive determinant of present and future tax levels while it may have been a negative influence on levels of taxation in past years.[4] However, to the extent that interest payments are made to foreign lenders, and to the extent that debtor government cannot tax these payments because of special features of the loan contracts, it will lose part of the tax base.[5]

### Institutional or social determinants

Much of the literature that has not concentrated on purely statistical relationships has called attention to more qualitative factors such as

(a)   the quality of the tax administration;
(b)   the resources that the country allocates to this function;
(c)   the honesty of the tax payers;
(d)   the degree of corruption among tax collectors which in turn may be influenced by the level of their wages;
(e)   the size of the penalties for non-compliance by the tax payers and for corruption by the tax administrators;[6]
(f)   the income distribution of the country;
(g)   the importance of the subsistence sector and of the parallel economy;
(h)   the attitude of the citizens toward the government which may be influenced by the quality of public services and by the efficiency with which tax revenues are spent;
(i)   the form of government, and so forth.

Many of these factors are difficult to quantify but are perceived to be of some importance in determining whether a country ends up with a high or low tax level. The extent to which taxes are evaded, or a large parallel economy develops, depends to a considerable extent on some of these factors.

### Tax policy determinants

Among these one should include the use of particular tax sources (for example, whether a country uses or does not use a value added tax; see Nellor, 1987), the number of taxes in the country's tax system,[7] the level of tax rates,[8] the use of tax incentives and tax expenditures in general, and so forth.[9]

Many studies have revealed that effective tax bases are often a small fraction of the potential or theoretical bases. For example, the effective base of the value-added tax is often less than 50 per cent of the theoretical base (see Aguirre and Shome, 1987). Even more extreme figures are obtained for income taxes, where, in some cases, the base falls as low as 10 or 20 per cent of the potential, and for import duties, where various exonerations and smuggling, combined with large non-taxed imports by the public sector itself, reduce the taxable base to a small fraction of what it could be (see Tanzi, 1987).

Much of this is known to those who are familiar with the literature on taxation in developing countries. Recommendations made by tax advisors aimed at raising revenue are normally related to these tax policy determinants. Thus, new rates on existing bases or new taxes are proposed, administrative changes aimed at reducing tax evasion are recommended, the authorities are advised to allocate more resources to tax administration and to increase the salaries of tax administrators. The need to reduce exemptions and to widen tax bases is highlighted, the need to increase the level of penalties is stressed, and so forth. In recent years, tax experts have often recommended that tax bases be broadened and that tax rates be reduced in recognition of the disincentive effects of high marginal rates and of the growing importance of unreported economic activities and tax evasion. A common belief has been that high rates are partly responsible for tax evasion.[10]

The determinants mentioned above may help explain the long-run or potential levels of taxation. However, they have not been able to explain more than a small fraction of the variation of tax levels in empirical cross-section studies. Furthermore, several countries have experienced wide fluctuations in tax levels in relatively short periods of time. These fluctuations could not entirely be attributed to changes in some of these determinants. For example, in Argentina the level of taxation, expressed as a percentage of GDP fell from almost 20 per cent in 1974 to about 13 per cent in 1975; it rose to over 23 per cent in 1980, fell again to 17 per cent in 1983 and rose again to 23 per cent in 1986. In Bolivia it fell from 8.9 per cent in 1981 to 2.8 per cent in 1983 and 2.9 per cent in 1984; it rose to 8.6 per cent in 1985 and to 14.4 per cent in 1986. In the Dominican Republic it fell from 17 per cent in 1975 to 9 per cent in 1982; it rose to almost 15 per cent in 1985. In Ghana it fell from 18.6 per cent in 1970 to 4.4 per cent in 1983 and rose to 14 per cent in 1986. In Madagascar it fell from 27 per cent in 1978 to 15 per cent in 1982. In Mozambique it fell from 16.7 per cent in 1983 to 8.5 per cent in 1985. In Sierra Leone it fell from 16.5 per cent in 1978 to 6 per cent in 1985. Some of these variations were due to movements of commodity prices which reduced export earnings,[11] but most of them were caused by other factors. A full explanation for these dramatic changes cannot be found in the behaviour of the traditional determinants of tax levels or in the deteriorating quality of the tax administration. More specifically, one must look at macroeconomic policies.[12]

This chapter focuses on these policies.

Government policies can affect tax revenue by changing the real value of the exchange rate, the degree of import restrictions, the level of public debt, the level of interest rates, the rate of inflation and by other means. These factors are important in determining the level of taxation at a given moment in time and in determining how that level changes over time. In many cases, substantial changes in tax levels can be traced directly or indirectly to these macroeconomic policies. This aspect has not received the attention that it deserves. In this chapter the relationship between major aspects of macroeconomic policies and tax revenue is discussed.

## Tax revenue and the level of the exchange rate and import restrictions

Those who follow closely the economic policies of developing countries must have observed the existence of an often negative relationship between a country's tax revenue and the real level of its official exchange rate. *Ceteris paribus*, an appreciation of the real official exchange rate – that is a fall in domestic currency units per unit of foreign exchange – leads to a decrease in the tax to GDP ratio. A much overvalued exchange rate implies a much lower tax ratio than would have existed otherwise.[13] There are several reasons behind this conclusion; some are related to direct effects of exchange rate appreciation and some are related to indirect effects.

### Direct effects of overvaluation

*Effect on import duties.*    The most direct link between the real value of the exchange rate and the level of taxation is the relationship between the level of the real exchange rate and the base on which import duties are calculated.[14] Import duties are for the most part levied with *ad valorem* rates and their tax base is determined by the value of the imported products. Therefore, given the official domestic volume of imports coming through official channels, the real value of imports, measured in domestic prices, falls as the exchange rate appreciates. If a country has plenty of foreign exchange and/or unlimited access to foreign loans, the fall in the domestic prices of the imported products associated with the overvaluation of the exchange rate might lead to a higher import volume which, if the price elasticity of imports is greater than one, may offset the negative revenue effects of the overvaluation. However, this is rarely the case especially over the longer run. Thus, a safe conclusion is that a developing country that lets its exchange rate appreciate is likely to experience an immediate and direct loss in one of its most important revenue sources.

*Effect on export taxes.*    The overvaluation of the exchange rate affects (directly) not only the revenue from import duties but also the revenue from other taxes. Take export taxes, for example. Since export taxes are imposed on export values expressed in domestic currency, the tax base for export taxes and thus the revenue from export taxes will fall as a direct consequence of the appreciation of the exchange rate.[15] Export taxes are less important than import duties. They account for about 5 per cent of total tax revenue for all developing countries and for 8 per cent for the poorest fourth.[16]

*Effect on sales and excise taxes.* In developing countries a large share of general sales taxes is collected from imports since in many of these countries, for a variety of reasons, much of the domestic production escapes taxation or is taxed at lower rates. For several countries for which this information is available, the share of total general sales tax revenue collected from imports often exceeds 50 per cent. For example, in Pakistan more than 70 per cent of the sales tax is collected at customs. Excise taxes are also often collected mostly from imported products (such as gasoline, tobacco, cars, televisions). So-called 'domestic' taxes on goods and services (including general sales taxes and excises) account for about 28 per cent of the developing countries' total tax revenue. Changes in the real level of the exchange rate affects these revenues as well. As the real exchange rate is allowed to appreciate, tax collection from general sales taxes and from some excises is likely to fall in real terms.

Developing countries rely heavily on taxes on 'tradable goods'. A high exchange rate lowers the value of these goods. In conclusion, the direct effect of the appreciation of the exchange rate on import duties, export taxes, and 'domestic' taxes on goods and services is likely to be important since these taxes account for 60 per cent of total tax revenue in developing countries.

## Indirect effects of overvaluation

The relationship just discussed between the exchange rate and tax revenue is the direct one. However, an overvalued exchange rate affects revenue also through several indirect channels. Some of these may be very important.

First the overvaluation of the exchange rate reduces, over time, incentives to produce export goods and to export. The volume of exports falls reducing the country's availability of foreign exchange. With less foreign exchange available, imports must be reduced. As a consequence, revenue from export taxes, import duties, domestic sales and excise taxes fall. To the extent that incomes are partly tied to exports, revenue from income tax will also fall.[17] Even if incomes are not directly tied to exports, the scarcity of foreign exchange will reduce domestic activities by reducing imports of raw materials and other inputs. This will negatively affect domestic income tax bases in the modern and, thus, the more easily taxable sector.

Second, overvaluation increases the probability of large future devaluations. Therefore, individuals are likely to take protective actions against that probable future event. One of these actions is to take their capital out of the country (capital flight). Another is to store their financial assets in dollar bills held within the country (currency substitution).

Capital flight and currency substitution (out of the reduced export earnings) will reduce even more the foreign exchange available for imports of goods and services. Therefore, these actions will reduce further the tax base.[18] If individuals expect that the overvaluation of the exchange rate will eventually lead to more restrictions on capital movements, they will have an additional incentive to attempt to take their capital out of the country while there is still time.

Third, the overvaluation of the exchange rate will often bring about restrictions on the movement of goods and capital, if none existed; or it will lead to further restrictions if, as is often the case, they were already there. Restrictions are inevitably associated with black markets for both foreign exchange and goods. These black markets reduce the level of official transactions and thus the tax base. Goods will often be smuggled into the country (sometimes with the collaboration of the customs agents) and will be sold in the black market where they will fetch high prices but will pay no taxes. Both import duties, sales taxes and even some income taxes will be lost as a consequence.

If the difference between official and black market exchange rates becomes large and if, as is normally the case in these circumstances, exporters are requested to yield to the government at the official rate the foreign exchange proceeds that they earn,[19] an incentive will be created for them to reduce production and/or to smuggle their export goods out of the country. Producers will often simply cross the frontiers with their goods and sell their products in neighbouring countries so that they can change in the black market the foreign exchange that they earn. In this way they can evade the export taxes and the 'implicit' taxes on their foreign currency earnings. This is an area where the Laffer curve is likely to have a relevance.

Fourth, an overvalued exchange rate accompanied by balance of payments difficulties eventually induces the government to restrict imports of manufactured consumer goods, as these are often considered less 'essential' and to favour the importation of raw materials and capital equipment because they will be considered 'essential' goods.[20]. The latter, however, are goods that have traditionally been favoured in the development strategy and in the trade policy of developing countries. In other words, the structure of imports will change in favour of goods with low or zero import duties and sales taxes and against those with high import duties and tax sales. This change in the structure of imports has been very costly in terms of tax revenue to many countries. Smuggling of goods subject to high duties will increase so that the ratio of official imports over total imports will shrink. This will induce losses in import duties and in domestic sales taxes. Taxes will continue to be levied on goods sold at low prices in shrinking markets.

Imports by the private sector will be squeezed out to accommodate lower-taxed or zero-taxed imports by public enterprises and by the public sector. Exporters' reactions will also inevitably affect revenue as exports would be discouraged by both the overvalued exchange rate and the lack of needed inputs. Producers will use their productive capacity (including land) to produce untaxed domestic or subsistence products. Or they may switch their production toward goods that can be smuggled out of the country more easily. In conclusion domestic activity and employment in the modern or official sector is likely to fall, reducing the tax base.

### Taxes and import substitution policies
Apart from the inevitable restrictions associated with an exchange rate that is becoming progressively more overvalued, restrictions on foreign trade imposed for other reasons (say, to provide protection to local industry) have implications also for tax revenue. It is an obvious point, but one that is often ignored, that the imposition of quotas and other import restrictions implies that the power to tax moves away from the government and toward those who get the import permits and the foreign exchange needed to pay for those imports. Thus, there is a kind of income redistribution from the government, which loses tax revenue, to the importers, who receive rent.[21]

The imposition of quantitative restrictions will also stimulate the domestic production of substitutes. However, domestic producers will produce substitutes at higher costs but because of their quotas will be able to sell their goods at higher prices. This will also happen if there are no quotas but there are import duties. The higher the duties, the higher the prices that can be charged for domestic substitutes. Therefore, in part, but only in part, the revenue loss to the government becomes an income gain to the producers. To a large extent, import substitution whether caused by quotas or import duties, will have redistributional effects as well as income-reducing effects because of the inevitable inefficiencies that it will create.[22] Furthermore, because of incentive legislation, the gains to the domestic producers are often not subject to income taxes. The net result is once again a fall in tax revenue.

There are two related issues that are addressed below even though they are strictly speaking, tangential to the main topic of this chapter: the impact of trade liberalization on tax revenue; and the impact of devaluation on the fiscal balance (as distinguished from the level of taxation) when a country has a large foreign debt. Both issues are important. A full treatment would require more space than can be allocated to them here.

### Trade liberalization and tax revenue
Because of current concern with incentive or structural aspects of economic policies, several countries have started on a road of trade liberalization and tariff

reform. As a result of this policy change, quantitative restrictions are progressively removed and are replaced by import duties. Furthermore, high import duties are often replaced by lower duties while goods that have been imported duty free (raw materials, capital goods) are at times taxed with lower import duties.[23] These reforms are often accompanied by devaluation in order to neutralize some of the impact of the policy of trade liberalization on the balance of payments and to bring the exchange rate more in line with a level consistent with some sustainable medium-term external position given the lower import barriers. In other words, the main equilibrating instrument for bringing the trade account into the desired balance becomes the exchange rate rather than the trade restrictions. The needed changes in the exchange rate almost always imply sizable devaluations.[24]

From the previous discussion it can be deduced that important revenue effects are likely to accompany these changes. Trade liberalization implies that the level of taxation may rise considerably in the typical developing country even when the nominal tariff structure is being reduced.[25] The specific impact would depend, of course, on the tax structure of the country, on the size of the real devaluation, on how restrictive the trade regime has been, on the details of the trade liberalization policies followed and, finally on the characteristics of the economy. It may be worthwhile to make a brief inventory of the positive and negative effects on tax revenue associated with a policy of trade liberalization with devaluation since some authors have argued that the net effect is likely to be negative.[26] Among the positive effects one should mention the following:

(i)      the replacement of quotas and other quantitative restrictions by tariffs;
(ii)     the reduction of duties from the prohibitive to a more normal range, that is the reduction occurs over a range of the demand curve for the imported product where the elasticity is likely to be greater than one. However, the devaluation *per se* will increase the domestic price of the product;
(iii)    putting low tariffs on previously exempted goods. In view of the large share of exempted goods (see Tanzi, 1987: 233) in total imports, this change is potentially very important in terms of revenue yield;
(iv)     the increase in the value of imports and in the domestic prices of the imported products because of the devaluation;
(v)      the likely reduction in smuggling;
(vi)     some positive effects, especially over the medium run, associated with increased efficiency in the economy;
(vii)    some positive effects associated with a possible change in the composition of imports in view of the decreased incentive to bias imports towards raw materials and intermediate products;
(viii)   some positive effects on tradable output, especially over the medium run, associated with the devaluation and the liberalization policy.

Among the negative effects on tax revenue one should recognize the possibility that, at least for some imported products, the combination of price increase due to devaluation and price reduction due to the reduction in import duties may result in a reduction in tax revenue. Furthermore, over the short run, trade liberalization with devaluation may reduce employment and output in some sectors (especially in the import-substituting sectors), enough to have some negative effect on tax revenue. However, these sectors are unlikely to have been contributing much to tax revenue.

A good case can be made that devaluation accompanied by trade liberalization is likely to result in a positive impact on tax revenue. The elimination of the overvaluation and of the import restriction should in most cases raise the share of taxes in GDP as well as improve the allocation resources. However, the overall effect on the fiscal balance rather than on tax revenue would depend on several other considerations such as first, the impact of devaluation on subsidies and public sector wages: does devaluation lead to increase in subsidies when the subsidized products are imported?; does it result in increases in public sector wages because the government tries to protect the income of government employees from the effect of devaluation? Second, if public enterprises depend largely on imported inputs, are these enterprises allowed to adjust the prices of the goods and services that they sell? Third if the country has considerable public debt, what is the effect of devaluation on the interest paid on the foreign public debt? And, if domestic debt is indexed, what will be the effect of devaluation on domestic interest payments?

In conclusion, there are many elements that point in different directions so that only a careful empirical analysis of each case could provide a reliable answer on the outcome. The opinion of this writer, however, is that for the majority of cases trade liberalization of the type outlined above would increase tax revenue and, possibly, improve the fiscal balance. The positive effect on the fiscal balance is, however, likely to be greater in the medium than in the short run.[27]

**Devaluation, external debt, and the fiscal balance**
The effect of devaluation (with or without trade liberalization) on the fiscal balance in the presence of a large public debt is a controversial and complex issue to which full justice cannot be done here.[28]

It has often been assumed (Dornbusch, 1987: 68) that devaluation leads to a widening of the fiscal deficits of those developing countries with large foreign public debts: 'The real exchange rate appears as a determinant of the deficit ratio, because the real value of the service of an external debt contracted in dollars will increase when the real exchange rate depreciates.'[29] While this is undoubtedly true, it is only part of the story since that statement ignores the impact of devaluation on tax revenue. It also ignores the effect of devaluation on government revenue from publicly owned mineral exports and the effect on government non-interest expenditure.

As shown earlier, given the tax structure of many developing countries, the positive impact of devaluation on tax revenue can be important. Of course if the government receives revenue from mineral exports made by publicly-owned enterprises the impact of devaluation on the domestic value of that revenue will also be positive. If the government receives foreign assistance fixed in dollars, the budgetary impact of devaluation will also be positive.

The conclusion as to the impact of devaluation on the fiscal deficit must be that one cannot generalize. As it was true for devaluation with trade liberalization, only a specific analysis of a country's situation can provide a reliable answer to the empirical question of whether its fiscal deficit will be reduced or increased by devaluation. The basic ingredients of such an analysis would be:

(i)     the extent to which the exchange rate had appreciated, and thus the extent of the needed devaluation;
(ii)    the source of the depreciation, that is, tariff reform, lower import restrictions, adverse terms of trade, deflationary policies and so on;
(iii)   the structure of the tax system and its dependence on traded goods;
iv)    the level of taxation and, thus, the absolute effect of devaluation on tax revenue;
(v)     the import content of public expenditure;
(vi)    the size of the foreign interest payment in dollar terms;
(vii)   the extent to which the government receives income (in dollars) from publicly-owned, mineral export-oriented activities and from foreign grants.

However, a country with a large foreign debt and, thus, with large payments for servicing that debt will often be forced to reduce its imports in order to generate the needed surplus in its trade account to service the debt.[30] In recent years imports have fallen considerably as a share of GDP in many developing countries with debt problems. To the extent that imports are important for determining tax revenue, the reduction in imports *per se* will have a depressing effect on tax revenue. The higher is the net interest payment on foreign debt and, thus, the needed reduction in imports, the greater will be, *ceteris paribus*, the fall in tax revenue. The fall in tax revenue may lead to a widening of the fiscal deficit if the government is unable to reduce public expenditure or to raise alternative revenue.[31] The widening of the deficit would lead to inflation and, perhaps, give a further incentive to capital flight.

Putting it in different terms the servicing of the foreign public debt requires both a surplus in the trade account and a surplus in the (properly measured) fiscal accounts. But, given the high dependence of the tax system on the external sector, the creation of a trade surplus through a reduction in imports may by itself make it more difficult to achieve the needed budgetary stance. Often, the government will rely on inflationary finance rather than on ordinary and non-inflationary revenue.[32] This may explain why several countries with large foreign debt have had a tendency to experience high rates of inflation unless (as in the Philippines) they continued receiving a substantial influx of foreign assistance that made it possible for them to maintain their level of imports or, as in the case of Chile, unless they changed the structure of taxation away from its dependency on imports.

In the face of a high foreign debt situation a country would be advised to restructure its tax system away from its direct or indirect dependence on imports. Taxes on non-traded goods and taxes on incomes and property will have to replace taxes that are import-related. Also, especially in these cases, public enterprises must become major revenue sources for the government rather than drains on government budgets.

## Tax revenue and inflationary policies

When the government contributes to inflation by financing part of its overall expenditure through money creation, it affects tax revenue in various ways. In developing countries where progressive income taxes collected on a pay-as-you-go system are not important, where specific taxes play a significant role, and where collection lags are generally sizable, inflation is likely to have a negative impact on real tax revenue.[33] In these countries there is little scope for 'fiscal drags' so that the effect of inflation on tax revenue is unambiguosly negative.

The existence of collection lags for all tax payments implies that, under inflationary conditions, there is likely to be a real revenue loss to the government that is a direct function of the rate of inflation, the size of the lag and the initial level of taxation. The longer is the collection lag, and the higher is the rate of inflation, the greater will be the percentage reduction in the pre-inflation tax level.

The impact of different lags and rates of inflation on the real value of one unit of tax revenue can be estimated by multiplying that unit by $1/(1+p)^n$ where p is the monthly rate of inflation and n is the collection lag, expressed in months. With the assumption that the elasticity of the tax system is unitary, the effect of inflation on the tax burden can be calculated by solving the following equation:

$$T^\pi = \frac{T_0}{(1+p)^n} = \frac{T_0}{(1+\pi)^{n/12}}$$

where, $T_0$ denotes that ratio of tax revenue to national income under zero inflation; $T^\pi$ denotes that ratio when the inflation is $\pi$; and n denotes the collection lag, while p and $\pi$ denote the rate of inflation on a monthly and on an annual basis, respectively.

Table 8.1    *Inflation and revenue from tax system[1] (ratios of total tax revenue to gross domestic product)*

| $\pi$ | $T_o = 0.1$ | | | | $T_o = 0.2$ | | | |
|---|---|---|---|---|---|---|---|---|
| | $n = 2$ | $n = 4$ | $n = 6$ | $n = 8$ | $n = 2$ | $n = 4$ | $n = 6$ | $n = 8$ |
| 5 | 0.099 | 0.098 | 0.098 | 0.097 | 0.198 | 0.197 | 0.195 | 0.194 |
| 10 | 0.098 | 0.097 | 0.095 | 0.094 | 0.197 | 0.194 | 0.191 | 0.188 |
| 15 | 0.098 | 0.095 | 0.093 | 0.091 | 0.195 | 0.191 | 0.187 | 0.182 |
| 20 | 0.097 | 0.094 | 0.091 | 0.089 | 0.194 | 0.188 | 0.183 | 0.177 |
| 25 | 0.096 | 0.093 | 0.089 | 0.086 | 0.193 | 0.186 | 0.179 | 0.172 |
| 30 | 0.096 | 0.092 | 0.088 | 0.084 | 0.191 | 0.183 | 0.175 | 0.168 |
| 35 | 0.095 | 0.090 | 0.086 | 0.082 | 0.190 | 0.181 | 0.172 | 0.164 |
| 40 | 0.095 | 0.089 | 0.085 | 0.080 | 0.189 | 0.179 | 0.169 | 0.160 |
| 45 | 0.094 | 0.088 | 0.083 | 0.078 | 0.188 | 0.177 | 0.166 | 0.156 |
| 50 | 0.093 | 0.087 | 0.082 | 0.076 | 0.187 | 0.175 | 0.163 | 0.153 |
| 60 | 0.092 | 0.085 | 0.079 | 0.073 | 0.185 | 0.171 | 0.158 | 0.146 |
| 70 | 0.092 | 0.084 | 0.077 | 0.070 | 0.183 | 0.168 | 0.153 | 0.140 |
| 80 | 0.091 | 0.082 | 0.075 | 0.068 | 0.181 | 0.164 | 0.149 | 0.135 |
| 90 | 0.090 | 0.081 | 0.073 | 0.065 | 0.180 | 0.161 | 0.145 | 0.130 |
| 100 | 0.089 | 0.079 | 0.071 | 0.063 | 0.178 | 0.159 | 0.141 | 0.126 |
| 120 | 0.088 | 0.077 | 0.067 | 0.059 | 0,175 | 0.154 | 0.135 | 0.118 |
| 140 | 0.086 | 0.075 | 0.065 | 0.056 | 0.173 | 0.149 | 0.129 | 0.112 |
| 160 | 0.085 | 0.073 | 0.062 | 0.053 | 0.171 | 0.145 | 0.124 | 0.106 |
| 180 | 0.084 | 0.071 | 0.060 | 0.050 | 0.168 | 0.142 | 0.120 | 0.101 |
| 200 | 0.083 | 0.069 | 0.058 | 0.048 | 0.167 | 0.139 | 0.115 | 0.096 |
| 250 | 0.081 | 0.066 | 0.053 | 0.043 | 0.162 | 0.132 | 0.107 | 0.087 |
| 300 | 0.079 | 0.063 | 0.050 | 0.040 | 0.159 | 0.126 | 0.100 | 0.079 |
| 350 | 0.078 | 0.061 | 0.047 | 0.037 | 0.156 | 0.121 | 0.094 | 0.073 |
| 400 | 0.076 | 0.058 | 0.045 | 0.034 | 0.153 | 0.117 | 0.089 | 0.068 |
| 450 | 0.075 | 0.057 | 0.043 | 0.032 | 0.151 | 0.113 | 0.085 | 0.064 |
| 500 | 0.074 | 0.055 | 0.041 | 0.030 | 0.148 | 0.110 | 0.082 | 0.061 |

In countries where the average lag for the whole system is long, the rate of inflation is high, and the initial level of taxation is also high, the absolute revenue loss, measured as a proportion of national income, can be very high.[34] For example, a country with a ratio of tax revenue to GDP equal to 30 per cent which faces a rate of inflation of 40 per cent per year will  lose 1.6 per cent of GDP in revenue if the lag is two months and 4.6 per cent of GDP if the average lag is six months (see Table 8.1).[35] With a six-month lag and inflation rate of 100 per cent per year this country would lose almost 9 per cent of its initial GDP in revenue (see Tanzi, 1978). Table 8.1 provides simulation results obtained solving the above equation for situations where the zero-inflation tax ratio varies from 0.10 to 0.40 per cent GDP, while the collection lag varies from two months (n = 2) to eight months (n = 8). Table 8.1 shows how quickly a country with an initially high

| $T_o = 0.3$ | | | | $T_o = 0.4$ | | | |
| --- | --- | --- | --- | --- | --- | --- | --- |
| $n = 2$ | $n = 4$ | $n = 6$ | $n = 8$ | $n = 2$ | $n = 4$ | $n = 6$ | $n = 8$ |
| 0.298 | 0.295 | 0.293 | 0.290 | 0.397 | 0.394 | 0.390 | 0.387 |
| 0.295 | 0.291 | 0.286 | 0.282 | 0.394 | 0.387 | 0.381 | 0.375 |
| 0.293 | 0.286 | 0.280 | 0.273 | 0.391 | 0.382 | 0.373 | 0.364 |
| 0.291 | 0.282 | 0.274 | 0.266 | 0.388 | 0.376 | 0.365 | 0.354 |
| 0.289 | 0.278 | 0.268 | 0.259 | 0.385 | 0.371 | 0.358 | 0.345 |
| 0.287 | 0.275 | 0.263 | 0.252 | 0.383 | 0.367 | 0.351 | 0.336 |
| 0.285 | 0.271 | 0.258 | 0.246 | 0.380 | 0.362 | 0.344 | 0.327 |
| 0.284 | 0.268 | 0.254 | 0.240 | 0.378 | 0.358 | 0.338 | 0.320 |
| 0.282 | 0.265 | 0.249 | 0.234 | 0.376 | 0.353 | 0.332 | 0.312 |
| 0.280 | 0.262 | 0.245 | 0.229 | 0.374 | 0.349 | 0.327 | 0.305 |
| 0.277 | 0.256 | 0.237 | 0.219 | 0.370 | 0.342 | 0.316 | 0.292 |
| 0.275 | 0.251 | 0.230 | 0.211 | 0.366 | 0.335 | 0.307 | 0.281 |
| 0.272 | 0.247 | 0.224 | 0.203 | 0.363 | 0.329 | 0.298 | 0.270 |
| 0.270 | 0.242 | 0.218 | 0.196 | 0.359 | 0.323 | 0.290 | 0.261 |
| 0.267 | 0.238 | 0.212 | 0.189 | 0.356 | 0.317 | 0.283 | 0.252 |
| 0.263 | 0.231 | 0.202 | 0.177 | 0.351 | 0.308 | 0.270 | 0.236 |
| 0.259 | 0.224 | 0.194 | 0.167 | 0.346 | 0.299 | 0.258 | 0.233 |
| 0.256 | 0.218 | 0.186 | 0.159 | 0.341 | 0.291 | 0.248 | 0.212 |
| 0.253 | 0.213 | 0.179 | 0.151 | 0.337 | 0.284 | 0.239 | 0.201 |
| 0.250 | 0.208 | 0.173 | 0.144 | 0.333 | 0.277 | 0.231 | 0.192 |
| 0.243 | 0.198 | 0.160 | 0.130 | 0.325 | 0.263 | 0.214 | 0.174 |
| 0.238 | 0.189 | 0.150 | 0.119 | 0.317 | 0.252 | 0.200 | 0.159 |
| 0.233 | 0.182 | 0.141 | 0.110 | 0.311 | 0.242 | 0.189 | 0.147 |
| 0.229 | 0.175 | 0.134 | 0.103 | 0.306 | 0.234 | 0.179 | 0.137 |
| 0.226 | 0.170 | 0.128 | 0.096 | 0.301 | 0.227 | 0.171 | 0.128 |
| 0.223 | 0.165 | 0.122 | 0.091 | 0.297 | 0.220 | 0.163 | 0.121 |

Source: Tanzi, 1978.
1. $\pi$ denotes the yearly inflation rate.
   $T_o$ denotes the ratio of total tax revenue to gross domestic product at zero inflation rate.
   $n$ denotes the average collection lag for the tax system.

tax rate (at zero inflation) and a sizable collection lag can experience a dramatic drop in the level of taxation when the rate of inflation accelerates.[36]

For a few countries for which over the years, the author has estimated the average lag for the whole tax system (Argentina, Jamaica, Morocco), the lag was found to vary between four and six months.[37] Large tax revenue gains are thus likely to accompany policies that reduce the rate of inflation or reduce the size of average collection lag, especially when the zero-inflation tax level would be high. This revenue-increasing effect associated with a slowdown of the rate of inflation was very important in the so-called 'heterodox' stabilization programmes of Argentina, Bolivia, and Israel. However, if the government has taken successful steps to reduce the impact of inflation on the tax system, the increase in the tax to GDP ratio associated with a fall in inflation is likely to be smaller unless the rate of inflation had been very high. In Brazil, for example, the impact of the Cruzado Plan on the ratio of tax revenue to GDP was smaller than in the other countries since Brazil had been more successful than the others in insulating its tax system from the negative effects of inflation.[38] Thus, that success became a negative factor during the Cruzado Plan.

The level of tax revenues is affected by inflationary policies also because some important excise taxes (tobacco, alcohol, and even fuel) and even some import duties are at times imposed with specific rates.[39] As these rates are often not adjusted in line with inflation, the government experiences revenue losses when prices are rising.

Inflation often brings about an appreciation of the exchange rate as the latter is not adjusted in line with the change in prices. Furthermore, the official rate of inflation may lag behind the actual or real rate if the government is regulating prices or if the price index is not fully representative. Therefore, the problem discussed on pp. 120–23 in connection with the exchange rate, are also relevant in this context. Furthermore, a few countries use administrative prices to determine the value of imports. These are price lists provided to customs officers which are changed only periodically. These prices are used to facilitate the task of determining import values. With inflation the prices in these lists tend to lag behind where they should be even though the exchange rate itself may be adjusting in line with the rate of inflation.[40]

Finally, a reference should be made to the prices that public utilities charge on the goods and services that they sell even though, strictly speaking, these are not 'taxes'. It is a common experience that these prices tend to lag behind the rate of inflation even when the official measure of this rate is reduced by price controls, overvalued exchange rates, and so forth. The countries' authorities often attempt to hold down the rate of inflation by not increasing public utility prices. Even when, at intervals, these prices may be brought into line with the price index there is likely to be some real revenue loss in between adjustments especially when the inflation rate is high.

This discussion, oriented toward developing countries, has highlighted the negative revenue effects of inflation on tax revenue. However, if a country is highly dependent on income taxes collected with progressive rates and withheld at the source, and if the acceleration in the rate of inflation is moderate, the country would experience inflation-induced revenue increases rather than decreases. This was the experience in many industrial countries in the 1970s. This is what is normally called the 'fiscal drag' in industrial countries.[41] Still the basic point of the chapter remains valid. Macroeconomic policies pursued independently of tax policy often have important and relatively direct influences on tax revenue and, through these, on the overall incidence of the tax system.

## Tax revenue and interest rate policies

Interest rate policies have also important and direct tax revenue implications. When interest incomes are paid by financial institutions, they can generally be checked with relative ease by the authorities and the taxes on them can be withheld at the source.

In many countries interest incomes represent the second major income tax and the second source of income tax revenue after wages. Therefore, a country's level of taxation will be affected positively when governments pursue policies that encourage savers to channel their financial savings to financial institutions. Often, however, governments attempt to maintain interest rates at levels which make them unattractive to savers. This is especially true in periods of high inflation.[42] Under these circumstances, one is likely to observe a progressive exodus of financial savings away from the financial institutions and towards difficult-to-tax domestic and foreign channels. This disintermediation will often have significant tax consequences. Which are these channels?

First of all there is always the option of the informal financial sector or the so-called 'curb market'. These markets are important in developing countries (see Chandavarker, 1986). Here, individuals avoid official institutions and borrow and lend directly from each other. As a consequence, the government loses part of its tax base.

Second, some individuals channel their savings towards the purchase of real assets, including durables and inventories, for which the implicit nominal rate of return is not taxable. This hoarding of real goods is costly to the country as well as to the tax administration.

Third, in many countries one observes the already mentioned process of 'dollarization' or currency substitution whereby savers channel more and more of their financial savings toward dollar bills physically held in the country. This reduces the seignorage that the country's monetary authorities can collect from currency creation and transfers that seignorage to the US Federal Reserve System. A recent survey by the US Federal Reserve Board indicated that a large proportion of all US dollar bills in circulation was probably held outside the United States. In Argentina some economists have estimated that in recent years the total amount of dollar bills in the country might have been as high as $5 billion.[43] In that country and in some other countries, payments for real estate transactions are routinely made in dollar bills, thus facilitating the evasion of taxes on property transfers.

Fourth, when real interest rates (after taxes) become unattractive, individuals have a strong incentive to take their money out of the country. In this case the tax base is essentially transferred to another country. In addition since the government will be unable to borrow domestically, it will rely more on foreign borrowing thus accumulating foreign debt. Thus, capital flight and a growing foreign debt may be two aspects of the same problem.[44] Since interest payments on externally-held debt are, by contractual arrangements, normally tax-free in the debtor countries (while the creditor countries can tax the earnings of commercial banks which receive the interest payments), there is a further transfer of the tax base. This transfer is in direct proportion to the size of the foreign debt. In some countries, it now represents a significant portion of the tax base.[45]

While interest incomes progressively vanish from the tax base, interest deductions by borrowers continue to be an important drain on tax revenue; those who make payments will continue to deduct fully these payments from their gross earnings in order to determine their taxable incomes. They will do so even when they borrow from the curb market or from abroad.

The savers of many developing countries have taken their money to the United States, where they can claim a 'non-resident alien' non-taxable status, or to so-called tax havens. At times they may have loaned the money back to enterprises that they control in their own countries anonymously through their foreign banks. The interest payments by these enterprises are then deductible for tax purposes.[46] The tax administrations of the developing countries often do not have the resources to ascertain whether the deductions claimed by the enterprises are reported as equivalent interest incomes by those who receive the payment even when these are paid domestically.[47]

In many developing (and developed) countries, debt management policy may have become another macroeconomic policy that has reduced the tax base. To encourage individuals to hold government bonds at lower rates of interest, the government has, in many cases, accorded to those bonds a tax-free status. As the size of the public debt rises as a share of national income, and as more and more private savings are invested in those tax-free bonds, the tax base is further reduced.

### Concluding remarks

This chapter has dealt with an aspect of taxation that has been largely ignored by the literature on the determinants of tax levels, namely, the impact of macroeconomic policies on tax revenue. Various policies have been discussed: those related to the exchange rate and to trade restrictions; those related to the financial market; and, those related to inflationary finance. These policies were shown to be important determinants of tax revenue. These are, of course, not the only policies that have these effects but they are probably the most important.

A more comprehensive analysis would have discussed the effects of other policies. For example, pricing policies that reduce the profits of private enterprises reduce taxes on profits. Wage policies that maintain wages above (below) the level that they would have reached without those policies have positive (negative) effects on wage taxes but negative (positive) effects on profit taxes. Furthermore, to the extent that high wages bring about higher unemployment, some additional negative effects can be identified. Rent control laws that reduce rental incomes also reduce the tax base for both income taxes and possibly property taxes. A large public enterprise sector that, because of pricing or other policies, does not make profits will also depress the level of taxation.

These examples indicate that this is a complex and important area that deserves much more attention than it has received so far. They also indicate that countries that wish to raise their level of taxation through tax reform may have limited success when they are at the same time pursuing macroeconomic policies that may largely neutralize the potentially positive effects coming from tax policy changes and from improved tax administration. In these cases those who were engaged in the tax reform may be blamed for the lack of success.[48] Tax reform is likely to be most successful in raising revenue in a stable or improving macroeconomic environment. When that environment is not stable, tax reform must be directed toward insulating the tax system from the negative shocks that may come from macroeconomic policy. For example, in situations where a large foreign debt is likely to reduce the volume of imports, or where the government insists in pursuing a policy that keeps the exchange rate overvalued, it would be desirable to reduce the dependence of the tax system on the external sector. In conclusion, good tax reform cannot be made if the macroeconomic situation is not taken fully into account.

One final comment may be appropriate. In our discussion we have dealt separately with various macroeconomic policies and have assessed their probable impact on tax revenue. This partial analysis approach, however, may not be appropriate in analysing concrete situations. In reality, the effects discussed above may occur jointly and may influence each other. For example, assume that devaluation leads to inflation, perhaps because of indexation arrangements in the economy.[49] In such case the positive effects of devaluation on tax revenue that were identified above may to some extent be neutralized by the negative effect of inflation on tax revenue. These interactions of policies must be kept in mind when the analysis used here is applied to a real world situation.

## Notes

1. For the Organization for Economic Co-operation and Development (OECD) countries the average in the 1980–85 period was between 35 and 37 per cent of GDP. For a few countries, in 1985 it exceeded 45 per cent of GDP (Belgium, Denmark, France, The Netherlands, Norway, Sweden). See OECD, 1987.
2. Some of this work was carried out in the Fiscal Affairs Department of the Fund (see Lotz and Morss, 1967; Chelliah *et al.* 1975; Tait *et al.* 1979).
3. It is peculiar that this important and obvious variable was left out of earlier studies. One reason may be that in those earlier studies it was implicitly assumed that the 'mobilization of resources' by the public sector is such an obvious desirable objective that governments would always try to fully exploit the 'taxable capacity' of their countries.

4.  See pp. 120–23 for qualifications to this statement.
5.  The level of foreign assistance is also an important determinant of the tax level. Imports under foreign-financed projects (grants or concessionary loans) are often not taxed.
6.  The combination of low wages for tax administrators and low penalties for transgressions on their part creates an environment which is not conducive to efficient and honest tax administration. In some countries the effective tax level is somewhat higher than the official tax level because of the bribes that tax-payers pay to the administrators to reduce their official tax payments.
7.  Some believe that the use of many taxes facilitates the increase in the level of taxation. Others believe that the higher is the number of taxes used, the lower is the tax ratio likely to be. There is a growing literature dealing with the relationship between tax structure and tax levels. (See Feenberg and Rosen, 1987.)
8.  The one relevant consideration is the validity of the so-called Laffer curve.
9.  To the extent that a country encourages some activities through tax expenditures (e.g., United States) rather than through explicit subsidies (e.g., Sweden), it will tend to show a lower level of taxation.
10. However, the theoretical literature on this issue is ambiguous.
11. See (Tanzi, 1986; Chu, 1987).
12. In particular cases natural calamities or social upheaval may play a significant role in reducing the level of taxation.
13. It should be stressed that this is true in developing countries and not necessarily in industrialized countries.
14. Import duties account for about 25 per cent of all the tax revenue of developing countries and for a somewhat larger percentage of the revenue of the poorer half among these countries. See Tanzi, 1987. Thus, what happens to import duties has an important impact on total tax revenue.
15. However, when the exchange rate appreciates, the 'implicit' taxes on exports rise when, as is often the case, exporters are required to relinquish their foreign exchange rate.
16. This, however, does not mean that exports are taxed less than imports. Much of the taxation of exports comes indirectly through the requirement that foreign exchange earnings must be ceded to the government at the official rate in conjunction with the overvaluation of the exchange rate.
17. In developing countries corporate income taxes are often closely associated with mineral exports (see Tanzi, 1987).
18. These actions will also reduce the income tax base directly. Often countries borrow to sustain, for a while, an overvalued exchange rate. The rich can escape the easily anticipated higher future tax liability by taking some of their money out of the country.
19. In this case the implicit taxation of exports becomes high even when there are no export taxes.
20. This policy makes the country and its tax bases also more vulnerable to adverse external shocks.
21. Unless the quotas are auctioned and they fetch prices consistent with their scarcity values.
22. It is assumed that infant industry arguments do not apply.
23. Perhaps the Chilean experience is the most relevant one in this context. But several other countries have started on the same road. For the Chilean experience, see Corbo 1988. For arguments in favour of a uniform tariff, see Harberger, 1988.
24. A large devaluation will often reveal that the existing import duties are much too high when imports are measured at the new highly depreciated exchange rate. It is thus likely to make more obvious the need to reduce existing duties.
25. Bovenberg has also shown that a reduction in export taxes accompanied by a depreciation in the exchange rate would raise tax revenue in Thailand. In other words, he finds some validation of the Laffer curve with respect to export taxes (Bovenberg, 1987).
26. If the policy of trade liberalization is seen as temporary, it may be associated with costs and other effects not analysed in this chapter (see Calvo, 1988).
27. For a less sanguine view of the impact of trade liberalization on the fiscal balance, see Blejer and Cheasty, 1988.
28. For a detailed discussion of the relationship between the budget and foreign debt, see Reisen

and Van Trotsenburg, 1988; see also Tanzi and Blejer, 1988. For a discussion of the Mexican experience, see Ortiz, 1988.

29.  On this basis some economists have been critical of IMF advice to countries to devalue in order to improve their external balances.

30.  It should be recalled that in this situation it is necessary that the public sector of the country transfers resources (interest payments) to foreign creditors, and that the private sector of the country transfers resources to the public sector. Thus, the trade account must be in surplus and the fiscal account (properly measured) must improve.

31.  Chile was very successful in raising alternative (non-inflationary) sources of revenue, especially through a broad based value-added tax (which is now among the most productive in the world) and through adjustments in the tariffs of the public enterprises. See Corbo, 1988.

32.  In this case high inflation may result and this will make it more difficult to ascertain the budgetary stance of the government as the conventional measure of the deficit will likely be in deficit but it will give indications that are not fully reliable. See Ortiz, 1988.

33.  See in particular Tanzi, 1977.

34.  If the initial level of taxation, as a percent of GDP, is lower the absolute revenue loss will also be lower. Therefore, it makes a difference whether a country starts with a high or low tax level.

35.  The results in Table 8.1 have been calculated using the above equation. See Tanzi, 1978, for details.

36.  The opposite will be true when the rate of inflation decelerates.

37.  In Argentina, the government took steps to reduce it so that the collection lag is now somewhat shorter. It is also likely to have changed, since those estimates were made, in the other two countries mentioned. This average lag is influenced by the different lags of the various taxes and by the relative importance of each tax (see Tanzi, 1977).

38.  This has been achieved by reducing the length of collection lags and by indexing the tax liabilities. However, complete protection against high inflation does not seem feasible since perfect indexation is not possible. For an analysis of these aspects within the Brazilian context and for the steps taken since 1985 to reduce the impact of inflation on tax revenue, see Giambiagi, 1987.

39.  Alcohol, tobacco, and petroleum products generate about 10 per cent of total tax revenue and more than 70 per cent of total excise taxes in developing countries, see Tanzi, 1987.

40.  The effects of inflation on tax revenue discussed here can be described as first round, or major effects. However, inflation can affect tax revenue in many other ways. For example, it is well known that inflation affects relative prices. If sectors that are differently taxed respond differently to the rate of inflation, tax revenue will be affected. Also, if government is controlling prices, it will be more successful in controlling the price of commodities (that are more heavily taxed) than the prices of services that are more lightly taxed. Also, inflation may have a negative impact on real income.

41.  For a detailed review of these aspects, see Tanzi 1980. Should the rate of inflation become very high in the industrial countries, they would also experience falls in the ratios of taxes to national incomes. The industrial countries collection lags are also significant (see OECD, 1983).

42.  This is especially the case when the tax laws do not make a distinction between real interest incomes and the part of interest payments that compensates the lenders for the erosion of their capital. Thus, as inflation accelerates, the net-of-tax real interest rates will fall even when the before-tax nominal rates are keeping up with the inflation rate.

43.  If this figure is correct, it implies that the yearly seignorage that Argentina was paying to the United States may have been at least $400 million at current rates of interest.

44.  The higher level of public debt is likely to signal a higher future level of taxation. This may cause even more capital flight and smaller domestic tax bases. See Ize and Ortiz, 1986.

45.  If the debt was domestic, in principle at least, it would have remained part of the tax base.

46.  This was a problem in Mexico until the recent tax reforms.

47.  US tax laws have come under criticism for facilitating this transfer of tax bases from developing countries to the United States. For a recent survey of this issue, see McLure, 1988.

48.  Falls in tax revenue are often attributed to 'deteriorating tax administration' when in fact they may simply be the consequence of misguided macroeconomic policies.

49.    In a recent analysis of high-inflation cases, Peter Montiel has concluded that 'nominal exchange rate shocks played the dominant role in triggering an acceleration of inflation'. See Montiel, 1988; see also Rodrigues, 1978.

# References

Aguirre, Carlos and Parthasarathi Shome, 'The Mexican value-added-tax: characteristics, evolution, and methodology for calculating the base', *IMF Working Paper* 87/21.

Blejer, Mario I. and Adrienne Cheasty, 'The fiscal implications of trade liberalization', Paper presented at the Istanbul Congress of the International Institute of Public Finance, 22-25 August 1988.

Bovenberg, Lans, 'Indirect taxation in developing countries: a general equilibrium approach', *IMF Staff Papers* 34, 2 June 1987.

Calvo, Guillermo A., 'On the costs of temporary policy', *Journal of Development Economics* 27, 1987.

'Costly trade liberalizations: durable goods and capital mobility', *IMF Staff Papers* 35, 3, September 1988.

Chandavarkar, A.G., 'The informal financial sector in developing countries: analysis, evidence, and policy implications', mimeo, 1986.

Chelliah, Raja, Hessel H. Baas, and Margaret R. Kelly, 'Tax ratios and tax effort in developing countries, 1969-71', *IMF Staff Papers* XXII, 2, March 1975.

Chu, Ke-young, 'External shocks and fiscal adjustments in developing countries', *IMF Working Paper* 87/48.

Corbo, Vittorio, 'Public finance, trade and development: the Chilean experience', Paper presented at the Istanbul Congress of the International Institute of Public Finance, 15-22 August 1988.

Dooley, Michael P., 'Capital flight: a response to differences in financial risks', *IMF Staff Papers* 35, 3, September 1988.

Dornbusch, Rudiguer, 'Impacts on debtor countries of world economic conditions', in *External Debt, Savings, and Growth in Latin America* Ana Maria Martirena-Mantel (ed.), IMF and Instituto Torcuato Di Tella, Washington and Buenos Aires, 1987.

Feenberg, Daniel R. and Harvey S. Rosen, 'Tax structure and public sector growth', *Journal of Public Economics* 32, 1987.

Giambiagi, Fabio, O' "efeito-Tanzi" e o imposto de Renda da Pessoa Fisica: um caso de indexacao imperfeita', *Revista de Financeas Publicas* XLVII, 371, July–September 1987.

Harberger, Arnold C., 'Reflections on uniform taxation', Paper presented at the Istanbul Congress of the International Institute of Public Finance, 22-25 August 1988.

Ize, Alain and Guillermo Ortiz, 'Fiscal rigidities, public debt, and asset substitution: The case of Mexico', *IMF Staff Papers* 31, 2, 1986.

Lotz, Joergen R. and Elliott R. Morss, 'Measuring "tax effort" in developing countries', *IMF Staff Papers* XIV, 3, November 1967.

McLure, Charles E., 'US tax laws and capital flight from Latin America', Working Papers in Economics E–88–21, Hoover Institution, April 1988.

Montiel, Peter, 'Empirical analysis of high-inflation episodes in Argentina, Brazil and Israel', *IMF Working Paper* 88/68.

Musgrave, Richard, *Fiscal Systems*, New Haven, Yale University Press, 1969.

Nellor, David, 'The effect of the value-added-tax on the tax ratio', *IMF Working Paper* 87/47.

OECD, *Income Tax Collection Lags*, Paris, OECD, 1983.

——*Revenue Statistics of OECD Member Countries*, Paris, OECD, 1987.

Ortiz, Guillermo, 'Public finance, trade and economic growth: the Mexican case', Paper presented at the Istanbul Congress of the International Institute of Public Finance, 22-25 August 1988.

Reisen, Helmut and Axel Van Trotsenburg, *Developing Country Debt: The Budgetary and Transfer Problem*, Paris, OECD, 1988.

Rodrigues, Carlos A., 'A stylized model of the devaluation – inflation spiral', *IMF Staff Papers* 25, 1, March 1978.

Sachs, Jeffrey, 'Trade and exchange rate policies in growth-oriented adjustment programs', *NBER Working Paper* 2226, 1987.

Seade, Jesus, 'Tax revenue implications of exchange rate adjustment', Paper presented at the Istanbul Congress of International Institute of Public Finance, 22–25 August 1988.

Tabellini, Guido, 'International tax comparisons reconsidered', IMF mimeo, 30 May 1985.

Tait, Alan, Wilfrid Gratz, and Barry Eichengreen, 'International comparisons of taxation for selected developing countries, 1972–76', *IMF Staff Papers* 26, 1, March 1979.

Tanzi, Vito, 'Inflation lags in collection, and the real value of tax revenue', *IMF Staff Papers* 24, 1, March 1977.

——'Inflation, real tax revenue, and the case for inflationary finance: theory with an application to Argentina', IMF Staff Papers 25, 3, September 1978.

——*Inflation and the Personal Income Tax*, Cambridge, Cambridge University Press, 1980.

——'Fiscal policy responses to exogenous shocks in developing countries', *American Economic Review* 76, 2, May 1986.

——'Quantitative characteristics of the tax systems of developing countries' in *The Theory of Taxation for Developing Countries*, David Newbery and Nicholas Stern (eds.), Oxford, Oxford University Press, 1987.

——and Mario Blejer, 'Public debt and fiscal policy in developing countries', in *Economics of Public Debt*, Kenneth Arrow and Michael Boskin (eds.), New York, St Martin's Press, 1988.

World Bank, *World Development Report 1988*, Oxford, Oxford University Press, 1988.

# 9 Fiscal policy, growth, and design of stabilization programmes

The objectives of IMF supported stabilization programmes include a balance of payments viable over the medium run, the promotion of growth under a stable economic environment, price stability, and the prevention of excessive growth in external debt. These objectives do not have the same weight, but each is important in stabilization programmes. A narrow interpretation of the Fund's role would emphasize the balance of payments objective and de-emphasize the others.

This paper deals with the role of fiscal policy in stabilization programmes, emphasizing the structural aspects of fiscal policies since, over the years, these have attracted less attention than has demand management. The Baker initiative of October 1985 called attention to their importance. The chapter does not discuss other elements of programme design, such as incentive measures implemented through the exchange rate, through import liberalization, through financial deregulation or through pricing policy, even though these structural elements are obviously important. In countries where institutions necessary for the effective use of other policies are not adequately developed, fiscal policy may be the main avenue to economic development and stability, although, unfortunately, political pressures, external shocks, and administrative shortcomings have frequently weakened government control over this instrument. Tax evasion, inflation, and the proliferation of exonerations have reduced the government's ability to control tax revenues, while political pressures, fragmentation of the public sector, and inadequate monitoring systems have undermined its ability to keep public expenditure in check. Far from being the stabilizing factor in the economy that it should be, fiscal policy has itself, in too many instances, become a major destabilizing force contributing to disequilibrium in the external sector.[1]

In recent years the connection between fiscal developments and external sector developments has been increasingly recognized. Some have gone as far as to suggest a 'fiscal approach to the balance of payments' that considers fiscal disequilibrium as the main cause of external imbalances.[2]

Although growth was always a primary objective of economic policy, the sustained rates of growth experienced by most countries until the mid-1970s (except for occasional and transitory periods of balance of payments difficulties) made it possible for the Fund, in negotiating stabilization programmes, to concentrate on the objective of stabilization in which it had more expertise and an accepted mandate. The increase in oil prices during the 1970s and especially the more recent debt crisis accompanied by the sharp fall in commodity prices brought about a new environment in which external sector disequilibrium could not be easily financed. This forced many countries to pursue (over longer periods than had earlier been the case) stabilization policies aimed at reducing external imbalances or the rate of inflation, policies that some critics considered as inimical to growth.

In the face of external shocks, some countries (for example, the Republic of Korea) succeeded in stabilizing their economies and in advancing once gain along the road of economic development. Others were less successful. When the need to pursue stabilization policies extended over several years, the short-run political costs of these policies began to loom larger than the longer-run economic benefits; political fatigue set in and some countries became restive under the harness of traditional stabilization programmes. The cries of critics that stabilization policies were inhibiting growth became louder and attracted a larger following. Critics advised policy-makers to abandon stabilization policies recommended by the Fund and to concentrate on growth, regardless of the consequences for the balance of payments and the rate of inflation. They espoused the position that inflation is a lesser evil than stagnation and that the external sector can be kept in equilibrium through quantitative restrictions and export subsidies, or by repudiating external debt obligations.

As already mentioned, stabilization and growth have always been legitimate policy objectives. Although in the past it was thought that at any given moment a country could focus on policies aimed specifically at one or the other of these objectives, the view that it is unwise to separate these objectives currently predominates. Stabilization programmes must pay attention to growth to ensure that stability is not won at the price of stagnation.[3] Growth policy must pay attention to stability to ensure that the pursuit of growth is not aborted by excessive inflation or by pressures on the external sector, as has happened in several cases in recent years. Growth without stability may be technically impossible over the longer run; stability without growth may be politically impossible except in the short run. This paper attempts to reformulate the fiscal design of stabilization programmes in order to emphasize the growth objective.

If stabilization were the only objective of economic policy, stabilization programmes could rely mostly on traditional demand-management policies.[4] Stabilization with growth, however, requires that demand-management policies be complemented by policies aimed at increasing potential output. Misguided structural policies have reduced potential output by misallocating resources and by reducing the rate of growth of the factors of production. They have thus been the main cause of stagnation and a contributor to economic instability. The design of adjustment programmes should integrate stabilization with growth, or demand-management policies with structural, supply-side policies.

### Fiscal policy and the design of fund programmes

Stabilization programmes can, in theory, emphasize either specific or general fiscal policies. For example, the country and the Fund could agree on a whole range of specific fiscal measures, such as changes in various taxes and tax rates and changes in specific public expenditures, subsidies, and public utility rates. These measures, however, would have to add up to the required adjustment in aggregate demand and supply. They must reduce the balance of payments disequilibrium and the rate of inflation to the desired level by reducing aggregate demand and by increasing aggregate supply. For identification I shall call this the microeconomic approach to stabilization programmes, an approach that explicitly recognizes both the demand-management and the supply management aspects of fiscal policy. It recognizes that fiscal policy changes usually affect not only aggregate demand but also aggregate supply.[5]

Alternatively, the country and the Fund could limit their agreement on a programme to general, macroeconomic variables. In the extreme version of this alternative, the Fund and the country might not even discuss specific fiscal policies, but would limit not only their agreement but also their discussions to the size of the fiscal deficit and to the expansion of bank credit associated with that deficit. If specific policies are discussed, it would be to assess their immediate impact on the size of the fiscal deficit and on aggregate demand.

In this approach, supply-side aspects of fiscal policy (what I have called the supply-management aspects) would be largely ignored. I shall call this the macroeconomic approach to stabilization policy. This approach implies that once the size of the deficit has been determined, the balance of payments consequences of that deficit have also been determined regardless of the specific measures that the country will employ to achieve the stipulated level of fiscal deficit.[6] Whether the deficit is reduced by raising taxes or by cutting spending, and regardless of the specific tax and spending measures used to achieve such a reduction, the balance of payments consequences are assumed to be the same.[7]

Although these alternative versions of the design of stabilization programmes have probably never been pursued in their pure form, over the years the formulation of stabilization programmes has been much closer to the macroeconomic than the microeconomic alternative,[8] in conformity with the common interpretation of the guidelines on conditionality.[9] Until recent years, stabilization programmes established fiscal ceilings on the basis of an implicit model that connected monetary expansion associated with the fiscal deficit to developments in the balance of payments. The countries themselves would then choose the specific ways in which the fiscal ceilings would be observed. Which tax rates should be changed, which new revenue measures should be adopted, and which expenditures should be reduced (or expanded) were left to the authorities to determine, although Fund missions did provide some advice based, where possible, on technical assistance reports. As Sir Joseph Gold put it 'performance criteria...must be confined to macroeconomic variables... The concept of "macroeconomic" variables involves the idea of aggregation...[and] includes the broadest possible aggregate in an economic category'. Gold goes on to state that 'the Fund should not become involved in the detailed decisions by which general policies are put into operation'. He concludes that 'specific prices of commodities or services, specific taxes, or other detailed measures to increase revenues or to reduce expenditures would not be considered macroeconomic variables' (Gold, 1979: 32–3).

Specific measures (such as the elimination of subsidies) were on rare occasions made performance criteria in Fund programmes, but the main reason for doing so was often deficit reduction and thus demand management.[10] Fiscal changes without direct and immediate bearing on the size of the fiscal deficit (say, revenue-neutral tax reforms) did not receive explicit attention in formal agreements, even though they might have a bearing on the efficiency of the economy. Changes that would increase the fiscal deficit in the short run but would have desirable supply-side effects on the economy over the medium run were not encouraged. The observance of the fiscal ceilings was the most essential fiscal element of a programme.

If the country wanted advice on its tax structure, on the structure of its public spending, or on their respective administration, it could request technical assistance from the Fund. No conditionality was attached to the provision or the use of this advice, although Fund missions occasionally used technical assistance reports to provide advice to the countries, especially on how to raise revenues.[11] Technical assistance has been the major channel through which the Fund has directly influenced the structure of tax systems and their administration and, to a lesser extent, the structure of public spending.

With important qualifications, this macroeconomic approach to stabilization programmes predominated until a few years ago. Starting with extended Fund facility programmes, however, Fund missions began paying more attention to structural aspects in general and specific fiscal aspects in particular,[12] and today much more attention is paid to structural (supply-side) elements in stabilization programmes. The transition from the macroeconomic to the microeconomic approach is, however, far from complete. The approach followed in negotiating stabilization programmes begins with an estimation of the required reduction in a country's fiscal deficit, given its balance of payments position and the foreign financing presumed to be available, and proceeds, separately and often *ex post*, to a discussion of specific policies.[13] The connection that is likely to exist, especially over the medium run, between the 'required' deficit reduction and the specific measures adopted to make that reduction possible is not accounted for in setting programme ceilings. For example, the removal of growth-retarding taxes is not encouraged if alternative revenue sources are not immediately available, as such a removal will immediately increase the fiscal deficit and, given the underlying model used, will presumably lead to a deterioration in the country's external position. Thus, the approach still goes from the macroeconomic to the microeconomic and much attention is focused on the size of the deficit and on its financing.

Nevertheless, recent Fund programmes have increasingly recognized that the specific measures through which fiscal deficits are reduced may determine, especially over the medium and longer run, whether a stabilization programme will have durable, beneficial effects on the balance of payments and on growth, or whether these effects will vanish as soon as the programme is over. An adequate macroeconomic framework (consistent with a viable balance of payments and with price stability in the short run) is a necessary, but not a sufficient, condition for growth and for stability over the longer run. Stability requires in addition efficient structural policies.

Should the Fund and the authorities focus mainly on macroeconomic fiscal variables, as has traditionally been the case? Or should they make specific fiscal policies of equal importance in a programme? Putting it more starkly, should the Fund be prepared to walk away from an arrangement with a country in which resources have been badly misallocated, thus reducing its growth potential, if an acceptable core of structural policies is missing even though the traditional macroeconomic framework appears adequate? Should Fund missions start the analysis of a programme by identifying such a structural core of required policies – that is, a set of specific supply-side measures – that must be implemented over the course of the programme before the macroeconomic ceilings are set?[14] The answers to these questions are not as obvious as they might appear at first, as convincing arguments can be presented on both sides.

A first argument in favour of continuing with the traditional, macroeconomic approach is that, at least in theory, this approach is objective. Whether or not performance criteria are satisfied is an issue subject, in most cases, to quantification and verification and thus beyond dispute.[15] As such, this approach reduces the uncertainty faced by authorities. They know that if the country satisfies the performance criteria it will obtain from the Fund the agreed financial support. And, once again, those performance criteria normally relate to macroeconomic variables.

A second, and perhaps more important, argument is that performance criteria based on ceilings imply less political interference by the Fund in the internal affairs of countries than do criteria related to specific measures. Authorities are likely to object to having to agree to modify a tax in a given way or to modify the level or pattern of public spending.[16] Critics who find present Fund conditionality too rigid are likely to object even more to what might be seen as an extension of that conditionality. Examples of this reaction exist in connection with Fund recommendations to eliminate or reduce subsidies. Many observers feel that these are political decisions that should be left to the authorities and that the Fund should at best offer only an opinion on them.

A third argument in favour of the traditional approach is that discussions at headquarters, require fewer and less specialized staff resources than do discussions of specific measures. For an institution concerned about its own budget, this is an important consideration. The design of a programme can be based on a relatively straightforward view of the relationship between fiscal deficits and balance of payments. Once some assumptions are made, it is far easier to decide what the size of a fiscal ceiling should be than to decide the details of specific policy changes and how these changes influence programme objectives.

A fourth argument, closely related to the preceding one, is that, at least in the fiscal area, it is far easier to write a letter of intent in which a country's formal commitments are couched in the form of general ceilings than to write documents that spell out formal commitments in terms of many specific policy changes. It is always difficult, for example to specify the precise requirements of a tax reform.

There are, however, arguments that caution against exclusive or excessive emphasis on traditional performance criteria that emphasize fiscal ceilings. They favour paying close attention to the microeconomic aspects of fiscal policy, such as the structure of individual taxes, the structure of expenditure, the allocation of investment, the prices charged by public utilities, and public employment. To avoid any misunderstanding on this issue I should emphasize here that the questions raised below about fiscal ceilings should not be interpreted as supporting Fund critics of conditionality. They simply call attention to the arguments (a) that a good stabilization programme must not rely exclusively on demand management and (b) that the ceilings used to serve demand management should not be set independently from the structural changes that the country is willing to make. The main justification for this change of emphasis is that, provided the supply response is not insignificant and occurs fairly rapidly, the more far-reaching the structural reform agreed to by the country, the greater will be that supply response (in terms of output, exports, capital repatriation, and the like). Such a supply response may imply that a less stringent demand-management policy may be necessary.

Problems have at times been encountered when ceilings have been imposed on macroeconomic variables. These problems are mentioned to indicate that a programme that relies exclusively on performance criteria related to macroeconomic variables may not be capable of providing the hoped-for results. First, the longer ceilings on macroeconomic variables are in use, the more ways countries learn to get around them. Ceilings are most useful when a country complies not just with the letter of an agreement but also with its spirit. Unfortunately, there have been instances in which countries have complied with the letter and defied the spirit of an agreement. They have engaged in operations aimed at circumventing the ceilings in order to draw resources from the Fund without making genuine adjustments. To deal with this problem, the Fund has been compelled, in some programmes, to increase the number of performance clauses related to the fiscal deficit. This has created a perception of excessive conditionality.

Second, the usual formulation of a stabilization programme may give the impression that the relationship between fiscal deficits and programme objectives, and especially their relationship with the balance of payments, is clear cut and unambiguous. In other words, it may give the impression of a single-valued functional relationship – that is, so much fiscal deficit implies so much deficit in the current account of the balance of payments. Unfortunately, our knowledge about important economic relationships (such as that between changes in the money supply and changes in prices, and that between changes in prices, changes in nominal exchange rates, and their effects on the balance of payments) is too limited to inspire excessive confidence about the precise level of the fiscal deficit required to achieve a given change in the current account of the balance of payments or in other economic objectives. The truth is that a given fiscal deficit may be associated with a range of balance of payments outcomes.[17]

Third, the ceilings may, in some cases, divert attention away from the basic objectives of economic policy. Meeting the ceilings may come to be seen, within the programme period, as an end in itself. During this period, programmes may be judged successful or not depending on whether ceilings are being met rather than on whether the ultimate objectives of the programme (durable improvement in the balance of payments, growth, price stability, and so forth) are being achieved.

Finally, and most important, excessive reliance on macroeconomic ceilings may divert attention away from the quality as well as the durability of the specific measures used by a country to comply with its performance clauses. Let me give some examples, starting with the question of the durability of the fiscal measure. The question to be raised is: Will a fiscal measure have a permanent impact on the fiscal deficit? Is, for example, a revenue increase or an expenditure cut of such a nature as to affect the deficit for years to come, or is it of a once-and-for-all type? This is an important question if the programme's objective is, as it should be, a permanent improvement in the economy.

Sometimes tax payments by enterprises have been advanced at the request of the government,[18] or public expenditures have been postponed (through the building up of arrears or through the postponement of inevitable expenditures)[19] so that the country can meet the fiscal ceilings and can, thus, make the next drawing. At other times, temporary sources of revenue (once-and-for-all taxes, temporary surtaxes, tax amnesties, sales of public assets, and so forth) have allowed the country to stay within the agreed ceiling without doing anything to reduce its underlying or core fiscal deficit.[20] At times governments have used up so much of their political capital in introducing these temporary measures that they no longer have the stamina to make the permanent and growth-promoting policy changes required to achieve durable adjustment with growth.

In addition to the question of the durability of the fiscal measures (will their effects survive the programme?), there is the important question of the quality (or, if one wishes, of the economic efficiency) of those measures. As far as short-term demand-management policy is concerned, whether a country reduces the fiscal deficit by raising revenue or by cutting expenditure is inconsequential.[21] It is also inconsequential whether it does it through the use of measures that have disincentive effects or through measures that do not have such effects. The stabilization programme will fail if the ceiling is not observed; it will not fail if it is observed through growth-retarding measures.

The above discussion should not be interpreted as arguing that stabilization programmes should no longer rely on demand management based on a macroeconomic framework that sets ceilings on relevant macroeconomic variables. In my view, the need for such a framework is too obvious to require justification. The discussion simply argues that this framework needs to be supplemented by measures aimed at ensuring that stabilization programmes are, first, durable and second, as growth-promoting as possible. Under present guidelines on conditionality, under which the Fund staff operates, the change advocated in this chapter might not be possible. A decision by the Executive Board of the Fund states that 'Performance criteria will normally be confined to (i) macroeconomic variables, and (ii) those necessary to implement specific provisions of the Articles or policies adopted under them. Performance criteria may relate to other variables only in exceptional cases' (International Monetary Fund, 1986: 27–8).

## Stabilization policy and economic growth
Growth-promoting stabilization policy requires that the reduction in the fiscal deficit be carried out through fiscal measures that are (a) durable in their effects and (b) efficient in their impact. In other words, the policies chosen must not self-destruct once the programme is over and must achieve their deficit-reducing objective with the least possible inhibition of economic growth.

The efficiency of fiscal instruments is important for growth, as much recent work on this issue has demonstrated. Work effort, exports, productive investment, saving, capital flight, foreign investment, and so on, can be affected by the choice of specific fiscal instruments.[22] These choices may play a large role in determining the amount of foreign resources a country will have available during and after the programme period. Thus, the relationship between changes in the size of fiscal deficits and changes in the ultimate objectives of economic policy, such as growth and stability, is inevitably influenced by the fiscal policy measures utilized. It can make a substantial difference to the growth prospects of a country if the fiscal deficit is reduced by eliminating a totally unproductive expenditure or by raising a tax that has strong disincentive effects, even though in terms of traditional stabilization policy (in terms of short-run fiscal deficit reduction) the result would appear to be the same. The more efficient the measures used to achieve a given deficit reduction, the greater will be the rate of growth, and, assuming an unchanged monetary policy, the lower will be the rate of inflation.

The implication of the above conclusion for stabilization programmes is obvious: provided that a country is willing to implement a considerable number of structural measures early enough in a programme so that the positive effects of these measures can be felt relatively soon, the Fund should be prepared to require less reduction in the overall fiscal deficit (that is, to require less austerity) than it would if the structural package were less far reaching or if the country delayed its introduction. Thus, the Fund should explicitly recognize, at the time it enters into an agreement with a country, a trade-off between quantity and quality of fiscal adjustment, a trade-off that would also be influenced by the timing of the introduction of the structural measures. This trade-off should be recognized and, possibly, formalized in programme design and negotiations.[23]

This is not the place to discuss in detail the quality of the fiscal measures that could form the structural core of a stabilization programme, but a few examples may help convey the importance of this issue. Suppose that an agricultural commodity of wide consumption (say, wheat, corn, or rice) has been subject to an export tax in a country negotiating a Fund programme. The elimination of this tax would reduce tax revenue and thus raise the fiscal deficit. This, in turn, would have monetary and consequently balance of payments implications, which the macroeconomic framework of Fund programmes would assess. But let us consider whether there are countervailing supply-side effects. The removal of the tax would raise the domestic price of the commodity and lead to a reduction in domestic consumption, thus making some additional supply available for exports.[24] In addition, the removal of the export tax would encourage producers to produce more of that product. When this additional production becomes available, exports will increase further. Since the availability of foreign exchange is always a key factor in a stabilization programme, focusing only on the demand effect (through the increase of the fiscal deficit) that the elimination of the tax will have, and ignoring the supply effect (through the incentive to produce and export more), is likely to introduce a bias against the elimination of that tax. It may thus possibly lead to programmes that require greater demand reduction than might have been necessary.[25]

Or suppose that some additional spending is carried out by the government to repair a road that facilitates the shipping of agricultural products out of the country. Here again the short-run negative effect on the balance of payments associated with the larger fiscal deficit is partly or fully neutralized by the positive effect associated with larger exports. These examples may be extreme but are far from rare. It would be easy to provide additional illustrations of the link between quantity and quality of fiscal adjustment. A perusal of stabilization programmes indicates that, despite an increasing awareness of these issues, political difficulties, guidelines on conditionality, and timing concerns have prevented their formal inclusion in Fund programmes.

In negotiating programmes, the Fund has attempted, with increasing frequency, to ensure that cutbacks in government expenditure are focused on less productive activities. World Bank guidance is sought in this connection. Nevertheless, obvious political sensitivities have limited the degree of Fund involvement in decisions on expenditure policy. As a result, the expenditure policies pursued have in several instances not been as supportive of the growth objective as they could have been.[26]

An examination of actual cutbacks in capital expenditure in various countries indicates that they have at times been borne by some of the more productive projects. To reduce the budget deficit, cutbacks have sometimes affected productive, externally financed projects despite the fact that loans for part of the total cost of the projects were highly concessionary. At other times, cutbacks have focused on productive, domestically financed, small-scale projects, while externally financed, highly visible, but less productive projects backed by important donors have been protected. Even where a core investment programme has been agreed between the country and the World Bank, higher implementation rates for lower-priority projects have often occurred.

A common feature of such policies has been the disproportionate cutback in expenditure on materials, supplies, and maintenance relative to other types of expenditure. As a result, roads, bridges, public buildings, irrigation projects, airports, and other public sector infrastructure have deteriorated by more than would have been necessary, notwithstanding the inevitability of certain adjustments necessitated by the debt crisis.[27] Inadequate maintenance eventually requires expensive projects for reconstruction of deteriorated plants and equipment.[28] In agricultural regions, impassable roads have drastically limited the impact of market-oriented policies aimed at encouraging increased agricultural production. Shortages of materials and supplies have also dramatically limited the productivity of public sector employees, whether in education, medical care, agricultural extension, or tax administration. Across-the-board cutbacks in expenditure have been common. Such an approach fails to address the enormous waste of expenditure in many politically sensitive but unproductive sectors, including defence spending. Significant cutbacks in public sector employment remain the exception. As a result, efforts to cut the public sector wage bill have typically resulted in a deterioration in real wages, often greatest among the higher-paid civil servants. The factors encouraging corruption, low productivity, and multiple jobs of civil servants have therefore been intensified.

Tax increases have in some instances included measures that can be expected to have detrimental effects on growth. This has at times occurred in countries that already have very high tax ratios. For example, on many occasions the rates of export duty have been raised (or an export duty has been imposed) following devaluation, on grounds that the exporters would enjoy some sort of 'windfall' profit. However, devaluations often simply offset past cost increases. Import surcharges have been levied, or the rates of import duties have been raised, for balance of payments and revenue reasons. As these surcharges have been imposed on products already highly taxed, they have, by increasing the differences between taxed and untaxed imports, increased distortions and reduced growth prospects.[29] Surcharges on the income taxes of individuals and corporations have often been used. Sometimes countries have raised payroll taxes or taxes on interest incomes with undesirable repercussion on employment, saving, and capital flight. In a few cases countries have levied taxes on expatriate employment, or have raised the rates of mining taxes, or have levied taxes on foreign exchange transactions, thus discouraging foreign participation in economic development.

The main point of this discussion is worth repeating. The impact of changes in fiscal deficits on economic objectives depends to a considerable extent on the quality of the specific measures employed. A change in the quality of those measures will change the relationship between the fiscal deficit and the balance of payments, especially over the medium and longer run. The required reduction in the fiscal deficit (the required austerity) needed to achieve a given effect on the basic objectives of economic policy will be more severe as less efficient measures are chosen. For this reason, stabilization programmes should systematically deal with microeconomic issues of public finance in addition to other structural policies. Programmes must include needed structural changes and must integrate them with the macroeconomic framework.

Several problems arise in connection with the implementation of the approach suggested in this chapter. They relate to (a) our knowledge of incentive effects, (b) timing considerations, and (c) political implications.

As to the first point, one could argue that not enough is known about the incentive effect of particular policies to place precise quantitative values on them. This is apparent, but irrelevant. Stabilization programmes often rely on exchange rate devaluation even though precise estimates of these responses are not available. They also rely on changes in real interest rates even though, again, the size of the response of financial (and real) saving to changes in real rates cannot be known with precision. The important point is to have a sense of the direction of the effects and some 'feel' for their size. If one waits for precise and objective quantifications of these effects, no formal agreement on a stabilization programme would ever be included.

As to the timing issue, one could agree that the choice of better policies would in time bring about a more efficient economy and higher rates of growth. But what about the present? Wouldn't, for example, the elimination or the reduction of an efficient tax or an increase in a highly productive government expenditure raise the deficit in the short run, thus necessitating more external or inflationary financing? A simple answer to that question is that important structural changes often bring with them immediate changes in expectations that can influence individuals and corporations to make further changes reinforcing their initial effects.[30] For example, changes that create an environment more favourable to the private sector may encourage individuals to repatriate capital, encourage foreign enterprises to invest in that country, and facilitate foreign borrowing. More foreign money is likely to be made available to countries pursuing structural reforms.[31] Still part of the answer is the fact that, as shown in the example of the export tax, some real effects will often occur early. If structural changes are made early in a programme, or even before its formal approval by the Fund, their supply-side effects would probably also occur within the programme's duration, so that the initial negative effect on the size of the fiscal deficit could be balanced by a positive effect in the latter phase of the programme. Reluctance to allow some initial expansion in the deficit through, say, the removal of inefficient taxes may contribute to the postponement of essential structural adjustment.[32] Finally, this timing question is not limited to these policies. For example, the existence of J-curve effects indicates that the same problem exists with exchange rate devaluation. Also, so-called ratchet effects may postpone the time when the impact of demand-management policies is felt on effective demand.

The proposed departure is not without political implications. The conditionality guidelines may have to be amended to make it possible for the Fund to include formally in a stabilization programme understandings about tax or expenditure reforms in the countries that approach the Fund for programmes and where there are significant structural distortions.[33] In some ways this would be a change more of form than of substance, because the Fund has already in recent programmes been involved in structural aspects and has tried to persuade some countries to implement particular policy changes. The countries' authorities may object to the proposed change, especially if they perceive it as additional conditionality without their receiving anything in return. Nevertheless, if they became aware that, at the time a programme is negotiated, there might be some trade-off between the size of the required macroeconomic adjustment on the one hand (the required austerity) and structural changes on the other, their possible objection to the proposed change might in some cases be less than one would assume *a priori*.

**Concluding remarks**
The above discussion indicates that, if at all possible, a more inductive approach

to determining the particulars of the fiscal policy required in stabilization programmes would be desirable. In this approach, in addition to identifying the range of adjustment needed at the macroeconomic level, the Fund, in cooperation with the country's experts, would make an inventory of the various changes in both the level and structure of taxes and of public expenditure that would be required to promote the country's growth objective.[34] It would have to take into account the importance that the country's authorities attach to such objectives as equity and the provision of basic needs. The task would then be to determine whether the proposed changes add up to a macroeconomic adjustment package that is consistent with the balance of payments objective. The structural adjustment would be made up of a basic structural core of fiscal measures representing a *sine qua non* for a programme. If this structural core did not add up to the macroeconomic adjustment assumed to be needed, the Fund and the local experts would look for progressively less efficient ways to add to revenues or to reduce expenditures. Should the country's economic difficulties be assumed to originate exclusively from excess demand (that is, if no major structural problems are identified), the negotiations would proceed along more traditional lines.

The country's authorities would be aware that there is a trade-off between the size of the needed demand constraint and the extent of the structural changes. They would know that the more daring and timely they are in introducing structural changes, the more flexibility they would have to be in demand-management. In essence, the programme would be made up of three elements, possibly all of major importance: the traditional macroeconomic framework with ceilings and targets; the structural core; and the investment core, which presumably would indicate, on the basis of World Bank recommendations, the minimum investment, as well as the allocation of that investment, consistent with both growth and balance of payments objectives.

One should not underestimate the difficulties, both technical and political, that a formal pursuit of this alternative would present; and one should recognize that this alternative would be considerably more labour intensive for both the Fund and the countries' experts and policy-makers. It is an alternative that requires further thinking before it can be fully implemented.[35] Initial experimentation in well-chosen and willing countries would be indispensable to a full assessment of its general feasibility and to an outline of the procedural steps to be followed.

It may be appropriate to conclude this chapter with a few highly personal thoughts on the political implications of the suggestions it contains.

While aggregate demand may grow independently of structural policies, so that a traditional stabilization programme would be sufficient in itself to bring about the needed reduction in that demand and thus the needed adjustment to the economy, it is more often the case that excess demand exists not (or not only) because demand has grown more than it should have, but because supply (including that of foreign exchange) has been constrained by misguided structural policies. For example, financial savings may have been reduced by constraints on nominal interest rates or by excessive taxation of interest income; this reduction may have constricted the supply of domestic financial savings available to finance the deficit and private investment in non-inflationary ways, and, because of capital flight, it may have reduced the availability of foreign exchange.[36] Agricultural output may have been reduced by low producer prices that necessitate the import of food. Agricultural exports may have been limited by excessive export taxes, by overvalued exchange rates, and by low prices paid to producers. Food supplies may have been limited by deteriorating transportation systems because of misallocation of public expenditures. In all these examples it is the supply that has been reduced, thus creating imbalances that, in time, manifest themselves as excessive demand. In these cases, demand-management policies alone would reduce the symptoms of these imbalances but would not eliminate the causes. Thus, stabilization programmes might succeed stabilization programmes without bringing about a durable adjustment unless the basic causes of imbalances are addressed.

One major difficulty in dealing with these basic issues is that the policies that I have called 'misguided' may be so only in an economic and not in a political sense. Public choice theorists would emphasize the fact that these policies may be quite rational, at least in the short run, if assessed from a purely political viewpoint.[37] They would argue that structural problems exist not necessarily because policy-makers made technical mistakes in their policy-making, perhaps because of poor economic understanding. Rather, public choice theorists would argue that through these policies policy-makers have tried to promote their own political objectives. Furthermore, the time horizon of policy-makers is generally so short that they do not take into full account the long-run implications of their policies on the economy. These policies create 'rents' for groups whose support the government needs in order to stay in power, even though they may in time reduce the level of income for the majority of citizens.[38]

If this public choice interpretation of economic policy is at least partly valid, and I do not know to what extent it is, it implies that policies aimed at structural reforms will often be resisted more than macroeconomic stabilization policies. They would be resisted because they would remove these rents from precisely those whose support the government needs and would thus reduce the leverage that the policy-makers have for staying in power. In part, structural reforms would reduce the *raison d' être* for the government in power. As a consequence, it would seem to follow from these theories that major structural reforms have the best change of being carried out when there is a major political change – that is, when a government that has long been in power is replaced by a totally different one – so that the political interests of the new policy-makers are not tied to existing structural policies. This public-choice inspired hypothesis should be amenable to testing. It seems to have some plausibility, but only a careful analysis of actual situations can assess its validity as a useful tool to explain changes that occur in economic policy.

## Notes

1. In this chapter the impact of fiscal developments on the balance of payments is emphasized. But, of course, the relationship is not unidirectional. In some cases fiscal disequilibrium may initially be created by developments in the balance of payments (say, a fall in export prices). In those cases the important question is whether the government should finance the shortcoming, or whether it should immediately or progressively lower domestic spending to reflect the lower real income of the country. On this, see Tanzi, 1986: 88-91; Tabellini, 1985; and Chu, 1987.
2. For the connection between the fiscal deficit and the balance of payments, see Kelly, 1982: 561–602. See also Tanzi and Blejer, 1984: 117–36.
3. This is particularly important in order to reduce over time the burden of the foreign debt of the countries.
4. But, of course, changes in the exchange rate, which have often been part of traditional stabilization programmes, have incentive effects in addition to their demand-management effect.
5. Over the years what I have called the supply-management aspect of fiscal policy has received far less attention than the more traditional demand-management aspect. To put it differently, price (or micro) theory was rarely integrated with income (or macro) theory. Fiscal policy based on the Keynesian framework normally concentrated on the effects of changes in tax levels and public spending levels on aggregate demand. Supply management is a relative newcomer to economic policy, even though it had been clearly recognized by Joseph Schumpeter in his classic book, *The Theory of Economic Development*, first published some seventy years ago. Supply management emphasizes the way the factors of production are used may be more important than their amounts. It emphasizes that growth requires not only that the factors of production keep growing at a desirable pace but also that they are allocated as efficiently as possible. If, for example, investment grows but is progressively channelled into less productive projects, the country's output may not grow.
6. Most of the formal models that link the fiscal deficit to the balance of payments follow this approach. In these models, it is the size of the macrovariables (such as the saving rate, the investment rate, the fiscal deficit) that plays the leading role. These variables are rarely disaggregated, so that the possibilities connected with better resource allocation are not explored.
7. It must be understood that even this macroeconomic approach will have to depend on specific measures to raise revenue or reduce spending.
8. The theoretical design of Fund programmes as generally interpreted has been much closer to what I have called the macroeconomic approach.
9. See, for example, Gold, 1979: 30–34.
10. For subsidies, one additional reason was their direct effect on the current account of the balance of payments when the subsidy encouraged the consumption of an imported commodity.
11. Technical assistance is provided by the Fund only at the request of a country's authorities.
12. The extended Fund facility was established in September 1974 to provide financial assistance in support of medium-term programmes for up to three years to overcome structural balance of payments maladjustments. The first request for this arrangement, by Kenya, was approved by the Fund in July 1975.
13. In actual negotiations, the sequence may not appear as described but in essence it is.
14. This might require a change in the conditionality approved by the Executive Board. Of course, whenever there is no presumption that resources have been badly misallocated, Fund programmes would continue to focus on a macroeconomic framework.
15. 'Performance criteria are always objective in order that a member will not be taken by surprise by a decision of the Fund to impede transactions under a stand-by arrangement. The member has maximum assurance, therefore, about the circumstances in which it can engage in transactions with the Fund'. Gold, 1979: 32.

16. A few programmes have made the total level of public expenditure a performance clause. This can be considered a departure from the traditional narrow interpretation of conditionality guidelines. Generally, the formal agreements have focused on the difference between public expenditure and revenue (that is, on the deficit).

17. Programmes recognize this problem by including (a) reviews to ensure that additional measures are taken to stay on track and (b) a commitment to take additional measures as needed.

18. A few years ago the government of a given country pressured a large foreign enterprise to advance tax payments for the next three years so as to allow the country to comply with the fiscal ceiling.

19. This is common with real wages for public employees that are at times reduced to unsustainable levels during the programme but bounce back to a more normal level when the programme is over. Permanent adjustment would more likely result from a reduction of the permanent public sector work force than from what is often a temporary reduction in real wages. On the issue of arrears in the payments of goods and services by the government, see Diamond and Schiller, 1987.

20. For a definition of the concept of core fiscal deficit, see Tanzi and Blejer, 1984: 119.

21. This is true regardless of the present level of taxation in the country.

22. The Fiscal Affairs Department of the Fund has produced a series of papers on this issue in the past few years. For specific studies of the relationship between export taxes and exports, see Tanzi, 1976: 66–76; Okonkwo, 1978; and Sanchez Ugarte and Modi 1987.

23. The potential output of a country is likely to grow if (a) the rate of investment grows while its average productivity and the average productivity of the other factors of production (labour, land, and so on) do not change; (b) if the average productivity of the factors of production increases owing to the removal of distortions, or to technological change, even though the supply of the production factors does not change. If the distortions have, as is often the case, reduced the country's ability to earn foreign exchange or have led to the misuse of the foreign exchange available, their removal will over time increase the flow of foreign exchange available to the country. In other words, the removal of the distortions would have the same effect as an increase in foreign lending to the country. It would thus reduce the need to constrain demand, as this need, in a typical Fund programme, is often a function of the scarcity of foreign exchange.

24. It should be recalled that an export tax on a commodity X can be decomposed in a production tax on X and a consumption subsidy on X. Thus, the removal of the export tax removes the subsidy to domestic consumption and removes the tax on production. Domestic consumption falls while production and, presumably, exports rise.

25. Of course, if the authorities propose to reduce the fiscal deficit through an increase in export taxes, then the negative supply-side effects of this policy would require even greater demand management than when these effects are ignored.

26. At this point it may be useful to state the obvious: government decisions are often influenced more by political considerations than by considerations of economic efficiency.

27. These expenditures are generally classified as 'current' rather than 'capital' expenditure. Therefore, the common view that stabilization programmes must protect 'investment' may not necessarily lead to the best policy. In some cases, the most productive expenditures are 'current' ones.

28. There is now a growing concern among some experts that the present reductions in fiscal deficits associated with these lower expenditures for maintenance of roads and other infrastructure will necessitate much higher expenditures (and thus higher deficits) in future years, as the lack of maintenance will require expensive rebuilding. This is again an example of the shifting of the fiscal deficit from the present to the future.

29. Imports subjected to import duties are often less than 50 per cent of total imports, so that substantial rate increases on the taxed imports are needed to generate significant tax revenue. Of course, as the rates go up so does smuggling.

30. This is particularly true when the attitude of the government indicates that these changes are not likely to be reversed soon.

31. It should be recalled that the Baker initiative is postulated on this assumption.

32.  Many structural changes can be made to be revenue neutral by removing some taxes (adding some expenditure) while at the same time adding some other tax (reducing some other expenditure).
33.  That is, some of the documents that reflect the formal understandings between the Fund and the country must spell out the details of the agreement between the two parties as to the tax modifications, changes in public expenditures, and so forth.
34.  Obviously, other structural aspects would also be considered.
35.  The full and formal introduction of structural changes in the theoretical design of Fund programmes should be considered one of the main challenges to our future research effort.
36.  For an analysis of the ways in which deficits get financed in developing countries and on the limits to those sources of financing, see Tanzi, 1986: 139–52.
37.  The literature on rent-seeking would support this view. See especially Buchanan, Tollison, and Tullock, 1980; Tollison, 1982: 575–602.
38.  For example, if agricultural prices are kept low in order to subsidize the real wages of urban dwellers, the government may acquire the support of the latter, but the cost may be a low rate of growth and increasing economic difficulties over the longer run. See, for example, some of the studies in Harberger, 1984.

## References

Buchanan, James M., Robert D. Tollison, and Gordon Tullock (eds), *Toward a Theory of the Rent-Seeking Society*, Texas A&M University, Economic Series, 4, College Station, Texas A&M Press, 1980.

Chu, Ke-Young, 'External shocks and the process of fiscal adjustment in a small open developing economy', *IMF Working Paper* 87/11, Washington, International Monetary Fund, 2 March 1987.

Diamond, Jack, and Christian Schiller, 'Government arrears in fiscal adjustment programs', *IMF Working Paper* 87/3, Washington, International Monetary Fund, 10 February 1987.

Gold, Joseph, *Conditionality*, IMF Pamphlet Series 31, Washington, International Monetary Fund, 1979.

Harberger, Arnold C. (ed.) *World Economic Growth*, San Francisco, California, Institute for Contemporary Studies, 1984.

International Monetary Fund, *Selected Decisions of the International Monetary Fund and Selected Documents*, 12th Issue, Washington, 30 April 1986.

Kelly, Margaret R., 'Fiscal adjustment and Fund-supported programs, 1971–80', *Staff Papers* 29, International Monetary Fund, December 1982: 561–602.

Okonkwo, Ubadigbo, 'Export taxes on primary products in developing countries: the taxation of cocoa exports in West Africa', unpublished, Washington, International Monetary Fund, 29 November 1978.

Sanchez-Ugarte, Fernando, and Jitendra R. Modi, 'Are export duties optimal in developing countries? some supply-side considerations' in *Supply-Side Tax Policy: Its Relevance to Developing Countries*, Via Gandhi (ed.), Washington, International Monetary Fund, 1987.

Tabellini, Guido, 'Fiscal policy response to the external shocks of 1979 in selected developing countries: theory and facts' unpublished, Washington, International Monetary Fund, 26 December 1985.

Tanzi, Vito, 'Export taxation in developing countries: taxation of coffee in Haiti', *Social and Economic Studies* (Kingston), 25 March 1976: 66–76.

——'Is there a limit to the size of fiscal deficits in developing countries?' in *Public Finance and Public Debt*, Bernard P. Herber (ed.), Detroit, Michigan, Wayne State University Press, 1985.

——'Fiscal policy responses to exogenous shocks in developing countries', *American Economic Review, Papers and Proceeding* (Nashville, Tennessee), 76, May 1986: 88–91.

—— and Mario I. Blejer, 'Fiscal deficits and balance of payments disequilibrium in IMF adjustment programs' in *Adjustment, Conditionality, and International Financing*, Joaquin Muns (ed.), Washington, International Monetary Fund, 1984: 117–36.

Tollison, Robert D., 'Rent seeking: a survey', *Kyklos* (Berne), 35, Fasc. 4, 1982: 575–602.

# PART 3

# TAXATION

# 10 Tax system and policy objectives in developing countries: general principles and diagnostic tests

Following the framework advocated by Richard Musgrave more than two decades ago (Musgrave, 1959), it has been standard procedure, in writing about the role of the government in non-centrally planned economies, to relate its actions to three broad objectives, namely, stabilization, redistribution, and allocation. These terms do not mean the same thing to everybody but acquire specific meanings in different places and times. Stabilization, for example, may be related to output, employment, balance of payments, or prices. Redistribution may be concerned with income changes among economic or social classes, regions, industries, sectors such as urban or rural, factors of production, races, sexes, or even age groups. Allocation does not imply the neutral use of resources, as it does in public finance textbooks written for advanced countries, but refers to a utilization of the factors of productions that presumably promotes employment, growth, or industrialization. In fact, in developing countries it could be replaced with the objective of growth or development.

Regardless of how important policy-makers consider these objectives, and of how they rank them, they may be able to influence them only if the policy instruments that they control are efficient. Such instruments may be associated with the financial system (such as the discount rate and reserve requirements), with the balance of payments (exchange rates, export subsidies, quotas, and the like), with regulations (such as price fixing), and, finally, with the public finances. The latter are the instruments of fiscal policy. Fiscal policy can be pursued through the use of taxes or public expenditure, in other words through tax policy and/or expenditure policy.

This chapter focuses on the use of taxes as potential instruments to be used, together with other instruments, to promote those economic and social objectives that the developing countries' policy-makers, rightly or wrongly, wish to promote. It attempts to answer the questions: What are the main characteristics of the tax system of the developing countries? Do these characteristics render these tax systems inefficient instruments of economy policy?[1]

The basic aim of the chapter is to describe the distinctive features of the tax systems of developing countries and to provide a simple framework for judging whether specific tax changes could make the tax system as a whole a better or worse instrument of economic policy and for assessing the efficiency of existing systems in the sense defined above. Thus, its emphasis is not on issues of efficiency raised by the theoretical literature on taxation.

Before discussing the tax structure itself, it may be worthwhile to single out some pertinent qualitative characteristics of the tax systems of developing (and developed) countries that, independently of the structure, largely determine how good these systems are.[2] These characteristics are desirable regardless of the tax structure itself. The following discussion reflects two assumptions: first, it is better to have few but efficient instruments to pursue economic policy rather than many inefficient ones; second, the government has significant control over the *statutory* tax system but, often, little control over the *effective* tax system. Tax laws can be changed but unless they are effectively administered and enforced those changes may be inconsequential.[3] Thus, it is imperative that changes made in the laws translate into changes in the effective tax system. Specific tests needed for carrying out a diagnosis of the tax system are outlined below.

## Qualitative characteristics of effective tax systems

To assess the degree of their efficiency in the sense indicated above tax systems are subjected in this section to eight diagnostic tests. A tax system that received high scores in these tests would, *ceteris paribus,* be presumed to have better qualities for use as an instrument of economic policy than one that received low scores.

*Concentration index.* In a good tax system a large share of total tax revenue would come from relatively few taxes and tax rates. Although it is difficult to say just how concentrated tax revenue should be, there are clear advantages when a large share of total revenue comes from few sources. With higher concentration the tax system becomes more transparent and more manageable. For example, it is easier in this case to do an incidence analysis and to assess its effect on income distribution, factor utilization, saving, and so on. Furthermore, whenever the need to increase or decrease revenue presents itself, the calculations to estimate the revenue effects of statutory changes (and the effects of these changes on income distribution and factor utilizations) are easier to make and to explain to policy-makers, legislators, and the public. When total tax collection is diffused among many small taxes, or when the collection from a given tax is diffused among many rates, as is often the case in developing countries, it becomes excessively difficult, if not impossible, to conduct a coherent tax policy. For example, the pursuit of stabilization policy through tax changes becomes considerably more difficult as it requires legislation and estimations involving many taxes. Under these circumstances, it is hard to make good forecast of the revenue impact of changes in statutory rates.

One could calculate a 'concentration index' that would measure the proportion of total tax revenue generated by, say, the three or four major taxes or tax rates. To do so the revenue from each tax and from each rate must be taken separately.[4] For example, if a 'general' sales tax has many rates, the revenue generated by each rate would be considered as a different tax source. For a schedular income tax, the revenue from each schedule would be considered as a separate tax. However, a global income tax might be considered as a single source of revenue in spite of its many rates.[5]

*Dispersion index.* A good tax system must not only have a high concentration index, as defined above, but must also keep low the number of low-yielding, nuisance taxes. A country can have a high concentration index, in the sense that a large proportion of total tax revenue comes from few sources, but still have a proliferation of minor taxes whose total yield is small.

That the problem of proliferation of small taxes is common can be seen by the following examples. In a Latin American country the tax office was recently collecting about 100 different taxes. A small Caribbean country is at the present time collecting 41 taxes – many imposed with multiple rates. Some European countries still use many taxes when those levied by state and local authorities are included. For example, Denmark uses 64 taxes, France 63, and Italy 41 (Commission of the European Communities, 1982.)

Small, nuisance taxes obfuscate the tax system, making its analysis difficult. Tax-payers face high costs of compliance as they have to comply with so many taxes; in some countries they have come to believe that they are overtaxed even when the tax level is not high. Tax administrators have to waste scarce administrative resources to go after these taxes and often the cost of collecting them exceeds the revenue intake.[6] Like fruit trees, tax systems must occasionally be pruned of unproductive and obsolete taxes if they are to remain healthy and productive. As with zero-base budgeting, the reason for the existence of a given tax must be periodically reassessed. If the *raison d'être* for the use of a tax is no longer there, the tax must be eliminated. One avenue of tax reform must, therefore, be the progressive elimination of small and unproductive taxes and, for taxes such as the general sales taxes (and perhaps even the income tax) the elimination of redundant rates. This change releases administrative resources that can be utilized to improve the administration of major taxes. Low yielding taxes often demand as much administrative effort as much more productive ones.

Therefore the average collection cost per unit of revenue for the whole tax system becomes much higher. It is surprising to find how many scarce resources are wasted on small and unproductive taxes.[7]

A 'dispersion index' could be calculated that would indicate the average share of total tax revenue accounted by these minor taxes. Thus, if 50 taxes generate only 10 per cent of total tax revenue the average contribution of these taxes is one fifth of 1 per cent. This is an unacceptably low proportion. By eliminating the smallest nuisance taxes the average contribution by small taxes could be raised.

As a general rule, a country should take a close look at any tax that does not raise at least, say, 1 per cent of total tax revenue.

*Erosion index.* The third general diagnostic test would assess the extent to which actual tax bases are close to potential ones. Erosion of tax bases is one of the major problems of the tax systems of developing as well as of developed countries. This erosion may originate from legal actions (tax holidays, personal exemptions and deductions, exoneration from import duties, zero rating) or from illegal actions (evasion, smuggling).

Whichever the origin, it often results in actual tax bases that are small fractions of their potential levels. For example, a general sales tax may end up being applied to only 10 per cent of total consumption; a global income tax may be applied to a similar proportion of national income; import duties may be collected from only 30–40 per cent of imports. Because of this erosion, in their search for revenue, countries are forced to apply high rates on the remaining taxable bases, and introduce additional taxes thus reducing the concentration index. High tax rates, of course, make the problem of evasion worse. These high rates, together with the many small taxes, aggravate the difficulties that tax administrators have and create disincentives which affect the economic performance of the country.[8] Furthermore, they make more difficult the achievement of horizontal equity as tax-payers in similar circumstances end up paying widely different taxes. One important measure of progress in taxation is, thus, the extent to which actual tax bases are being brought closer to their potential level.

This change would allow a progressive reduction of high tax rates without affecting revenue. As countries develop, the 'erosion index' for particular taxes must be reduced to an absolute minimum.[9]

*Collection lags index.* A fourth test relates to collection lags. In recent years some attention has been paid to the fact that, in many countries, tax payments may be delayed much beyond the time when they should be made (Hirao and Aguirre, 1970; Tanzi, 1977). These delays may result from long allowable lags (legal lags) or from tax-payers' abuses (delinquency lags). In other words the law itself or, more often, administrative regulations allow the tax-payer to pay his taxes a long time after the particular event that created the tax liability took place (earning of income, selling of product, importation, and so on).

Furthermore, the tax-payer may delay the payment beyond the time when it is due because of low or even insignificant penalties connected with such action.[10]

Legal lags can be long for incomes from capital sources. For these, lags of two years are common even in some industrial countries.[11] Delinquency lags can be of almost any length. The author was recently told by a director of taxation of a given country that in that country a tax-payer could delay paying taxes for up to ten years with almost no penalty and no interest charges. When such delays are possible, the tax system cannot be efficient, regardless of how well designed it may be in theory. In such a case, for example, it becomes very difficult to increase tax revenues in the short run through changes in statutory rates.[12] Furthermore, the ratio of tax revenue to GNP will become highly sensitive to the rate of inflation, falling when inflation accelerates and rising when inflation slows down (Tanzi, 1977).

One of the fundamental objectives of tax reform must therefore be the progressive reduction of collection lags to some feasible minimum.[13] Prompted by the effects of high rates of inflation, some progress has been made in many countries in recent years. However, much remains to be done.[14]

*Specificity index.* Another test for the diagnosis of the soundness of a tax system is the degree to which it relies on specific (*ad rem*) taxes. In many countries such taxes continue to play an important role in connection with import duties and excises. Recommendations aimed at their removal have often been resisted, at times for good reasons and more often for bad ones. The following are some of the reasons given for the retention of specific import duties.[15]

1.  As *ad valorem* duties are often very high, importers undervalue their imports and in doing this they often get the cooperation of foreign suppliers. Attempts to obtain reliable price lists from foreign governments are often unsuccessful. Proposals to place customs officials in the main foreign countries or to get price information in other ways are frustrated by budgetary limitations. Attempts on the part of customs officials to compare the prices declared by one importer with those declared by others often lead to poor results because importers collude and declare identical (low) prices.
2.  It is difficult for the government to prove undervaluation in a court of law. Thus penalties cannot be imposed. When penalties can be based on more objective criteria, as with specific duties, they can stand up more easily in court.
3.  When duties are specific, importers lose interest in undervaluing their imports; therefore, import statistics improve and better economic policy becomes possible.[16]
4.  With better price statistics, specific duties can occasionally be adjusted more closely in line with actual price changes, that is, they can be indexed in an informal way.
5.  With specific duties, the quality of imported products improves because the tax does not increase with the value. This may not be desirable for consumer goods – as more expensive products will be preferred over less expensive ones – but it may be beneficial to the country for machinery and raw materials.
6.  Clearance of goods from the docks is facilitated by specific duties, because

only physical characteristics, and not values and qualities, need be determined. Given the limitation of dock space and of trained inspectors in many countries, this is an important consideration.

7.  Specific duties may hide the very high levels of some duties; therefore, the government may have more freedom of action in changing the level of specific import duties.

8.  Finally, the prices of some products fluctuate so often and so wildly that no price list can satisfactorily keep up with them.

Similar reasons are often advanced for the use of *ad rem* taxes for excises. For these, the main advantages mentioned are: the lower administrative skills required for them, the difficulty of getting price information, the reluctance of governments to make explicit the equivalent *ad valorem* tax rate, and the belief that *ad valorem* taxes are inflationary.

Some of these reasons have much validity, others less. And some (such as, for example, the presumed inflationary effect of *ad valorem* taxes) are just plain wrong. The basic issue is that, when countries experience inflation, revenue from specific taxes falls. Adjustments to the specific rates (to keep the real revenue from these taxes constant) are often delayed for political reasons; when they are finally made they are seen by tax-payers as substantial price increases. Because these adjustments become politically more and more difficult to make, the elasticity of the tax system is reduced. The higher the share of total tax revenue collected from specific taxes (that is, the higher the specificity index), the more negatively affected will be the total tax revenue from inflation. A good tax system must minimize recourse to specific taxes. The more developed a country is, the less excuse it will have to rely on these taxes. Of course, the higher the rate of inflation, the greater price the country will pay for doing so.[17]

*Objective index.* Another test that can be applied to the tax system of a country is the extent to which taxes are being levied on objectively measured bases.

The casual observer may believe that income taxes always apply on clear and objective measures of income; that sales taxes apply to clear measures of sales; that import duties apply to objective values of imports, and so on. Acting on this belief he might analyse the impact of these taxes on the economy, basing his analysis on theories about their incidence, their effect on incentives, and so on, learned from public finance textbooks. However, in many developing countries, incomes, imports, sales, property, and the like, may have objective or true values totally different from those on which the taxes are actually calculated. This is not just an issue of evasion which implies that the tax-payer himself knows exactly what the objective tax base is. Rather, in some countries record keeping and accounting standards may be so poor that the tax-payer himself would be unable to assess his sales or income.

Thus, presumed values replace actual ones and the distinction between, say, income taxes and sales taxes becomes far less sharp. A concrete example is the so-called minimum tax on corporations used by many African countries. This tax is supposed to be an income tax but is imposed as a percentage of the turnover of the corporation.

Although this again would be a difficult enterprise, it would be useful if an index could be developed whereby the proportion of total tax revenue derived from truly objective bases could be estimated. In the absence of such an index, at least an impression should be formed as to the extent to which guesses or 'guesstimates' (as, for example, with 'presumed' incomes or with other *forfait* taxes) have replaced actual measurements.[18]

*Enforcement index.* When tax compliance is not enforced, the divergence between the statutory and the effective tax system may become so large that the legal tax system loses its meaning. In this case the correlation between legal changes and effective changes may be so low that the effects of legal changes on the effective tax system can no longer be predicted. Furthermore, the incidence of the tax system becomes impossible to determine. Thus, the tax system ceases to be a potential instrument of policy.

Little attention has been paid to the structure of penalties for non-compliance in developing countries (see Sisson, 1981). In some countries the payment of taxes becomes almost a favour on the part of the tax-payers, as the consequences of non-compliance are insignificant. When effective penalties exist, together with a good chance that evaders will get caught, tax systems are potentially more efficient policy tools.

Evasion can be reduced by higher penalties or better administration. Penalties can generally be increased without any pecuniary costs to the government. Better administration, on the other hand, often requires additional spending. Because of these considerations some have recommended that the fight against evasion should be fought with higher penalties rather than with better administration. As a cynic might put it, 'evaders should be hung with a probability that approaches zero'.

There are several problems with this approach. First, when penalties are too high, often they are not applied. Second, even if the pecuniary costs to the government may be low or zero,[19] there are other costs (political, social) associated with high penalties that cannot be ignored.[20] Thus, the best policy is one that accompanies reasonable penalties with better administration through improvement of assessment and collection procedures, registration of taxpayers, use of computers, better audits, and so on. Tax policy and tax administration must go hand in hand if a better tax system is to be achieved. A property penalty structure is a necessary ingredient for both.

Although it would be impossible to provide precise quantitative indices of penalties and enforcement measures in general, this is an area where even collection of basic information would be helpful. For example, how many tax-payers are audited? Indicted? Jailed? How many returns are inspected? How many premises are visited by tax inspectors? Comparative information would be useful.

*Cost-of-collection index.* Finally, one would want to look at the cost of collecting tax revenue. Clearly, *ceteris paribus,* the lower the cost of collection the better the tax system. Little research has been done on this important aspect of taxation. We do know, however, that overall the ratio of collection costs to revenue raised ranges from, perhaps, as low as 2– 3 per cent in some countries to some 7–8 per cent in others. Furthermore, on a tax-by-tax basis, we do know that that ratio has at times exceeded 100 per cent. By and large general sales taxes and foreign trade taxes are far less expensive to collect than income taxes. Thus comparison of collection costs must take into account the structure of the tax system. But it must also take into account the size and the geographic configuration of the country, the number of inhabitants, literacy rates, and accounting and book-keeping standards. Perhaps a meaningful approach would be one that compares collection costs across countries for categories of taxes (incomes, sales) but it would still be useful to know how the overall index of cost of collection changes with economic development.

In conclusion, regardless of its structure, the tax system of a country will be deemed more efficient when it has:

(i)     a high concentration index;
(ii)    a low erosion index;
(iii)   a low collection lag;
(iv)    a low specificity index;
(v)     a high objectivity index;
(vi)    reasonable penalties, and, finally,
(vii)   a low cost of collection.

Only when the tax system satisfies these requirements to some extent can it perform its role of a policy instrument for the achievement of multiple objectives. Otherwise, its only function will be that of raising revenue.

We turn now to the structure of the tax system to assess how that structure relates to policy objectives. For each type of tax we ask what other objective could it influence in addition to the obvious one of raising revenue. For the rest of this chapter the discussion centres on practical considerations rather than on purely theoretical ones. Although we shall not raise again the issues discussed above, they must be kept in mind throughout the following discussion.

**Taxes on foreign trade and internal consumption**

The principal objectives that these taxes can satisfy with a relative degree of efficiency are the following: they can generate considerable revenue;[21] they can discourage the consumption of particular products if there are religious, social, economic, or other reasons for doing so; they can provide protection to specific domestic activities; and to the extent that the government does not wish to use the exchange rate to influence the balance of payments, they can be used toward achieving this objective in the short run; however, in the long run, the exchange rate is a far more efficient instrument for controlling the current account of the balance of payments as import taxes inevitably handicap exports by allowing the exchange rate to remain overvalued and by increasing the costs of inputs. We shall divide these taxes into five categories and discuss them separately. These categories are: a general sales tax; a general (flat-rate) tax on imports; excise taxes; import duties; and export taxes.[22] Each has its own function in the sense that, if it is properly designed, it is relatively more efficient as an instrument directed toward a specific objective rather than toward other objectives.

*Role of a general sales tax.* Although in most cases all taxes on consumption (whether related to domestic or imported products) will generate revenue, the *main* role in relation to revenue generation should be played by a general sales tax. To be most efficient in this role such a tax should be levied at a uniform rate on as broad a base as possible. The base must include the duty-paid value of imports and exclude exports. In practice, however, general sales taxes are often levied with multiple rates although this creates considerable administrative complications (especially for the now popular value-added taxes), and although the available evidence indicates that little is gained in terms of equity by having multiple rates (see Gandhi, 1979). Furthermore, the efficiency of this tax as a revenue instrument is further reduced by the fact that, in most countries, the actual tax base is a fraction of the potential tax base. This erosion results from evasion as well as from policies aimed at making it an instrument of social and economic policy by exempting many products and activities.

The function of discouraging the consumption of particular items or of making the consumers of those items pay for particular costs associated with their consumption should be left to the excise taxes. In this way the government will have two potentially efficient instruments rather than one relatively inefficient one. Even though the base for the general sales tax should be broad, some well-defined products could be exempted for administrative or social reasons (basic goods, school books, medicines). The basic rate that the government would choose for this tax would depend on revenue needs and on how broad the tax base is. The narrower the base, the higher that rate must be to generate the same revenue. In this connection, it must be remembered that the higher the rate the greater will be the incentive toward evasion.[23] To the extent possible, the base should include services, and especially those sold by public enterprises.[24] Some of the value added generated by the process of distribution should also be included. Furthermore the tax should avoid, or at least limit, cascading. For these reasons a value-added tax is preferable to other forms of general sales taxes.

. A broad-based general sales tax levied with a single rate on a broad base has important characteristics that other taxes do not have: it can generate large revenue with hardly any lag so that it is little affected by inflation;[25] the revenue effect of a rate change is immediate; the policy-makers can easily calculate, with an acceptable degree of accuracy, how much revenue will be generated by a given, modest change in the rate; and almost any legislator, regardless of training, can immediately visualize the impact of a rate change. For example, the impact of a change from, say, 10 to 12 per cent can be easily estimated and understood. Therefore, this tax lends itself quite well as an instrument of stabilization policy which requires a change in revenue within a short period of time. Clearly its comparative advantage is, *vis-à-vis*, the objective of stabilization and revenue generation.

*Role of a general tax on imports.* Once a general sales tax (which taxes internal production as well as imports) is in place, is there any reason to have a general tax on imports? The main economic role of such a tax should not be to generate revenues, although it inevitably will do so. Rather, it should be to reduce imports in the short run when the balance of payments is in disequilibrium and the government does not yet wish to change the exchange rate, and to provide a generalized and minimum level of protection to all domestic economic activities.[26] If this tax is levied on the totality of imports with a flat *ad valorem* rate, it will be simpler to administer and will be a flexible and efficient instrument of policy. It will be easy for the government to change it and to estimate the revenue, and, perhaps, even the balance of payments effects of rate changes.[27] Like the general sales tax, this tax will also have the good feature of generating tax revenue immediately as it can be collected without lags. Obviously, if the government should not wish a change in total tax revenue, but it still wished to discriminate against imports, it would be easy to neutralize the revenue effect from this tax with a change, in the opposite direction, in the rate of the general sale tax. Of course, since the latter has a larger base, the opposite change in the rates would not be equal. The main administrative difficulty of this tax is the evaluation of imports.

*Role of excise taxes on consumption:* In addition to the general sales tax, which would affect all consumption (except that exempted for very special reasons), there will be scope for taxes on the consumption of some products. Three important reasons for excise taxes are: to discourage the consumption of particular products; to give more equity to the taxation of consumption; and to make the consumers of some products pay for costs associated with their provisions or their use but not normally incorporated in the price of the product. Therefore, differential tax rates could be levied on some products. The less useful or essential a product is considered to be, the higher could the rate be.[28]

These rates would apply regardless of whether the product is locally produced or imported. If the reason for imposing these taxes is that the product is not essential, there would be no reason to discriminate in favour of locally produced products and against imported products. Many countries have attempted to discourage luxury consumption through the use of import duties. The problem with this approach is that a high duty on the import of a luxury product stimulates the domestic production of that product by giving it excessive protection.

Thus, the duty often leads to a reallocation of resources toward the domestic production of luxury products. The consequence of this is that the government loses revenue, conspicuous consumption is not reduced, and resources get allocated in socially undesirable ways.

There are other reasons, besides the luxury of products, for using excise taxes. For taxes on petroleum products, the main reason is to make the users of roads pay part of the costs of building and maintaining the roads. For alcohol and tobacco taxes, the reasons often have to do with religion or health or other social costs connected with their use. The main point is that as long as the government wishes to influence the pattern of consumption, it can do this more effectively through excise taxes than through other taxes. Excise taxes must be levied on prices that, for domestic products, are gross of general sales taxes, and, for imported products, are gross of import duties (that is, on duty-paid import values).

*Role of customs duties with differentiated rates.* Once a general tax on imports is in place, accompanied by a general sales tax and by differentiated internal excises on specific products to discourage luxury consumption or to promote other objectives, is there any reason to have differentiated rates on imports? There is only one important reason and that is to provide protection to those particular activities that the government wants to encourage or (when a general import duty is already in place) that it wants to encourage more than others.[29] In this case, as the duty is being used to perform just one function – that of providing protection rather than raising revenue, discouraging luxury consumption – the protection granted to domestic activities is not accidental, but the government can decide precisely how much protection it is willing to grant to particular activities and can thus set the tariff accordingly. It is unlikely that in this situation the government would want to give the highest protection to the production of luxury products, as is often the case when the discrimination against these products is done through the use of import duties.[30]

The coordination of domestic indirect taxes (sales, excises) with import duties has proven to be one of the most difficult areas of tax reform in developing countries. It is fair to say that little, if any, progress has been made in this area. The reason for this lack of success is clearly that the objectives sought by tax experts in these reforms are often not shared by the policy-makers.[31] Yet, this is, perhaps, potentially the most important area of tax reform in developing countries.

*Role of export taxes.* Export taxes have been imposed for a variety of reasons besides the obvious one of generating revenue. Some of these are:

(i)   to keep down the domestic prices of some products (rice, sugar, meat) considered particularly important to industrial workers and to consumers with low incomes;[32]

(ii)  to stimulate the local production and/or the export of more elaborate products that use domestic raw materials as inputs;[33]

(iii) to induce producers to produce better crops whenever several qualities or grades of the same product can be produced (as with coffee) by putting export taxes (or higher tax rates) on poorer qualities;

(iv)  to sterilize windfall profits associated with a devaluation; and

(v)   to get some tax revenue out of the agricultural sector.

In theory a tax on the export of a commodity is equivalent to two different components: a tax imposed on the production of the commodity, and an equal subsidy to the local consumption of that commodity. Consequently the higher the export tax, the higher is the implicit production tax and the implicit subsidy to the local consumption of the commodity. The result of this is that production is discouraged by the implicit tax while the local consumption of the commodity is encouraged by the implicit subsidy. The actual reaction of consumption and production to these effects will of course depend on their elasticities. In general the higher the elasticities the more damage the export tax is likely to cause to production and exports. For this reason export taxes may often be second-best instruments for achieving the objectives specified above. Thus, it would be wise to maintain a sceptical attitude *vis-à-vis* the usefulness of these taxes.

## Taxes on income
### Role of personal income taxes
Taxes on personal incomes should be levied for two major reasons: first to provide revenue and, second, to bring some equity in the distribution of the tax burden among income classes. All governments try to make their tax system progressive and the most efficient instrument for doing so is *potentially* the personal income tax. It is helpful to think of the income tax as being made up of three basic instruments of economic policy, namely, the exemption, the first rate, and the higher rates.[34]

The first of these instruments, the exemption, can be used to promote two objectives. It can be calibrated to exclude people with incomes deemed too low to justify taxation. It would be kept high enough to limit the number of tax-payers to a level consistent with good administration. When this exemption is too low, the tax administration may find itself engulfed by an excessive number of tax-payers who cannot possibly be checked. There have been cases of countries where a drastic reduction in the exemption level increased the number of filers to such an extent that the administration of the tax literally broke down.

Thus, a general rule should be: the poorer the tax administration of the country, the higher the level of the exemption. As tax administration improves, the level of the exemption can be reduced. This level, however, should in any case be related to the per capita income of the country. In many countries, however, the need to relate the exemption to the per capita income of the country has not been recognized, so that the former has often been excessively high, thus reducing potential revenue. A general rule should be the following: the lower the administrative capacity of the country and the country's per capita income, the higher (as a multiple of per capita income) the level of the exemption should be.[35]

The second of the basic instruments that make up the income tax, the first rate, can in a way be considered as the analog, *vis-à-vis* the income tax base, of the general sales tax. Its function should be mainly to generate revenue and it should be increased or reduced, as the need arises, for this purpose alone. In most countries a large proportion of total income tax revenue originates from the first rate, so that what happens to it is of particular significance for revenue.

The third of the basic instruments of the income tax, the progressive higher rates, should be utilized mainly for equity reasons. High rates rarely generate much revenue but they may be important for making the tax systems more progressive and, presumably, more equitable. Or, perhaps, for making it look more progressive than it actually is. These rates should not be changed mainly for revenue reasons, although obviously, when they are changed, there will be revenue effects.

To satisfy the equity objective income taxes must insure that: individuals with the same overall income pay identical taxes provided that they are in the same familial status (such as, married or single, number of children). This characteristic is referred to as horizontal equity; individuals with higher over-all incomes must pay a larger proportion in taxes than individuals with lower incomes; this characteristic is referred to as vertical equity.

There seems to be a growing consensus that the marginal income tax rate should not exceed 50 per cent. However, these rates should be reached at meaningful levels. As a general guideline one could, perhaps, suggest that the marginal tax rate be reached at the average level of income of the richest 1 per cent of the population, say, somewhere between 15 and 20 times the country's per capita income.[36]

Public finance experts generally agree that horizontal and vertical equity is achieved more easily with a global (or unitary) that with schedular income taxes. Many developed countries today have global income taxes and the trend among developing countries is to move from schedular to global income taxes. In the original theory of schedular income taxation that one finds in the Italian or French literature of the early part of this century, the various incomes were supposed to be taxed first with proportional rates that ignored the particular situation of the individuals (in other words, they were not 'personalized'); then the various incomes were supposed to be aggregated and subjected to a progressive income tax. In this way, the government could discriminate, if it wished to do so, among various types of incomes (such as from dependent work, from land) on social or other grounds (for example, on the grounds of differential evasion) by having different proportional rates on the schedules. However, once the incomes were aggregated, they would all be taxed with the same progressive rates. Today differential tax treatment of different kinds of incomes is often introduced through special deductions granted to particular incomes. Thus in some countries incomes from wages receive higher deductions than other incomes.

### Role of taxes on enterprises

In addition to the taxes on the income of individuals most countries tax the incomes of legal entities (such as corporations).[37] This makes income taxation not truly global because it introduces a schedular element. Of course with a system of full integration, whereby all the income of enterprises were assumed to be distributed to the shareholders (regardless of whether full distribution actually took place), there would not be any need to have separate taxation of the income of enterprises. However, full integration is very difficult in any country. In developing countries, there is the additional complication that the owners are often foreigners so that they cannot be taxed on their personal income. This means that often the enterprises are taxed with a separate tax.

The main objective of taxes on enterprises is clearly revenue generation although equity is also important. In view of the international mobility of capital, the applicable rate should not be out of line with the rates prevailing in other countries. This rate should be lower than the marginal rate on the income of individuals and, if a lower rate on low levels of profits exists, it would apply on a level of income comparable to the one at which the individual's marginal income tax rate applies. The basic rate on legal enterprises can be reduced or increased to induce more or less retention of profits on the part of the enterprises. Because of the considerable lag in the collection of this tax and of the variability of the tax base (profits), this is not a good instrument for bringing about changes in government revenue in the short run.

## Taxes on property

To varying degrees most tax systems rely on property (besides consumption and income) as a tax base. Property taxes can, in theory, promote both revenue and equity objectives. Urbanization seems to be an important determinant of their importance as very often these taxes are tied with local finances, as real properties benefit directly from local expenditures. Attempts to personalize property taxes in the form of net wealth taxes have been largely unsuccessful. This is a pity because a net wealth tax could be a powerful instrument for income redistribution. Countries with highly uneven income distribution and with a large concentration of wealth should attempt to have productive property taxes, especially when their income taxation is inadequate. But experience indicates that not too much should be expected from this tax source.[38]

## Concluding remarks

The experience of industrial countries shows that it is very difficult to use the tax system as an instrument for achieving economic and social goals. Political obstacles frequently stand in the way of tax measures designed to accomplish non-revenue objectives. When such measures are adopted, administrative constraints make them difficult to implement.

In developing countries, where political, social and administrative obstacles are often much greater, tax systems are likely to be even less effective as policy instruments. This has led many tax experts to argue that the only function of the tax system should be the raising of revenue. It is argued that other goals can be pursued through the expenditure side of the budget. There are at least two problems with this point of view. First, the obstacles that render the tax systems relatively inefficient instruments of economic policy do not disappear on the expenditure side. It is a bit naive to believe that what cannot be done on the tax side can be done, in the same environment, on the expenditure side. There is now considerable evidence to indicate that expenditure policy is likely to be equally ineffective.[39] Second, whatever experts think, policy-makers will continue to attempt to use the tax system to achieve goals that they deem important. For these reasons tax experts cannot abdicate their responsibility to see that the tax systems change in ways that improve their effectiveness as instruments of economic policy.

The design of any tax system will have to deal with two major problems: conflicts of objectives and the gap between the statutory and the effective tax system. Much of the available literature has emphasized the first of these problems. The present chapter has emphasized the second. It has provided various indices for evaluating tax systems. These indices have been discussed in isolation (one by one) and particular aspects of the tax structure have been singled out as being important in connection with policy objectives. This approach, while useful, has left out the question of whether these indices could in some cases conflict among themselves. The basic challenge that tax experts will continue to face is this: Can tax systems be reformed in ways that increase their effectiveness as instruments for policy-makers while at the same time retaining some of the characteristics that economists consider desirable?

## Notes

1. The concept of efficiency used here is Tinbergen's; an instrument is efficient when a relatively modest change in it brings about a noticeable effect in the objective that the policy wants to influence (Tinbergen, 1952).
2. Elsewhere the author has analysed the quantitative aspects of the developing countries' tax systems. See 'Quantitative characteristics of the tax systems of developing countries' in Newbery and Stern's *Modern Tax Theory for Developing Countries*.
3. This statement, of course, does not ignore the political difficulties often encountered in changing these laws.
4. Thus, information usually available that gives revenue aggregated by major tax categories is useless for this purpose.
5. An international index of tax concentration could be developed whereby the actual concentration indices of various countries could be correlated with various determinants (such as per capita income, level of taxation). Actual and estimated indices could then be compared. This has been the standard procedure in the literature on international comparisons of tax levels. (See Lotz and Morss, 1967; Chelliah *et al.* 1975; Tait *et al.* 1979; Tanzi, 1968.)
6. Sometimes the cost of collection is several times the revenue generated.
7. It is necessary to point out that some taxes are levied for reasons other than revenue.
8. In developing countries these high rates may also provide incentives to substitute the production of non-taxed activities (including subsistence activities) for taxed ones. This substitution may have serious effects on production as many developing countries have found out in recent years. Because of high taxes as well as the high taxation implicit in price controls, in some African countries unofficial or parallel activities (including subsistence) have progressively replaced official ones.
9. The problem of erosion, though more serious in developing countries, is not limited to them. The current interest in flat-rate taxes in many countries is nothing but an attempt to reduce erosion and rates at the same time. Little research across countries has been done on tax erosion. For a comparative analysis of income tax erosion in six industrial countries, see Tanzi, *Individual Income Tax and Economic Growth: An International Comparison*, Baltimore, Johns Hopkins University Press, 1969. It would be useful to develop international indices of tax erosion for given taxes (such as income, general sales, imports). The erosion index may change systematically in relation to variables such as per capita income, urbanization, structure of total production.
10. These 'penalties' are at times negative when the rate of interest charged by the authorities is below the rate at which the tax-payer can lend the tax money due.
11. The OECD has studied this problem for its member countries (OECD, 1983).
12. This means that a country entering in a stand-by programme with the Fund will often have no choice but to rely on excises and other tax sources to generate additional revenue through rate changes as these taxes have much lower lags.
13. For three countries for which the author has been able to estimate the average collection lag for the whole system, the lag has averaged between four and six months. Given a yearly rate of inflation of, say, 30 per cent – the present average for developing countries – the revenue loss due to this lag would be about 10 per cent of total tax revenue. This means that these countries could raise the level of their tax revenue by about that percentage by eliminating these lags.
14. The determination of the average lag for the tax system of a country is a difficult task as the needed information is rarely readily available. The average lag is likely to be related to the level of economic development, the structure of the tax system, and the country's experience with inflation. Its importance, of course, increases with the rate of inflation. Research in this area

is very limited undoubtedly because of the difficulty of getting information. However, the return to this research is likely to be substantial. Just as for erosion and concentration, it should be possible to develop measures that assess the timeliness of tax collection in various countries and relate them to particular objective variables.

15. These reasons are listed because they are generally not as well known as the reason for *not* having specific taxes.

16. On the other hand, they may be tempted to overvalue imports in order to increase costs and thus be able to reduce income tax liabilities, transfer foreign exchange abroad, or be able to justify higher prices when price controls are in existence.

17. There is no comparative study assessing the specificity index across countries.

18. This should not be interpreted as a criticism of these methods of taxation. In many cases there is simply no realistic option. It only means that as a country develops one would expect that more objective criteria progressively replace less objective ones.

19. They are not zero if penalties require prison terms or lengthy judiciary procedures before they can be applied.

20. Of course, there is always the possibility that they will be abused for political reasons, that is, that they will be directed toward political opponents.

21. On the average they generate at least 60 per cent of the total tax revenue of developing countries (see Tanzi, 1987).

22. To the extent that subsidies are negative taxes the discussion that follows is relevant to them also.

23. High rates could stimulate the self-consumption of output as a sales tax generally applies only when the product is sold.

24. In some developing countries, imports and the output of public enterprises constitute the two major bases for the imposition of consumption taxes.

25. In some countries the collection lag for this tax is as short as one month.

26. Of course this assumes that the value of all imports can be accurately determined. When that is not the case even a general *ad valorem* single-rate tax will result in differentiated tax treatment among imports and consequently in differential protection. Policy-makers in developing countries often argue that the generalized inefficiencies that exist in their economies justify some minimum level of protection for most activities. Thus, regardless of how sceptical one is regarding the benefits from protection, as long as policy-makers believe that it is needed, they will search for suitable instruments to pursue this policy.

27. This tax should not be confused with that now in use in several countries which is generally a surtax only on the products that are already subject to import duties. The tax under discussion would be applied to all imports with no exception.

28. If efficiency considerations alone were important, products with low elasticity of demand might be singled out for heavier taxation. This is the standard recommendation made by optimum taxation literature (see Stern, 1983). For these products, too, it must be recalled that high rates bring about such things as evasion, underground or subsistence production.

29. The effect of an import duty is equivalent to that of an equal tax on the consumption of that product combined with an equal subsidy to the production of the product.

30. The level of protection on a particular activity is obviously not measured by the nominal import duty. When the domestic value added of a product is small, and inputs carry a low or zero tariff, a relatively small tariff on the product can imply a very high level of (effective) protection to the domestic activity. One can generalize that consumption is affected by nominal tariffs while production is affected by effective protection.

31. This is in part undoubtedly due to the inability of the experts to explain fully the objectives of the reform to the relevant policy-makers.

32. This reason has justified export taxes on rice in Thailand and on meat in Argentina and Uruguay.

33. Thus, a country may tax the export of cocoa but not that of candies or chocolates, or that of coffee beans but not that of instant coffee.

34. This is an idealized view of an income tax. In reality, the structure of most income taxes in developing countries is more complex than that. Because of this complexity it becomes very

difficult to utilize the existing income taxes toward the objectives for which this tax is theoretically best. Thus, its structure must change in the direction of the idealized view described above if it is to become a more useful instrument of economic policy.

35.  In rich industrial countries the exemption is likely to be a small fraction of per capita income. In poor developing countries it is likely to be several times the per capita income.

36.  In general the worse the tax compliance, the less desirable is it to have income taxes that, on paper, are highly progressive. In such a situation more proportional taxes minimize the divergence in effective tax rates for individuals with similar incomes.

37.  In fact, in developing countries the taxation of the income of enterprises generates much more revenue than the taxation of the income of individuals.

38.  In developing countries, capital accounts for a much larger share of total income than in industrial countries. Furthermore, income from capital sources is, in the case of individuals, more difficult to tax than income from wages and salaries.

39.  See Tanzi, 1974, for an early elaboration of this point and for some statistical evidence.

# References

Bird, R.M., 'Assessing tax performance in developing countries: a critical review of the literature' 34, *Finanzarchiv* 2, 1976.

Chelliah, R., H.J. Baas, and M.R. Kelly, 'Tax ratios and tax effort in developing countries, 1969-71' 11, International Monetary Fund, *Staff Papers* 1, 1975.

Commission of the European Communities, *Inventory of Taxes*, Luxembourg, Office for Official Publications of the European Communities, 1982.

Gandhi, V. 'Vertical equity of general sales taxation in developing countries', Washington, International Monetary Fund, mimeo, 1979.

Hinrichs, H.H., *A General Theory of Tax Structure Change During Economic Development*, Cambridge, Harvard University Press, 1966.

Hirao, T. and C. Aguirre, 'Maintaining the level of income tax collection under inflationary conditions' Washington, International Monetary Fund, *Staff Papers* July, 1970.

Lotz, R.J. and E.R. Morss, 'Measuring "Tax Effort" in developing countries', 14, Washington International Monetary Fund, *Staff Papers*, November, 1967.

Musgrave, R., *The Theory of Public Finance*, New York, McGraw-Hill, 1959.

Newbery, D. and N. Stern, *Modern Tax Theory for Developing Countries*, IBRD 1987.

Organization for Economic Co-operation and Development (OECD), *Income Tax Collection Lags*, Paris, OECD Studies in Taxation, 1983.

Sisson, C., 'Tax evasion: a survey of major determinants and policy instruments of control', Washington, International Monetary Fund, mimeo, 1981.

Stern, Nicholas, 'Optimum taxation and tax policy', Washington, International Monetary Fund, *Staff Papers* 31, 2, June 1984.

Tait, A.A., W.L.M. Gratz, and B.J. Eichengreen, 'International Comparison of Taxation for Selected Developing Countries, 1972-76' 26, International Monetary Fund, *Staff Papers*, 1, 1979.

Tanzi, V., 'Comparing international tax "Burdens": a suggested method', *The Journal of Political Economy*, 76, 5, September/October, 1968.

Tanzi, V., *Individual Income Tax and Economic Growth: An International Comparison*, Baltimore, Johns Hopkins University Press, 1969.

——'Redistributing income through the budget in Latin America,' Banca Nazionale del Lavoro, *Quarterly Review*, 1974.

——'Inflation, lags in collection, and the real value of tax revenue' International Monetary Fund, *Staff Papers* 24, March, 1977.

——'Quantitative characteristics of the tax system of developing countries' in D. Newbery and N. Stern, *Modern Tax Theory for Developing Countries*, IBRD, forthcoming, 1987.

Tinbergen, J., *On the Theory of Economic Policy*, Amsterdam, North Holland, 1952.

# 11 Comments on 'Tax policy and economic growth in developing nations', by Alvin Rabushka and Bruce Bartlett

## Introduction

The objective of the Rabushka and Bartlett study is to test the popular supply-side thesis that marginal tax rates are very important for the economic performance of developing as well as developed countries. The study consists of three chapters: one on taxes, one on what the authors call 'implicit taxes', by which they mean the sets of policies that interfere with economic activities as they would be carried out by the market mechanism, and a chapter which presents some statistical results of correlations between growth and several variables, including tax variables.

The first chapter surveys some literature on taxation in developing countries. It also cites some statements made by recent as well as past economists concerning the role of taxation in economic development. The argument is made that as the economies of industrial countries at the time of Adam Smith were similar to those of the developing countries today, some of the statements of classical economists have validity in today's developing world. Although the literature covered is quite extensive, some important contributions are not mentioned. This may give some readers the impression that the authors may have been a little biased in their coverage. For example, several books which over the years have tried to relate taxation to economic growth are not mentioned. Furthermore, Rabushka and Bartlett did not have available many of the unpublished reports related to tax systems of developing countries, especially the ones written in international institutions. One could make the argument that these reports have been more influential in transforming tax systems than the published works.

Be that as it may, I think that they have a point when they argue that the effects of high taxation, and especially of high marginal tax rates, were pretty much ignored in much, if not in all the literature on taxation in developing countries. Why was this? Although the authors do not speculate on these reasons, I should like to synthesize the basic thinking that characterized much of the writing in recent decades. I am sure that Rabushka and Bartlett would not disagree with my synthesis although others might.

## Traditional views on taxation and development

First, there has been the traditional view that in developing countries high incomes do not originate from work effort or entrepreneurship; they are assumed to reflect mostly inherited wealth. Thus, they are more in the nature of rents than of genuine incomes. As a consequence, they could be taxed away with little negative effect. Second, that high incomes inevitably result in high consumption and/or capital flight. Third, that in any case the government can generate a high rate of saving for the country by raising taxes while holding down its own consumption. In this way, whatever negative effects high marginal tax rates might have on individuals' propensity to save could be more than compensated by higher government saving. Fourth, because of lack of know-how and entrepreneurship in the private sector, the government had to take the initiative in carrying out investment. The government was seen as the engine of growth in the economy. Fifth, the negative effect on labour supply could be ignored because of the overabundance of labour. Some influential studies assumed that the supply of labour schedule was perfectly elastic at a subsistence level of wages. Sixth, that private investment in desirable sectors could be stimulated through the use of specific tax incentives, so that low tax rates on corporate income were not necessary. Seventh, that in any case there was little solid evidence that marginal tax rates were important in determining the propensity to save, to invest, or to supply greater effort.

Many of these assumptions were prevalent throughout much of the literature on economic development and taxation until recent years. One should, however, be careful not to suggest that all authors accepted these assumptions. There are several who would object to being identified with some of the assumptions.

These assumptions have proved faulty in a number of ways. First, in developing countries large incomes are often more the result of what Rabushka and Bartlett call implicit taxes, than of property ownership. In many developing societies today it is more important to have access to subsidized credit, to scarce foreign exchange at the official exchange rate and to import licences, or to be able to produce behind a protective wall than to own property. The return to property ownership in the form of such things as rents, profits, interests is often sharply reduced by price control regulation and other similar policies so that property ownership is no guarantee of large incomes. Rents based on government policies have replaced rents based on property ownership.

Second, the assumption that high income inevitably results in high consumption has been challenged in various theories of the consumption function. Some of these challenges are as relevant for developing countries as they are for industrial countries.

Third, with the benefit of hindsight, it is easy to show that governments have been unable to resist pressures for higher public consumption, or for politically determined investment projects. Thus, in many countries the increase in the tax burden that took place over the years did not result in higher public saving, as had been anticipated, but in higher public consumption. Furthermore, whatever public investment did take place, it was often misallocated resulting in very low or negative rates of return.

Fourth, it has become obvious that governments do not have a monopoly over know-how or entrepreneurship. A country without entrepreneurs in the private sector is not going to produce them in the public sector. And, by the same token, Adam Smith's basic contention that when people do things for themselves they become more productive and more enterprising has been recognized to be valid in many countries today, including in a more glaring fashion in some centrally planned economies.

Fifth, it has been recognized that even though the overall labour supply may be abundant, as evidenced by the existence of a high rate of unemployment, it is rarely abundant for particular skills. Trained workers are as scarce in labour abundant economies as they are in economies with overall labour scarcity.

Sixth, the argument on whether one can stimulate more investment by low corporate tax rates or by investment incentives is still a debatable one. Even within the United States today there are well-known economists who have argued that the 1986 tax reform will discourage investment as it traded some investment incentives for lower rates. I myself prefer lower rates, coupled with the elimination of many incentives as the existence of incentive legislation often leads to abuses and corruption. I must, however, recognize that this point is open to debate.

Finally, while in the past it was often argued that there was no evidence that high marginal tax rates had any effects on the propensity to save, invest, and work harder, in recent years more and more studies using sophisticated techniques have shown that taxation may in fact have some negative effects.

## What supply-side economics should mean in developing countries

Recognizing that this change in views has taken place, and I wish to emphasize that not everybody will agree that it has, what is its implication for economic policy? It would seem that it would argue for a reduced role for the public sector in the economy. Or looking at it from the other side, it would argue for a greater role for the market. This, of course, does not mean that the public sector should disappear or that free enterprise should take care of everything. It does mean, however, that we should scrutinize more than we have in the past what the public sector does, shifting perhaps the burden of proof from the market to the public sector. It must be the latter that must justify its intervention rather than the former having to justify its role. A change in this direction would require several (relatively sequential) steps. In my view the first and foremost of these steps would be paying a lot of attention to what Rabushka and Bartlett call implicit taxes. This is where the major problems are. Rabushka and Bartlett are right in emphasizing the role of these implicit taxes and I am glad that they allocated a whole chapter to them.

To reveal my bias, I felt that Chapter 2 was the most interesting and important of the three chapters. The developing countries must start dismantling quotas and import restrictions; must let exchange rates move toward equilibrium; must free their financial markets; must remove price controls, and in general they must reduce the government's role in investment and trade decisions. All these policies breed corruption, misallocation of resources, and eventually lead to reactions on the part of the private sector which come in the forms of underground economic activities, or black markets. In these circumstances individuals focus their energies toward what has been called rent seeking activities rather than toward productive activities. As these reactions become important, they imply that the government loses its grip over the economy but, even though it cannot any longer control what happens in the economy, the damage has been done. These policies bring about a random pattern of rents and taxes which become the main determinants of income distribution. These implicit tax rates can be extremely high and far higher than any rates that are associated with the tax system itself.

As the first step described above is taking place, the government must begin to pay closer attention to the level and the composition of public expenditure. Although the level of public expenditure in developing countries is much lower than industrial countries, in the majority of developing countries it is too high in relation to their current revenues. Therefore, policies in the spirit of supply-side economics must aim at reducing public expenditure. The role of public enterprises must be reduced, except for natural monopolies. Some of these enterprises must be privatized if they have an economic justification; or they should simply be shut down when they have proved to be inefficient. The role of subsidies must be reduced and in some cases eliminated. Investment must be carefully scrutinized to see that it meets criteria of profitability, and so forth.

It is only when the ratio of public expenditure to GDP begins to fall that I would pay serious attention to the proposals made by some supply-siders to reduce tax burdens. Given the present size of fiscal deficits, the developing countries need all the tax revenue that they can get. However, one does not have to wait to bring about changes that are revenue-neutral, or that may even enhance the overall level of revenue. These changes could come in the form of wider bases taxed with lower marginal tax rates. In some cases the reduction in rates may be almost costless in revenue terms. This may happen when the maximum marginal tax rate on personal incomes is reduced as this rate produces very little revenue. In making these tax reforms, one would want to pay particular attention to the taxes that are most damaging in terms of the efficiency of the economy. These are not the personal income taxes, as some supply-side economists believe, but the foreign-trade taxes. High export duties and high import duties have far more damaging effects than the existing maximum marginal tax rates on personal income. A reform of the tax system that aims at reducing export taxes and very high import duties must take priority over one aimed at reforming income taxes. But, of course, especially in connection with export taxes, the revenue losses must be compensated by gains in some other taxes.

### Supply-side economics and tax policy
Let me now comment more closely on supply-side policies advocated in the tax area. I am clearly a sympathizer of these policies. However, I feel that I have a kind of intellectual vested interest to see that we do not destroy the credibility and the potential effectiveness of these policies by making extravagant claims for them.

One big mistake that we could make is to go to developing countries and tell them, as some enthusiastic advocates have actually done, to sharply reduce taxes before the other changes that I have mentioned above have been made. I was glad to see that the paper by Rabushka and Bartlett does not recommend this, or at least I do not think it does. Some of those who have made these recommendations simply do not know much about how the economies of developing countries function, and they do not show a full understanding about the interrelationships between balance of payments, budgets, rates of inflation, and so forth. Recommendations that may be effective or at most innocuous in advanced countries can prove to be harmful if applied to developing countries without the proper caution.

In countries where fiscal deficits can be financed mostly by foreign borrowing or monetary expansion, and where, under present circumstances, foreign borrowing is extremely limited, tax reductions made ahead of the other changes mentioned above would aggravate all the current problems, as they would inevitably lead to higher inflation and greater balance of payments difficulties. Some supply-siders may believe that cutting taxes will somehow immediately reduce government expenditure, but look at what has happened in this connection in the United States and in the United Kingdom. If President Reagan and Prime Minister Thatcher were not able to cut government expenditure, in spite of their firm commitment to such an objective, what would make us believe that this would happen in developing countries? Or do we still believe in the Laffer curve? That tax cuts would be self-financing?

Let me now go back to the maximum marginal tax rate on income taxes. This is the variable which, reflecting a cultural bias on the part of some writers, has attracted the most attention. There has been a belief that reducing this rate will bring about all sorts of economic miracles. I favour a reduction of this rate in developing countries, mainly because I see it as a nuisance, and do not recognize for it any particular redeeming value. However, the maximum marginal tax rate of the personal income tax is hardly as important a variable as it is made to be.

Its reduction in the absence of the other changes that I have mentioned above would not have significant permanent effects, even though it may have some beneficial short-term effects such as raising stock market indices where stock markets exist. For sure, its reduction will not raise the rate of growth of a country by any measurable amount. It should be reduced because it would not cost much in terms of revenue loss, and it might do some marginal good. However, the cut in that rate will still not provide individuals with foreign exchange to import needed inputs or credit to make worthwhile investments, and it will not increase profits when prices are controlled and many activities operate at a loss.

The maximum marginal tax rate affects very few people. In fact, the average total revenue from all personal income taxes in developing countries is only about 2 per cent of GDP, and the revenue from the marginal tax rate is miniscule. Let me give you some data: in Brazil, Jamaica, Kenya, Korea, Malaysia, the Philippines, and Thailand, for which this information is available, less than 1,000 tax-payers were subject to these rates. In Thailand, the Philippines, and Korea, the figure is less than 20 tax-payers. I know that one argument that will be made about this statement is that the rate itself must have affected the base, so that people will not earn income because of the high rate. Well, my answer to that is 'maybe', but I am a sceptic. It is more likely that the base has been affected by tax evasion and by all the bad policies I mentioned above.

By the way, the Rabushka and Bartlett figure for the threshold income at which the maximum rate becomes operative strikes me as being too high. Available income distribution statistics for developing countries indicate that, on the average, an individual with an income which is 15 times the per capita income of the country is in the top 1 per cent of the income distribution. A majority of developing countries have per capita incomes of less than $1,000. Therefore a threshold figure of $20,000 implies that very few people would be affected by these rates, even legally.

Going back now more directly to the paper by Rabushka and Bartlett, I am not surprised by the inconclusive results in Chapter 3 for the reasons that I have stated. Taxation, though important, is hardly the most important policy in developing countries, and the personal income tax is hardly the most important element of taxation. Perhaps the importance of the maximum marginal tax rate is symbolic. It can be thought of as a proxy for the other policies. If Hong Kong has prospered, maybe it is not because of the low marginal tax rates on incomes, but because of all the other policies it has followed. In this connection, it might be worthwhile to mention that in 1973 Uruguay cut the maximum marginal tax rate on personal income all the way to zero. In fact, the country simply abolished the personal income tax but no great prosperity followed. The reason was, perhaps, simply that many of the other policies did not change.

Let us think of supply-side policies as those policies aimed at removing all the obstacles on the way to growth. There are many of these obstacles and they are of differing significance. Under present circumstances the marginal rates of the personal income tax are not among the most significant obstacles in developing countries.

# 12    A review of major tax policy missions in developing countries

## Historical background

The provision of technical assistance for national tax reform must be a phenomenon that dates far back in history. I am sure that during the Roman or some other empire there must have been tax experts who 'assisted' the newly conquered territories in reforming their tax systems. In this chapter I concentrate on more recent assistance provided by outsiders, as individuals or as parts of organizations, in response to requests from independent countries.[1]

As far as I have been able to determine, the first modern example of such independent technical assistance is a report written for the government of Cuba in the 1930s by Professors Seligman and Shoup. An apocryphal story tells that the Cuban government was so incensed by the message of the report that it ordered the Spanish version of it burned. After World War II, Carl Shoup engaged in the first major postwar attempt at reforming the tax system of another country. In 1949, as director of the commission to study the tax system of Japan, Shoup recommended, *inter alia*, the introduction of a value-added tax. This was a pioneering and daring recommendation, since no country at that time had such a tax and little was known about it.[2] The fact that the Japanese introduced a value added tax only in 1989 shows that Professor Shoup was ahead of his time. At least 50 countries now have such a tax.

Also ahead of its time was Nicholas Kaldor's recommendation of an expenditure tax, made to India and Sri Lanka. The tax was introduced in India in 1957 and in Sri Lanka in 1959. As an observer put it somewhat diplomatically, in India 'the imposition of the expenditure tax was the subject of considerable public controversy and aroused strong opposition'.[3] It was repealed (in India) in 1962 when the finance minister who had introduced it was replaced. It was reintroduced in 1964 when that same finance minister regained his post, and it was repealed for good in 1966. It had generated an insignificant amount of revenue and a significant amount of administrative and political headaches. The experience of Sri Lanka was similar: it also experimented twice with the tax. Goode reports that 'in 1967, when proposing repeal of the expenditure tax – after a second trial – the Minister of Finance of Sri Lanka characterized it as 'unworkable and impractical in an economy like that of Sri Lanka'.[4] The opposition to the tax at times took a violent turn. As yet no country has introduced an expenditure tax, although various official or semi-official studies in the United States, the United Kingdom, Sweden, and Ireland have recommended it.[5]

At about the time that Kaldor was advising India and Sri Lanka, Professor Shoup was engaged in another major attempt at reforming the tax system of a country. In 1958 he submitted his report to the government of Venezuela. Written by a working group that included some of the best-known public finance scholars of the time, the report was published as a book that came to influence much of the thinking in this area.[6] It served to educate those in Venezuela and elsewhere who were interested in tax reform.[7] What it did not do, however, was reform Venezuela's tax system, even though some of its recommendations were eventually enacted. Not until 1967 did major legislative changes take place, and it is not clear whether any of them originated from the Shoup Report.[8] Many of the report's recommendations were not followed; more important, some of the subsequent changes, especially in the area of tax administration, went against the spirit of the Shoup Report. An IMF mission there in the early 1980s found many areas in which regress rather than progress had taken place since 1958.

Together with Nicholas Kaldor and Carl Shoup, perhaps the best known and most influential name in tax reform of developing countries is that of Richard Musgrave. He came to be identified with major attempts at tax reform in Colombia (1969) and Bolivia (1977).[9] In both cases Musgrave directed outstanding groups of public finance specialists and in both, but especially that of Colombia, the resulting volumes became standard works in the field of taxation in developing countries. Both reports were very good, as one would have expected from the quality of the authorship.[10] The concrete results, however, as measured in terms of their impact on the nations' tax systems, have so far been very different.

Caesar might have summarized the Bolivian experience as follows: They came, they studied the tax system, they wrote a good book, they left, nothing happened. A few years ago a visitor to Bolivia was unable to locate anyone who had either read the report or had a copy of it. Perhaps he talked to the wrong people, or, more likely, those who had participated in the Musgrave Commission (many Bolivians did so) were no longer in government. In Colombia, on the other hand, the Musgrave Report played a large role in one of the major tax reforms of recent decades. Several factors contributed to this positive outcome; perhaps the most important was the involvement of various Colombians.[11] Some of the main actors in the 1974 Colombian tax reform had worked with the Musgrave Commission. Four of the eight-member commission were Colombians, as were the two advisors and the secretary and coordinator. Eleven of the 23 members of the technical staff were Colombians. Many of them became or remained influential in the Colombian government and were behind the 1974 reform. Some became ministers; others served as commissioners of internal revenue. As a consequence that reform had a large domestic content. It was brilliant in conception and very innovative, although perhaps too ambitious. It has not survived the test of time well.

Shoup, Kaldor, and Musgrave have not been the only actors in the tax reform scene. Others include Oliver Oldman, Richard Bird, and Malcolm Gillis (all of whom played a large role in some of the reforms already mentioned), Milton Taylor, Gerson da Silva, Roy Bahl and Charles McLure. These experts were often, though not always, parts of teams organized by the Harvard International Tax Program, by the OAS–IDB Joint Tax Program, by the US Internal Revenue Service or Agency for International Development (AID), by the United Nations, and occasionally by other groups. Milton Taylor and Gerson da Silva were associated with the OAS–IDB Joint Tax Program;[12] Oldman, Bird, and Gillis were associated with Harvard; Roy Bahl has been closely associated with AID. Chile, Egypt, Argentina, Panama, Brazil, Peru, Indonesia, Jamaica, Liberia and a few other countries have received much attention from outside experts. Major tax reform has taken place in Jamaica and Indonesia.

The Indonesian effort represents an interesting experiment. Led by Malcolm Gillis, under the umbrella of Harvard University, with the Indonesian government covering the costs, it has involved in one way or another most of the current leading public finance experts with some knowledge of developing countries (and even some without) as well as a large investment in money by Indonesia and in time by Professor Gillis.[13] It is a reform far more daring in scope than almost anything attempted before.[14] It has transformed the Indonesian tax system and may serve as an example for other countries. Serious administrative problems have, however, developed along the way, threatening some of the policy changes. At this time it looks promising, but it is too early to tell whether it will stand the test of time well.

A similar experiment has been carried out in Jamaica, by another large group of leading scholars, financed by AID and led by Roy Bahl. Because the reform is not yet complete, no conclusions can yet be drawn. In this chapter I define a successful tax mission as one that results in reform of the tax system of a country along the lines proposed by the mission. Obviously such a definition suffers from two potential problems. The first is the time horizon to consider before one assesses the success of the mission, and the second lies in attribution to the work of the mission of all future changes that are consistent with its recommendations. Both problems can affect any assessments that are made.

## Common characteristics of tax reform attempts

It is perhaps foolhardy to attempt to sort out some of the common characteristics in these many and varied attempts. I am sure that most of those engaged in these enterprises would object to any common characterization, and they would be right, since all attempts reflect individual and sharply distinct efforts. Still, common denominators among several can be found. I will try to list a few.

### Experimentation

It would seem that a developing country with few resources is the least likely place in which one would want to experiment, yet we find several examples. An extreme version was Kaldor's attempt at introducing an expenditure tax in India and Sri Lanka. Another example was Shoup's proposal for a value-added tax in Japan after World War II. These are the most visible, but not the only, examples. It takes many years to work out all the administrative implications of new taxes and to find solutions to anticipated as well as unanticipated hurdles. The value-added tax is still being modified within the European Economic Community, and many problems (as for example the taxation of financial activities) are still without a solution. One can imagine the difficulties that the Japanese administrators would have faced in 1949 if they had gone the route recommended by the Shoup mission. Most public finance experts still shudder at the administrative complications that an expenditure tax would face if introduced in an advanced country such as the United States. The problems faced by the administrators of India and Sri Lanka are well documented.

### Cultural biases

Regardless of the attempts on the part of experts to remain immune from cultural biases, such biases inevitably occur, in either technical or social form. The changes recommended to the developing countries often reflected the values (such as progressivity is good; the tax system *must* redistribute income) of the experts rather than of those receiving the advice. The belief that objectives are universal and that if something is good in Washington, New York, or London, it must be so in La Paz, Bogota, or Delhi, predominated. This meant that the advice given often had objectives that did not necessarily reflect those of the governments receiving it. Also it meant that the experts were not necessarily concentrating on the most important taxes. Compare, for example, the attention paid to income taxes, or even to capital gains taxes, with that paid to foreign trade taxes, which still contribute the lion's share of tax revenues in many developing countries.

### Optimism about what taxation can do

There were at least two sides to this characteristic. The first was an overoptimistic and, with the benefit of hindsight, perhaps naive view of the development process. Earlier attempts equated more taxes with more government saving and thus with more development expenditure. This expenditure was in turn believed to promote more growth. Tax reform was therefore identified with tax increase, and was seen as a step toward accelerating the rate of growth. Fuat Andic, in reviewing the report of the Musgrave Commission for Colombia, summarizes its 'general methodological approach' as follows:

Decide upon the target rate of per capita income growth. Translate the rate into the required rate of capital formation on the basis of a rough estimate of the so-called marginal capital–output ratio. Determine the share of public investment based upon developmental requirements; this will determine the requirements for public saving. (Andic, 1973: 164).

The idea that governments were also capable of wasting resources was not fashionable. Today, of course, we run the opposite risk: that of coming to believe that governments cannot do anything right. I would not be surprised if one of the main objectives of future tax reforms becomes a reduction in the tax ratio.

Second, there was often an implicit belief that many of the distortions that prevailed throughout the economy were the natural result of underdevelopment rather than of public policy. A similar belief was associated with the distribution of income; the *normal* working of the market of a developing country was believed to promote an uneven income distribution. As a consequence, taxes should be neutral in their impact on prices, and should promote a more even distribution of income. Many of the tax reformers were willing to sacrifice simplicity to achieve these objectives of neutrality and equity. During much of this period the equity that concerned the tax reformers was vertical; hence the emphasis on progressive taxation. The fact that progressive taxes could create or aggravate problems of horizontal equity has not attracted much concern until recently. None of the many tax incidence studies done for developing countries had much information about the dispersion of the tax burden *for individuals in the same income classes*. They all had information about the average burden by income classes.

Unfortunately, in many countries, the distortions in relative prices, as well as the effects on income distribution associated with taxes, paled in comparison with those brought about by other government policies. In the majority of developing countries, one finds that government policies directed toward such things as exchange rates, capital movements, import restrictions, pricing of public services or agricultural outputs, interest rates often distort relative prices to such an extent that whatever improvement one can get from the tax system is of marginal relevance. If this improvement comes at the cost of other objectives, including that of simplicity and ease of administration, then one must wonder whether it is worth it.[15] In many of these countries the distribution of income that results may be more the product of government policies than of the private ownership of factors of production. Those who, because of political or other connections, manage to get access to scarce foreign exchange, import licences, subsidized credit, or manage to have a quota imposed upon the importation of a product which they produce domestically, end up with huge incomes which may bear little relationship to whether they own specific factors of production.[16] Access to public favours often becomes more important in determining incomes than access to property, and the income distribution comes to reflect 'who one knows' as well as 'what one owns'. Thus, the great preoccupation with capital gains, with wealth taxation, and with highly progressive income tax rates that characterized many of the tax reform proposals may have been based on a somewhat unrealistic view of the economies to which they are addressed.

## Fashions

During certain periods, some recommendations enjoy a greater vogue than others. Intellectual fashions have appeared and disappeared over the past three decades. For example, in the 1950s and 1960s unification of schedular income taxes became the vogue. In that period it would have been difficult to find a report that did not propose a global income tax. In the 1960s and 1970s, the OAS – IDB programme actively promoted the introduction of suspense or 'ring-type' sales taxes. Today, more reports recommend a value-added tax. Perhaps these changes are the result of a learning process, whereby new alternatives come to be seen as genuinely better than earlier alternatives. On the other hand, they may simply result from fads.

## Comprehensiveness of proposed changes

Most of the tax reform attempts aimed at changing the whole tax system rather than just parts of it. In theory this comprehensive approach is preferable to one that aims at modifying only part of the existing system, because of the interconnection of the various parts: it is difficult to reform domestic indirect taxes without reforming foreign trade taxes, and so on. In practice, however, one runs the risk that in attempting to get too much one gets nothing. Comprehensive reform is much more unsettling than partial reform. Even when a strong claim can be made that in terms of the objectives of taxation the tax system that would emerge from the reform would be clearly superior to the one that it would replace, one must pay attention to the transition costs. These costs are often ignored in the Paretian approach to policy. Option B may be better than A once we reach it. The trouble is that if the transition costs are high, we may never get to B. The more comprehensive is the reform, the more demands are likely to be made on the administrators who will have to administer the new system as well as on the politicians who will have to legislate the new tax laws. There is just so much change that the tax administration of a country or its political body can accommodate. There is also the concrete danger that the government will not go along with the whole package but will pick and choose among the comprehensive proposals. In the process it may even reduce the quality of the tax system rather than increase it. Finally, the current government may be out of power before the reform process is completed, since that process will require a long time, and the new government may wish to institute its own reform.

*Excessive emphasis on 'Policy'*

A final aspect, of perhaps greater importance than all the others mentioned earlier, is the emphasis in the tax reform on 'policy'. Administration has often been the stepsister of the tax reform process. This emphasis was inevitable when the advisers were general economists rather than tax experts. In an important Latin American report, for example, at least three of the five-man tax mission consisted of well-known economists who had practically no background in taxation and even less in taxation in developing countries.[17] But the emphasis can be found in reports written by public finance experts.

One of the countries in which technical assistance in taxation seems to have been highly successful is Chile. This country received assistance from the United Nations, the Internal Revenue Service of the United States, Harvard, and the Organization of American States. A major part of this success can be attributed to the fact that tax reform efforts were pursued at the same time that major improvements in tax administration were being enforced vigorously. In those countries where technical assistance concentrated mainly on the reform of the tax structure, and where tax administration was considered only incidentally, the results were much less favourable.

## Requirements for the success of tax reform

In the previous section I speculated briefly on some of the shortcomings common to many, but by no means all, tax reform efforts promoted by outsiders over recent decades. That discussion also points in the direction of the requirement for a successful tax reform. I will now briefly outline some of these requirements.

As I look over the experience of this period, there are some obvious aspects to the success of tax reform in some countries and not in others. If I had to list the basic ingredients that make for a successful tax reform I would include the following:

*Government with a long horizon.* Genuine tax reforms require time as well as the commitment of the country's government, which will have to use up some of its political capital in order to bring about changes in the system, especially when the benefits from the tax reform are widespread, while its costs are concentrated among specific groups that can get organized and oppose it. The cost rises when these groups become politically powerful and organized. There is thus always a cost and a risk for a government in engaging in tax reform. This brings two consequences. One is that such a process will be started and will be continued only when a government has a long time horizon in front of it. The costs of the reforms are always immediate; the benefits are almost always spread over the future. The rate of discount that the government will use to make the benefit–cost evaluation of the reform will often be determined, or at least will be influenced, by how long it expects to remain in power. If a government expects to be out of power relatively soon, it will apply a very high discount rate to those benefits and will have very little interest in pursuing a genuine, as distinguished from a demagogic, tax reform.

*Pressure of a politically powerful domestic mentor.* Of equally great importance is the fact that when one talks about 'the government' one really should be talking about one or perhaps a few powerful figures who have the stamina, the interest, and the vision to push for the reform and to stay with it over a period that is likely to extend over years. A government that remains in power but whose members keep changing will have less chance of seeing a major reform accomplished. We have reviewed experiences, as in India with the expenditure tax, where taxes disappeared when their mentor lost his job. On the other hand, when a powerful political figure (within a government with a long time horizon) retains an interest in the reform, and adopts it as his own creation, there is a better chance of its success.

*Recognition that reform is more than a change in policy.* As previously indicated, the reforms that succeeded were those in which great importance was paid to administration. Successful tax reform requires an equilibrium between political objectives, tax policy changes, and administrative development. All of these have to move together. When political objectives overtake the other two, we often have demagoguery. In that case the government is not genuinely interested in tax reform but only in scoring political points. When policy moves alone, while the other two elements do not move, we have aborted reforms. Successful tax reform must not overemphasize the theoretical aspects (or tax policy aspects) while paying little attention to the more mundane, but perhaps more important, administrative aspects. Tax reformers must realize that making tax policy recommendations is only the first step, albeit a necessary one. These recommendations must be translated into tax laws, regulations, reorganization of tax offices, changes in administrative procedures, preparation of lists of tax-payers with relevant addresses, redesigning tax forms, modification of penalities, new audit concepts, new training of administrative personnel, taxpayer education, and so on.[18]

One mistake that foreign experts have often made is to go to a country, write a report, and leave, under the assumption that once policy changes have been proposed, the government will see their wisdom and will take over and carry the torch the rest of the way. In most cases, nothing will happen. What this means is that the group of tax reformers must include more than tax policy experts. It must also include tax administrators, and especially tax administrators with an intimate knowledge of the specific country. There are areas in which a tax administrator who is good in one place can also be good in other places, but there are other areas in which this translation of skills from one place to another does not work.

*Adaptation of reform to domestic economic conditions.* There is a story about a tax expert who provided advice to several American states. After he wrote the first well-received report for a given state, he decided that its analysis and recommendations were equally applicable to other states. When he received requests for similar studies from other states, he took the old report, changed the name of the state and some of the statistical material, and sent it to the new clients. I have not heard such a story concerning technical assistance provided to countries, but the story has a message. Some experts may convince themselves that particular recommendations have merit independently of local conditions. If this happens, they may not make as great an effort as desirable at adapting their tax proposals to local conditions. Such adaptation often requires close knowledge of the country's economic, political, and social conditions. This requires the need for substantial domestic participation in the reform process; or, alternatively, the need to spend very lengthy periods of time in a country. One does not learn much by studying the existing tax laws, as actual practice may be very different from the law. And one does not learn very much by looking at the available and often questionable statistics. The limited quantity of statistics available and their often poor quality means that much of the advice provided will be based on intuition or guesses, and these will be good only when the expert really understands the country. Obviously, this understanding often requires the knowledge of the country's language and customs.[19]

*Support from the country's tax administration.* Successful reforms require not only an intimate knowledge of the country's economic, political, legal, and social structure, but also the support of those who are currently administering the tax system. Reforms are unlikely to succeed when little attention is paid to those who will administer the new taxes or when the latter see the reform as something imposed by outsiders. At times good proposals may be blocked for totally unanticipated reasons. For example, in one country the recommendation to reduce the role of excise taxes and to expand that of broader taxes was blocked mainly because the head of the excise tax department would lose power as a consequence of loss of personnel assigned to these taxes. What the tax advisers had ignored was the fact that this gentleman was a special adviser to the prime minister, and thus had enough power to prevent the change.

The point is that all tax reforms bring with them not only changes in the burden of taxes on tax-payers but also changes in the relative power of the different parts of the tax administration. These shifts in power cannot be ignored by those who are recommending the reform since the affected individuals often have the power to make or break the reform. The civil servants of the countries must become part of the act and must have input. One reason why a traditional recommendation of most experts – to use import taxes only for protection and to transfer their function of discrimination against non-essential goods to the domestic indirect taxes – has rarely if ever been followed is that it would lower the relative influence of the customs administration. In many countries customs administrators are powerful enough to be able to block such reforms.

## Notes

1. By agreement with the chairman of the scientific committee in charge of the 41st Congress of the IIPF, no mention is made in this chapter of the role of the Fiscal Affairs Department of the International Monetary Fund (IMF) in tax reform. I wish to thank Milka Casanegra, Carlos A. Aguirre, and Peter Griffith for valuable advice. The views expressed are personal, and should not be construed as official IMF views.
2. See Shoup Mission 1949. It should be noted that the report was requested by the Supreme Commander for the Allied Powers. Since Japan was then under occupation, this technical assistance did not reflect a request from an independent government.
3. See Khanna, 1964. 9:360.
4. See Goode, 1984. 5.
5. See US Treasury Department, 1977; Meade, 1978; Lodin, 1978; Commission on Taxation, 1982.
6. The Commission to Study the Fiscal System of Venezuela included, in addition to Carl Shoup, John Due, Lyle C. Fitch, Sir Donald MacDougall, Oliver S. Oldman, and Stanley S. Surrey. See Shoup, 1959.
7. Writing in 1968, Oldman referred to the fact that 'the Shoup Report is still considered a principal reference work on the tax problems of less developed countries', and 'the impact of the Report in other countries ought not to go unnoticed'. See his Introduction to Gittes, 1968.
8. See Gittes, 1968.
9. Both reports were later published by the International Tax Program of Harvard Law School. See Musgrave *et al.*, 1971; Musgrave, 1981.
10. For reviews of the Colombia Report, see Tanzi, 1972; Andic, 1973.
11. This tax reform is surveyed in Tanzi, 1975 and CEPAL, 1977.
12. Milton Taylor led OAS–IDB Joint Tax Program missions to Panama, Colombia, and Peru during the 1960s. The resulting publications are OAS–IDB 1964, 1965, 1969. The OAS–IDB Joint Tax Program was very active from the early 1960s to the mid-1970s. Three conferences that it organized had much influence, especially in Latin America. See Joint Tax Program 1965a & b, 1973.
13. The extent of Gillis' involvement is indicated by the fact that he learned the Indonesian language over this period.
14. *Inter alia*, the reform has included the introduction of a value-added tax, the elimination of most incentives, and an extreme simplification of the income tax. The value-added tax has just one rate (10 per cent) and the income tax just three rates (15, 25 and 35 per cent respectively).
15. The same comment applies to the policy recommendations that originate from the optimal taxation literature.
16. There is now a growing literature on rent seeking and its impact on income distribution.
17. The report is OAS–IDB, 1969. The three economists included an internationally known macro theorist and two prominent monetary economists.
18. A recent example should suffice to show the importance of this point: after a country introduced a value-added tax it realized that it did not have an updated list with addresses of tax-payers, and when it tried to contact the tax-payers by using the old list, more than 80 per cent of the letters sent came back undelivered.
19. How customs can differ is indicated by the fact that in a certain country I was told that it would be considered morally wrong for a tax inspector to report to his superiors the name of a tax-payer who has tried to bribe him; the inspector is only expected to politely decline the bribe offer.

## References

Andic, Fuat M., 'Fiscal reform in Colombia: a review article', *Finanzarchiv* 32, 1973.

CEPAL, *La reforma tributaria en Colombia, revista de hacienda*, July–September 1977.

Commission of Taxation, 'First Report of the Commission on Taxation', *The Irish Banking Review* December 1982.

Gittes, Enrique F., *Income Tax Reform, the Venezuelan Experience*, Cambridge, Mass., Harvard Student Legislative Research Bureau, 1968.

Goode, Richard, *Government Finance in Developing Countries*, Washington, DC, Brookings Institution, 1984.

Joint Tax Program, OAS/IDB/ECLA, *Fiscal Policy for Economic Growth in Latin America*, Baltimore Johns Hopkins Press, 1965a.

—— *Problems of Tax Administration in Latin America*, Baltimore, Johns Hopkins Press, 1965b.

—— *La politica tributaria como instrumento del desarollo*, OAS, 1973.

Khanna, K. C., 'An expenditures tax in India', *Bulletin for International Fiscal Documentation*, September 1964: 353–6.

Lodin, Sven-Olof, *Progressive Expenditure Tax – An Alternative?* Stockholm, Liber Förlag, 1978.

Meade, J. E., *The Structure and Reform of Direct Taxation*, London, Institute of Fiscal Studies, 1978.

Musgrave, Richard A., *Fiscal Reform in Bolivia*, Cambridge, Mass., Harvard Law School, International Tax Program, 1981.

Musgrave, Richard, and Gillis, Malcolm, *Fiscal Reform in Columbia*, Cambridge, Mass. Harvard Law School, International Tax Program, 1971.

OAS-IDB Joint Tax Program, *Fiscal Survey of Panama*, Baltimore, Johns Hopkins Press, 1964.

—— *Fiscal Survey of Colombia*, Baltimore, Johns Hopkins Press, 1965.

—— *Estudio Fiscal del Peru*, OAS, 1969.

Shoup, Carl (Director), *The Fiscal System of Venezuela, A Report*, Baltimore, Johns Hopkins Press, 1959.

Shoup Mission, *Report on Japanese Taxation*, 4 vols., Tokyo, General Headquarters, Supreme Commander for the Allied Powers, 1949.

Tanzi, Vito, 'Fiscal reform in Colombia: the report of the Musgrave commission', *Inter-American Economic Affairs*, 28, 1972:71–80.

—— 'The 1974 Colombian tax reform: description and evaluation', mimeo, 1975.

US Treasury Department, *Blueprints for Basic Tax Reform*, Washington DC, 1977.

# 13 Potential income as a tax base in theory and in practice

The theoretical literature on taxation has relied on neutrality and equity as the two basic criteria for choosing taxes. The grounds on which these criteria are based are different. Neutrality is an objective criterion based on strictly economic (that is, efficiency) grounds. Equity, on the other hand, is a subjective criterion based on grounds (social and/or political) that are not strictly economic nor, one could say, scientific. For a long time the income tax scored quite high on both of these criteria. On equity grounds it was often considered as the most equitable of all taxes; and on efficiency, or neutrality, grounds its 'theoretical superiority ... over indirect taxation was accepted as virtually axiomatic'.[1]

More recently, however, a growing dissatisfaction with the income tax is evident. At the professional level doubts have been raised in recent important studies as to whether this tax really scores as high as it has been traditionally assumed on grounds of both equity and efficiency.[2] And, at the popular level, the degree of acceptance that this tax enjoyed for a long time has been eroding as indicated by the results of recent surveys of tax-payers' attitudes *vis-à-vis* taxes.[3] This recent disenchantment has led to proposals that would change the nature of income taxation by either exempting saving or by making income taxation more 'comprehensive'.[4] At the same time a highly theoretical branch of public finance has been dealing with the difficult problem of designing an optimal income tax structure that would trade equity and efficiency in a socially optimal way.[5]

This chapter deals with some of these issues but in a somewhat indirect fashion. In particular it argues that some of the shortcomings attributed to income taxation result from the established custom (in both theory and practice) of defining income as an *ex post,* or historical, concept rather than as an *ex ante,* or 'potential', one. The latter is often more difficult to measure than the former. However, this does not explain why this concept, in spite of few exceptions, has been practically ignored in theoretical discussions that have never shied away from dealing with far less measurable concepts. Besides, it will be argued that if certain conventions are adopted, the measurement of potential income, while still very difficult, might not be as intractable as one might assume; it is for example, now routinely measured at the macroeconomic level[6] and has had some practical applications in a few countries.

### Income concept and equity

The public finance literature has for a long time assumed that the equity criterion is satisfied when taxes are based on 'ability to pay'. This principle has even found its way into some political documents. For example, Article 53 of the Italian Constitution states that: 'Everyone shall contribute to public expenditure in proportion to his ability to pay.' To make this principle operational as a guide to taxation, one basic, though not sufficient, step must be a definition of what constitutes ability to pay. According to Musgrave, 'through the last century income came to be accepted more or less generally as the proper index of ability to pay'.[7] Today the identification of a tax-payer's ability to pay with income remains, in spite of some doubts, fairly general. For example, Pechman has written that 'the close association between a person's income and his or her taxpaying ability is commonly accepted';[8] and Goode that 'if A has more income than B, it seems reasonable to say that A has greater ability to pay taxes (than B)'.[9]

After postulating the connection between ability to pay and income, most textbooks in public finance proceed to define income 'as accretion to wealth, or increase in net worth plus consumption during a given period'.[10]Thus, the income that is presumed to measure ability to pay is implicitly assumed to reflect actual revenues of the tax-payer adjusted to include accrued capital gains, imputed rental value for owner-occupied houses and fringe benefits. This concept of income does not include leisure[11] or the income foregone when property (such as land, buildings) is left unutilized or is underutilized. Furthermore, when used in practice, it has not included accrued capital gains and has rarely included the imputed rental value of owner-occupied houses.

There are alternative ways of defining income. Regardless of which definition is accepted, however, it can be considered either in an *ex post* (after the fact) sense, or in a potential or presumptive sense. The *ex post* interpretation is the one normally implied or assumed in the literature.[12] According to it, income can only be measured at the end of the period and thus reflects an actual, or historical, concept. Also the relationship between income and total resources – both human and non-human – that the individual had available over the period is ignored. The implicit assumption is that either the individual will always use his resources fully and efficiently, or the individual has no social responsibility to use his resources fully and judiciously but rather, as Roman law used to put it, he can 'use and abuse' his resources any way he wishes. Thus, if over the period the individual has generated an income, Y, the question is not asked whether he could have generated an income, $Y + \Delta Y$, given the total resources that he had available. The income forgone ($\Delta Y$) when resources are left unutilized is not considered part of the base on which depends ability to pay.

There is a conceptually different way of looking at income, however. It is a way that assigns to the individual some social responsibility that gives a more specific meaning to the principle of ability to pay. In fact, income could be defined as the earnings that the individual could be expected to generate over the period by the socially acceptable 'full' and judicious use of his total resources. It is, therefore, an index of ability to earn, assuming a normal or average effort. We shall refer to this concept as potential income but it must be emphasized that by potential we shall not mean the maximum income that an individual could generate but simply the normal income that can be expected if his real resources are fully used and if he is holding a full-time job for which has has been trained. Naturally, factors beyond the individual's control (such as weather, strikes, illnesses) can at times bring about a divergence between the income expected (at the beginning of the period) and the one that actually materializes even when the individual has used all his resources fully and judiciously. Divergences attributed to these factors would have to be considered in a practical system of taxation based on potential income but they can be ignored, for the time being, in our theoretical discussion.

Potential income can exceed or fall short of actual income. It will exceed actual income whenever the individual's effort or judgement is superior to the average. For example, the individual works more than the conventional 40-hour week or he invests his assets in particularly risky investments. It will fall short of actual income when his effort or initiative is lower than the average.

On the basis of these two definitions of income let us assume that an individual with the ability, the resources, and the opportunity to earn, say, $20,000 in a given year chooses to remain idle or to leave his assets underutilized or unutilized so that his actual income is zero. Should the base for the income tax be actual or potential ability to pay? Should it be zero or $20,000? This is a question that the literature on income taxation has rarely raised but that is clearly a key and relevant question.[13] This question is central to the discussion of whether consumption or actual income should constitute the tax base. It follows that 'the major choice' for the best index of ability to pay is not that 'between [actual] income and consumption'[14] but that among (a) actual income, (b) potential income and (c) consumption. Here the Hobbesian argument is as relevant to the choice between (a) and (b) and between (b) and (c) as it is to the traditional choice between (a) and (c). Ignoring (c), should the tax-payer be taxed on the basis of what he could contribute to the national pie, or on the basis of what he actually contributes?[15] Thomas Hobbes addressed this question when he wrote:

> What reason is there that he *which laboreth much* ... should be more charged than he that, *living idly,* getteth little and spendeth all he gets, seeing the one hath no more protection from the commonwealth than the other?[16]

To remain theoretical let us assume that the citizens of a newly formed country, imitating the Italians, have included in their constitution an article that states that taxes must be based on ability to pay. They have also identified ability to pay with income. Let us also assume that they have agreed on the amount of total taxes that they need to raise and that a special census has surveyed the skills of the various citizens as well as the productivity of their real assets (such as land) so that 'potential' income has been assessed for all citizens. Would such a country want to tax actual or potential incomes?

If actual incomes were taxed, the country would be faced with the following problems and/or issues:

1.  Citizens with a strong work ethic might end up subsidizing the consumption of public goods by those who value leisure more. This distinction could carry over to the use of land and other resources. The more leisure-oriented individuals might put their land to uses (such as hunting) that do not generate actual income.
2.  If part of the tax revenue is used for human capital development (education, health, training) or for real investment, the productive capacity of the country will increase. This capacity will be reflected in increases in potential incomes and thus in (potentially) higher ability to pay. However, this increased potential could be partly dissipated if some tax-payers let their actual incomes fall below their potential. In a situation of this sort, where potential incomes are partly the result of productive public expenditures, the argument for basing ability to pay on potential, rather than on actual, income will be stronger as it will be supported by a benefit-received criterion for taxation.

    Both of these arguments support the contention that, on equity grounds, potential income may be a better tax base than actual income.[17] Furthermore, if citizens have some economic sophistication, they would recognize at least two non-equity grounds for preferring potential income.
3.  Citizens would realize that the use of actual income as the tax base would be associated with greater excess burdens than the use of potential income. This efficiency argument is discussed in the following section.
4.  They would realize that total revenue would be indeterminate, as some individuals, in trying to avoid taxes, would change their behaviour thus making their actual incomes differ from their potential. If substitution effects prevail, total actual incomes could be well below potential and taxes collected lower than expected.

## Income concept and efficiency

The excess burden of taxation is highly dependent on the elasticity of the tax base with respect to the tax rate. If the base is perfectly inelastic, there is no excess burden. This is the reason why a poll tax is considered such a good tax from an efficiency point of view[18] and why an income tax may not be a good tax.[19] A poll tax, however, is highly inequitable unless it can be graduated with respect to ability to pay. If potential income is considered a good index of ability to pay, and if it could be measured, it could be used to develop a system of progressive income taxation, which, while respecting society's ethical judgement about progressivity, would have some of the characteristics of a poll tax as far as efficiency is concerned.

To present the argument in the simplest fashion let us proceed with the example of the newly established country where a special census has determined the potential income of all tax-payers. Let us also assume that, on the basis of the ethical judgement of the citizenry, the country has established the desired progressivity of the tax function,

$$T_i = f(Y_{p_i})$$

which relates the tax payment, T, of a tax-payer, i, to his potential income, $Y_p$. Presumably, although not necessarily, the tax would be progressive. In Figure 13.1, which is tridimensional, this relationship is shown by the curve

$$T_i = f(Y_{p_i})$$

in the T, $Y_p$ plane. The tax payment is exclusively a function of potential income and not of actual income. Figure 13.1 shows also, in the $Y_p$, $Y_A$ plane, the relationship between potential and actual income for the tax-payers. The $Y_p$ axis measures potential income and the $Y_A$ axis measures actual income.

If actual and potential incomes were always equal, all the tax-payers would be placed along the 45-degree line in the $Y_p$, $Y_A$ plane of Figure 13.1. However, as potential incomes would be defined in relation to some average or normal index of effort (such as, average workweek, average rate of return to capital), and as random factors (weather, strikes, illnesses) might interfere, in reality one would expect some, presumably random, dispersion around the 45-degree line. Other factors may and often do bring about dispersions around the 45-degree line that are not random but systematic, with the result that the actual incomes of some groups of tax-payers fall below their potential incomes. A brief digression on these factors is necessary at this point.

We shall distinguish three such factors: basic inefficiency in the economy; existence of high marginal tax rates and their interaction with various welfare programmes; and tax evasion. The first and third of these factors are particularly, but not exclusively, relevant to developing countries while the second is of greater relevance to industrial countries.

Developing countries are characterized by markets that are often inefficient and 'fragmented'[20] and by income tax systems with widespread evasion (especially for incomes other than wages and salaries). Although the inefficient use of resources relates to all types of inputs, it is particularly serious for real assets. Some of these assets are used far less efficiently than others and, in some cases,

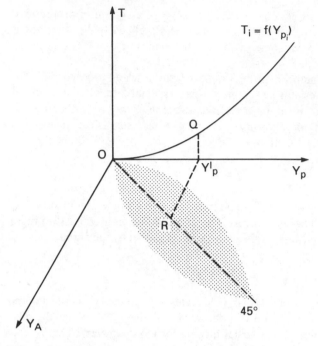

*Figure 13.1*

as with land and often even with buildings, these assets may be left totally unutilized so that their actual income falls to zero.[21] As economies develop and become less fragmented, the variance of the rates of return of particular assets around the national average is likely to decline. This occurs because the economies become better integrated, the flow of information increases and assets are better utilized. As this happens, and in the absence of other factors, the relationship between actual and potential income should improve for the majority of economic agents. In terms of Figure 13.1, more and more economic agents would move toward the 45-degree line. Developing countries are also characterized by widespread tax evasion which brings systematic divergences between actual incomes *as reported to the tax authorities*[22] and potential incomes. Evasion is rampant for incomes from wealth and progressional activities and much less so for wages and salaries.

As markets are much more efficient in industrial countries and as tax evasion is somewhat less widespread, actual incomes and potential incomes should be highly correlated in these countries. However, new factors may create divergences. These factors are mainly the high marginal income tax rates and the (often untaxed) subsidies and transfers to the officially unemployed and to other particular groups who meet various means tests. These factors may induce or even force some individuals to forego work in favour of compensated leisure. This is one aspect of supply-side economics. For these individuals incomes actually earned can fall (especially when subsidies and transfers, in cash or kind, are significant and not taxed) substantially below the incomes that they could have earned, given their skills and abilities. Several recent reports have called attention to this problem and part of the recent criticism of income taxation is based on the belief that these disincentive effects are important.

As already indicated, in the presence of any of the factors mentioned above the dispersion around the 45–degree line will not be random but systematic. For some groups, actual income would systematically fall below potential income.[23] Therefore, many of the dots in the graph would be placed to the northeast of the 45–degree line. If tax liabilities were made to depend exclusively on potential income, once the latter was known, the tax payment would be determined regardless of the individual's level of actual income. Therefore, the individual, who through extra effort and risk received, in any given period, an actual income that exceeded his potential income, would not pay any extra tax. While the income tax would satisfy the equity criterion by being progressive with respect to the level of potential income, the marginal tax rate with respect to the actual income would in fact be zero. Of course, a zero marginal tax rate creates a powerful incentive to extra effort.

Let us consider the $Y_p$, $Y_A$ plane in Figure 13.1: an individual with a potential income indicated by point R, on the 45-degree line, and by $Y_p'$ on the $OY_p$ axis would pay taxes equal to $Y_p'Q$ regardless of the level of his actual income. Of course if $Y_A' > Y_p'$, then the average tax rate, measured against his actual income, would fall. Given $Y_p'$, the greater is the excess of $Y_A'$ over $Y_p'$ the lower will be the average tax rate as defined above. This could be expected to provide incentives to the individual for increasing actual income.

As the individual would, over the short run, not be able to alter his potential income, he would see the tax payment as a kind of poll tax and would attempt to reduce its burden by increasing the level of actual income over his potential income. Over the longer run, however, the individual might be able to alter his potential income by altering the size and quality of the resources on which potential income would be based. Therefore, if the progressivity of the tax *vis-à-vis* potential income were very great, the tax could still have disincentive effects over the long run, as it could induce people to acquire skills associated with lower potential earnings; there could be fewer brain surgeons and more taxi drivers. But these effects, if they did exist, would be less serious than for a tax levied on actual income.

### The practical use of potential income
The foregoing theoretical discussion argues that potential income provides a more attractive tax base than actual income. On both equity and efficiency

grounds a strong case can be made in favour of potential income.[24] However, the question whether practical difficulties make these results irrelevant for the real world taxation of income must be addressed.

Although largely ignored in standard public finance literature, the taxation of potential income has attracted some attention in the literature on economic development and in the practice of taxation. A few practical examples and proposed applications of the use of this concept are outlined below.

### Taxes on potential output of land

The literature on economic development has, at times, singled out the 'absentee landlord' for his negative role in the modernization of traditional agriculture and for leaving idle potentially productive lands. This criticism has often been accompanied by proposals to tax land on its potential output rather than on its actual output.[25] These proposals have not been made for administrative reasons. Simply, it was argued that the taxation of potential income would promote better utilization of scarce resources; and no one has the right to withhold valuable and scarce resources such as land from full productive use. Clearly, the implication of taxing the potential output of land is that ability to earn (potential income) rather than ability to pay (actual income) has been seen as the proper basis for agricultural income taxation.

Taxes on the potential output of agricultural land were introduced in Uruguay in 1960 and in Colombia in 1973. They were also proposed in Chile in 1964 and again in 1968.[26] Similar taxes have been in use in France and in a few other countries that at some stage have been under French influence, such as Morocco. A brief description of some of these taxes will bring out their most salient features.

*Uruguayan land tax of 1960.* This tax was introduced as part of the new income tax that became effective in 1961.[27] The income tax was levied on the global income of tax-payers but different rules applied to the determination of each category of income. Agricultural income was determined as follows: a relatively good physical cadastre provided knowledge about property ownership. It was then determined that a hectare of average productivity would produce a certain quantity X of beef and a certain quantity Y of wool. Each year the government would determine, on the basis of market information, the current price of beef, Pb, and wool, Pw. Therefore the gross income of the average hectare, R, was assumed to be

$$R = Pb(X) + Pw(Y) \qquad (1)$$

Multiplying R by the number of hectares that a person owned, the total gross income could be obtained, under the assumption that all the land of this individual was of average quality. In order to take into account quality differences among lands, the law relied on the values at which the land had been assessed (fiscal cadastre). These values were used to provide relative and not absolute values. Thus, a hectare that had been assessed at twice the average hectare would be given a weight of 2, one that had been assessed at half the average hectare would be given the weight of 0.5. Therefore, the gross income of a hectare other than an average one would be

$$R = [Pb(X) + Pw(Y)] . K \qquad (2)$$

where K is the ratio between the assessed value (at the time the tax was introduced) of the specific hectare and that of the average hectare. From this gross income the tax-payer could deduct rental payments (if he did not own the land), which could not exceed a given percentage of gross income; extraordinary losses associated with calamities (floors, fires); and expenses for particular improvements.

This tax proved to be relatively productive especially in the earlier years after its introduction. Basically it was a simple tax to administer. The major shortcoming, which eventually came to be exploited by those groups most affected by it, was the accuracy of the fiscal cadastre that had been used to determine the relative value of each parcel of land. As the assessed values had been far out of date at the time the tax was introduced, with different lands having been assessed at different times, it was easy for opposition groups to criticize the tax and organize efforts aimed at progressively reducing the overall burden of this tax and changing its character.

*Colombian land tax of 1973*. This law stipulated that farmers should declare a minimum net income of 10 per cent of the assessed value of the land (net of superstructures). Only in the presence of calamities would this income be assumed to be zero. In February 1974, under pressure from agricultural interests, the government issued a decree stating that such calamities had been present in the whole country during the year 1973 so that no payment was made in 1974 on 1973 incomes. The governments also amended the law to create various loopholes that in future years would have sharply reduced the tax liability. In 1974 a more comprehensive legislation was introduced. This legislation is discussed on pp. 203–4.

*French taxation of agricultural income*. In France agricultural income is taxed through a *forfait* system that is available to all farmers small or large.

> The goal [of this system] is not to estimate the [actual] income of a particular farmer in his particular circumstances, but to estimate the average income per unit of surface (or other unit of measurement) for all farms of the same category in one area, whatever

the particular circumstances.[28] Each year a Departmental Tax Commission estimates the average net income per hectare for each kind of farm activity and for each agricultural region. This estimated average income is then multiplied by the number of hectares that a farm allocates to that particular activity to determine the estimated income of that farm.

*Moroccan taxation of agricultural income.* A few countries that, at some stage, have been under French influence have taxes somewhat similar to the French. One good example is provided by the Moroccan agricultural income tax.

The present Moroccan agricultural tax was established in 1961 to replace the *tertib*, a tax of longstanding that had been one of the major taxes during the protectorate period. This tax affected all agricultural properties, of which there were, and still are, about 2 million.

The *tertib* was an annual tax on agricultural production. A commission composed of representatives of the commune where the property was located, of the tax service, and of tax-payers determined each year the normal average yield per hectare for each kind of agricultural product for each area. This was done by actually analysing the production of a given year and carefully noting the results. Once the representative average production per hectare, per tree and per cow had been established this was generally applied to all agricultural producers in the region. They were then required to pay the tax according to this average figure. The *tertib* was criticized for being inefficient, expensive and inequitable. The tax base was gross production and there was no adjustment of the tax for personal situations. There was, thus, no tax exempt minimum and no account was taken of family status or of costs of particular farms. In addition, the *tertib* only taxed actual production, failing to levy unutilized land. This tax was administratively expensive as it required a fairly large survey of cattle, trees and crops for each area and for each year.

After 1961 the current agricultural tax replaced the *tertib* and attempted to correct the major defects of the previous tax. The new tax was still levied on the basis of annual production, taking into account fertility of land, number of trees and cattle per hectare; however, it also applied to unutilized and underutilized lands, since the basis became potential, rather than estimated or actual, production. Potential yield tables were established in 1961 for every province and for every agricultural product. However, instead of basing estimates on a census as had been originally planned, potential production was temporarily based on the average yield in kind calculated for the *tertib* during the ten years preceding 1961. This average yield in kind was adjusted for price changes over the ten years in order to obtain the agricultural tax base in *dirhams* for 1961. It was expected that the tables for potential production would be updated periodically by local rural tax agents upon the recommendations of commissions which would be convened throughout the country to help in the updating when necessary. In fact, this updating was only done in 1978 by which time the bases were very much out of date.

The Moroccan tax on agricultural income is progressive (with marginal rates ranging from 0–20 per cent) and with an exempt minimum introduced to avoid taxing agricultural tax-payers with very low incomes. In 1977, 211,056 tax-payers reported incomes above the exempt minimum. Unlike the French (and the Uruguayan) tax, this tax is a separate one and not part of the regular income tax.

## Taxes on potential income from capital

There are few examples of countries that have taxed capital (rather than just land) on a potential income basis rather than on an actual income basis. In some cases this has been done for purely administrative reasons when the direct estimation of actual income was difficult. In these cases the objective was the measurement of actual income rather than its replacement by a different concept. The best-known examples are provided by Israel with the *tachshiv*[29] and by France with the *forfait* applied to business enterprises,[30] but the practice is also used in Latin America.[31] In other countries, however, the specific intention was to tax potential, rather than actual income, for equity as well as for efficiency reasons.

*Colombia's 'presumptive' income tax:* The tax reform of October 1974 introduced, among many changes, a system of income taxation based on a presumed rate of return on the value of property. This innovation was expected to contribute to the objectives of the reform that were: (i) an increase in revenue; (ii) a fairer relative contribution of wealth and labour to taxation; (iii) a better use of resources and particularly of land; and (iv) a reduction of tax evasion by wealthy individuals. The Colombian authorities were optimistic that the use of the concept of presumptive income would force tax-payers to put their properties to income-earning activities.

Under the reformed system, it was assumed that for tax purposes, the net income (*renta liquida*) of a tax-payer, including the imputed rent for residences and farms used by the tax-payers, should be at least 8 per cent of their net wealth (*patrimonio liquido*) at the end of the year that preceded the taxable one. The imputed rent was assumed to be equal to 10 per cent of the excess of the assessed value of the residence (or its costs if this was higher) over Col$300,000. Thus, residences assessed at less than Col$300,000 were exempt. Net wealth was the assessed value of gross wealth less outstanding debts. This presumed income was imputed to the individual even if, in fact, the actual income received (including imputed rent) was less than 8 per cent. A few exceptions were made for particular circumstances, such as those related to activities which required the growth of slow-growing trees, cattle raising, activities in sectors where prices were controlled. The 8 per cent was presumed to be the average rate of return that ought to be obtained by the judicious use of wealth. The marginal tax rate on the excess over 8 per cent would be zero.[32]

This tax, while clever, can be criticized on various counts. First, it was not clear why 8 per cent was chosen as the average figure for the presumed rate of return on property value; second, why should this figure, even if right, be assumed to remain the same from year to year?; third, individual circumstances were considered only up to a certain point so that, through no fault of their own, the 8 per cent average might have been too high for some and too low for others; fourth, and most seriously, the base for the calculation of presumptive income was available assessments. As these were neither closely related to market values nor a constant proportion of those values, potential problems were introduced from the beginning. This was the same problem encountered in Uruguay and Morocco with the land tax; finally, and somewhat related to the previous point, net wealth does not include just real property but also financial assets (including bank deposits and securities), as well as other personal belongings (such as cars). To the extent that the assessed value of financial assets is much closer to their market value than the assessed value of real properties, the concept of presumptive income introduces a bias against the holding of financial wealth and this bias may have negative consequences for the development of financial deepening.

After a relatively successful introduction, the Colombian presumptive income tax did not perform as well as had been hoped. The reasons were several: pressure groups brought about legislative changes that reduced its coverage; inflation introduced the need for frequent reassessments; the administration failed to meet this need so that the property values used to estimate the income became obsolete; and inflation increased the nominal values of outstanding debts thus reducing even more the tax base.

*Capacity taxation*
Following the Indian experience with the taxation of manufacturing units on a presumptive basis, Pakistan introduced during the 1960s a system of taxation based on capacity (that is, potential output) rather than on actual production. It was thought that this system would stimulate output by reducing the average tax rate on enterprises using their capacity more fully. This system of taxation is not, strictly speaking, related to income but rather to output. Conceptually, it is not different from a proportional tax on the potential gross output of land.[33]

Capacity was defined as 'the rate of production that can be reasonably attained in the short run, given a fixed plant and equipment'.[34] The three factors that were used to determine annual production capacities were '(1) estimates made by manufacturers themselves, (2) machine ratings, and (3) past production data'.[35] The outputs associated with these capacity estimates were then levied with excise taxes. An actual output lower than the capacity output would increase the tax burden on the enterprise, thus reducing its income.

A tax on potential value added of enterprises in developing countries has also been proposed but never applied.[36] This proposal borrows the basic idea from the tax on potential output of the agricultural sector and applies it to the manufacturing sector. It involves the following steps:[37]

(i) the government would have to survey the various enterprises once a year and determine how much they would produce if they were fully utilized;
(ii) on the basis of the estimated full-capacity output, the value of that output would be calculated;
(iii) from the estimate of the value of potential output, actual inputs from other firms would be subtracted (that is, only what the firm actually buys from other firms, and not what it would buy at full capacity would be deducted); and
(iv) the difference would be taxed at a certain rate.

The basic criticism of this type of taxation is a practical one: 'the determination of capacity remains an arbitrary exercise, no matter how much expertise and ingenuity are applied'.[38]

## General conclusions
The first two sections of this chapter argued that from a theoretical point of view, based on both equity and efficiency considerations, a tax system based on potential income might be more desirable than one based on actual income. A few applications of this concept in some countries were discussed. These examples indicate that the concept of potential income has not been totally ignored in the practice of taxation. It might be believed, *a priori*, that administrative difficulties would be too great in the application of the concept of potential income. However, one must make a distinction in this respect between developing countries and industrial countries. To say that the concept of potential income is difficult to apply is not necessarily the same thing as saying that this concept is more difficult to apply than that of actual income. One must remember that the taxation of actual income in developing countries has not been successful. In these countries, the measurement of actual income for many activities may be as difficult as, and perhaps even more difficult than, that of potential income. Therefore, at least for developing countries, administrative considerations alone do not automatically argue against the use of potential income and in favour of that of actual income.

The use of income taxation based on some presumptive criteria in several developing countries attests to the difficulty of estimating actual incomes in these countries. However, in view of the widespread belief that the proper income tax base is actual income, in most cases through presumptive taxation, the government was trying to tax actual rather than potential income. In other words, apart from a few cases the reference concept has been actual income.

Once it is realized that we must not compare the taxation of potential income with the *ideal* taxation of actual income, then the relevant question becomes: which of these two concepts would be easier to tax and which would more nearly conform to equity and efficiency criteria?

In developing countries the answer to this question is not obvious. However a few suggestions can, perhaps, be ventured. As far as the taxation of agricultural income is concerned, potential income would surely be the preferred concept. In this case the alternative of taxing actual income is often not feasible. But, of course, if potential income were to be taxed, countries should be prepared to allocate to the administration of this tax more resources than have generally been allowed. Only in this way would some of the problems discussed above, in connection with the Uruguayan and Moroccan experiences, be avoided. Perhaps the concept of potential income could also be extended to the taxation of buildings but, again, good cadastral values would be necessary.[39] In addition, the concept of potential income, perhaps intended as minimum reportable income, could be applied to professional activities. Such an approach is already in existence in a few countries (Portugal, Tunisia, Morocco and Costa Rica).[40] Wages and salaries, on the other hand, could still be taxed on the basis of actual income as in developing countries these incomes are easy to determine and it is unlikely that wage earners would abandon their jobs in order to receive welfare payments.

In industrial countries the situation is somewhat more complex. Here resources are probably allocated more efficiently. Furthermore, on the basis of administrative considerations, actual income has an advantage over potential income as it is easier to measure. In these countries the concept of potential income would have to be applied with far more discretion than in developing countries.

As far as wage income is concerned, a simple rule could be that a fully employed worker is deemed to be receiving an income equal to his potential. Therefore for the majority of people receiving income from wages, a shift to a concept of potential income would imply no change from the current situation. Only when there have been periods of inactivity or when an individual has moved from a high-paying to a low-paying job would the individual be required to provide an acceptable justification (illness, strike, shutdown) for such inactivity or change. In the absence of such a justification, the taxable income of the individual could be raised to the level that he would have reached had he been fully employed during the year or had he retained the higher-paying job. For incomes from capital sources, one possibility could be to impute to the properly assessed value of the property a rate of return comparable to that of government bonds for that year, which is a rate of return available to all tax-payers. Imputed rent could also be determined in this way. Even the income of public corporations could be determined in the same way, by simply imputing to the undepreciated capital of the corporation a rate of return equal to that of government bonds. If the corporation's actual earnings were higher, the corporation would benefit. If these earnings were lower than the bond rate, the corporation would be penalized.

The above ideas are just suggestions of possibilities. It is clearly very easy to raise objections to these suggestions and it may be equally easy to improve on them. It must be recalled that when income taxation was first proposed, experts raised many questions as to the feasibility of using this concept and some thought that it would never work. However, in view of the changing current attitude *vis-à-vis* income taxation, and in view of the fact that often these objections are related to the lower efficiency in the use of resources that is brought about by high marginal tax rates, the taxation of potential income might be a possibility in the future. If potential income came to be accepted as the proper concept, I am sure that many ways could be found to measure it in a more acceptable fashion than outlined above. Therefore we should not reject the concept until we have really convinced ourselves that it is unusable. On the basis of the attention that we have paid so far to potential income, it seems to be premature to reject it.

## Notes

1. Arnold C. Harberger, *Taxation and Welfare,* Boston, Little, Brown and Company, 1974:25.
2. See especially, US Department of the Treasury, *Blueprints for Basic Tax Reform,* Washington DC, US Government Printing Office, 17 January 1977; and Institute for Fiscal Studies, *The Structure and Reform of Direct Taxation,* Report of a Committee chaired by Professor J. E. Meade, London, Allen & Unwin, 1978.
   It is worthwhile to recall that in 1914 Edwin R.A. Seligman, in his encyclopedic book on income taxation, had already raised serious doubts about this tax and had concluded that 'to assert...as is often done by superficial thinkers, that the income tax is the fairest of all taxes, is to maintain an untenable position' *(The Income Tax: A Study of the History, Theory and Practice of Income Taxation at Home and Abroad,* 2nd ed., New York, Augustus M. Kelly Publishers, 1970:17.
3. Advisory Commission on Intergovernmental Relations, *Changing Public Attitudes on Governments and Taxes,* Washington DC, various years. In March 1972 only 19 per cent of the total US public thought that the federal income tax was the worst (that is, least equitable) tax. By May 1980 this proportion had risen to 36 per cent.
4. In addition to the two studies cited in note 2, see *What Should be Taxed: Income or Expenditure?,* Joseph A. Pechman (ed.), Washington DC, The Brookings Institution, 1980; and *Comprehensive Income Taxation,* Joseph A. Pechman (ed.), Washington DC, The Brookings Institution, 1977.
5. See, for example, J.A. Mirrlees, 'An exploration in the theory of optimum income taxation', *Review of Economic Studies* 38, 1971:175–208.
6. However, the difference between the macroeconomic concept of potential income and that of measured income is due to unemployment, while at the microeconomic level, which is the one of concern in this chapter it may be due to other factors.
7. Richard A. Musgrave, *The Theory of Public Finance: A Study in Public Economy,* New York, McGraw-Hill, 1959:94.
8. Joseph A. Pechman, *Federal Tax Policy,* 3rd ed., Washington DC, The Brookings Institution, 1977:54.
9. Richard Goode, *The Individual Income Tax,* rev. ed., Washington DC, The Brookings Institution, 1976:17.

208    *Public finance in developing countries*

10.    Richard A. Musgrave and Peggy B. Musgrave, *Public Finance in Theory and Practice*, New York, McGraw-Hill Book Company, 1973:225.
11.    This omission was the basis for Little's famous critique which, according to Harberger, 'destroys any theoretical presumption of the superiority of direct over indirect taxation' (Arnold C. Harberger, *op. cit.*, p.26).
12.    After the present chapter was completed, Richard Goode brought to my attention a paper by Professor Alvin Warren of the Pennsylvania Law School entitled 'Would a consumption tax be fairer than an income tax?', *The Yale Law Journal* 89, 6, May 1980. That article also compares an *ex post* with an *ex ante* concept of income but reaches somewhat different conclusions from the ones reached in this chapter.
13.    An early reference to potential income, when the difference between actual and potential income is due to leisure, is found in Abba Lerner, *The Economics of Control*, New York, The Macmillan Company, 1944:237. Another more recent reference which deals, in a somewhat more abstract fashion, with some of the issues raised in this paper is M.G. Allingham, 'Towards an ability tax', *Journal of Public Economies* (North Holland Publishing Company) 4, 4, November 1975:361–76. Of relevance is the already cited paper by Alvin Warren.
14.    Musgrave and Musgrave, *op.cit.*, p. 205. Material in brackets added by author. Interestingly enough while potential income has been largely ignored by the public finance literature, it has not been ignored by the literature on economic development. Furthermore, the concept has been used in some practical experiences. See pp. 200–205.
15.    It must be pointed out that when tax-payers are taxed on the basis of actual income, a very wealthy individual who kept his wealth in a non-income generating form (cash, jewels, paintings, idle land) could have a high level of consumption without paying income taxes. For this reason some have argued that consumption, rather than income, should be the basis for taxation. Others have argued in favour of supplementing the taxes on income with taxes on wealth. However, as long as wealth taxes are proportional, they cannot perform the same redistributive role as income taxes.
16.    Thomas Hobbes, *Leviathan*, II, 1651 (italics added by author). While Hobbes has usually been cited regarding the choice between a tax based on income and one based on consumption, the above quote indicates that his real concern was with the choice between potential and actual income.
17.    However, as pointed out in Alvin Warren's paper and as stressed in a comment to this paper by Richard Goode, the taxation of income based on a potential concept implies a significant and, for some, perhaps, an intolerable interference with personal liberty. As Goode puts it 'what would be done about the person with superior earning capacity who decides to write poetry, enter a religious order, or spend years in unsuccessful efforts to invent a new devise or process?' Goode argues that this would be particularly so for potential income from human capital. In this view what may appear as highly equitable from a social or collective viewpoint might be seen as inequitable from an individualistic or personal viewpoint.
18.    But even a poll tax may become inefficient if tax-payers can migrate.
19.    Although the available empirical evidence is not yet as clear cut as one would wish, many experts now believe that high marginal income tax rates reduce tax-payers' willingness to work hard, to save and to invest in risky ventures.
20.    The term is Ronald I. McKinnon's. See McKinnon, *Money and Capital in Economic Development*, Washington DC, The Brookings Institution, 1973, for many examples of underutilization of resources in developing countries.
21.    As many surveys of capacity utilization in developing countries have shown, plants too are often used at a small fraction of their full capacity rate.
22.    Though not necessarily as earned.
23.    This is the basis for the current belief on the part of some economists that a reduction in income tax rates will increase total output and, possibly, total tax revenue.
24.    It must be repeated, however, that an argument can be made, and has been made, against a tax on potential income on the grounds that it might be seen as interfering with personal liberty.
25.    See Dino Jarach, 'El impuesto a la renta normal potencial de la tierra', *Cuaderno de Finanzas Públicas*, 5, Programa Conjunto de Tributación, Washington DC, undated. See also Federico Herschel, 'Taxation of agricultural and hard-to-get groups', in Richard Musgrave and

Malcolm Gillis, *Fiscal Reform for Colombia, Final Report and Staff Papers of the Colombian Commission on Tax Reform*, Harvard Law School, 1971, Part II, chap. 6.

26. Richard M. Bird, *Taxing Agricultural Land in Developing Countries*, Cambridge, Mass., Harvard University Press, 1974; and Roberto Junguito and Guillermo Perry, 'Evaluación del Regimen de Renta Presuntiva' in *La Estructura Fiscal Colombiana*, eds Sebastián Arango Fonnegra, Jaime Bueno Miranda and Florangela Gómez de Arango, Bogotá, Colombia, 1979:241-72.

27. I owe this description to Carlos Aguirre.

28. Harvard Law School, International Tax Program, World Tax Series, *Taxation in France*, Chicago, Commerce Clearing House, Inc., 1966:633. The words in brackets have been added by the author.

29. See Professor Arye Lapidoth, 'The Israeli experience of using the Tachshiv for estimating the taxable income', *Bulletin for International Fiscal Documentation 1977/3*, 31, International Bureau of Fiscal Documentation, Amsterdam: 99–106; and Harold C. Wilkenfeld, *Taxes and People in Israel*, Cambridge, Harvard University Press, 1973.

30. Harvard Law School, *Taxation in France*, see note 28.

31. Raynard M. Sommerfeld, *Tax Reform and the Alliance for Progress*, Austin, University of Texas Press, 1966: 156-7.

32. A detailed analysis of the Colombian experience with this tax is contained in Roberto Junguito and Guillermo Perry, op. cit. (see note 26), pp. 241–72.

33. For a good description and evaluation of this tax see Sijbren Cnossen, *Excise Systems: A Global Study of the Selective Taxation of Goods and Services*, Baltimore, Johns Hopkins Press, 1977, chap. 6.

34. *Ibid.*, p. 76.

35. Cnossen, op. cit., p.76.

36. See Vito Tanzi, 'The theory of tax structure development and the design of tax structure policy for industrialization', *Fiscal Policy for Industrialization and Development in Latin America*, David T. Geithman (ed.), Gainsville, University of Florida, 1974: 48–67.

38. Cnossen, op. cit., p.79.

39. As the share of capital in national income is much higher in developing countries than in industrial countries, limiting the use of potential income to capital incomes would cover a higher proportion of total income in the former than in the latter countries.

40. For a proposal to tax the potential income of professionals see Tanzi, 'Taxation, educational expenditure, and income distribution', and 'Comments' by Arnold Harberger and by Alfonso Celso Pastore in *Financiamiento de la Educación en América Latina*, eds Mario Brodersohn and Maria Ester Sanjurgo, Mexico, Fondo de Cultura Económica, Banco Interamericano de Desarrollo, 1978: 233–54.

# 14 Import taxes and economic development

## Introduction

Historically, taxes on foreign trade have been very important in practically all the countries of the world. At present, however, their use in industrial countries is limited while they still provide the bulk of revenues in developing countries. As recently as 1913 these taxes accounted for about 50 per cent of federal tax revenue in the United States. This proportion is still found today in several developing countries. In view of the importance of these taxes, it is rather surprising that they have received little attention on the part of public finance scholars.[1]

This chapter surveys some of the main issues related to the imposition of import duties in developing countries.

## The changing importance of import duties in developing countries

In spite of some decline in their relative importance, import duties are still the most important single source of tax revenue in developing countries.

Table 14.1 provides data on tax revenue (as percent of GDP) for 100 developing countries. The table also breaks down tax revenue among its major components. Import taxes accounted, on the average, for 26 per cent of total tax revenue or for 4.3 per cent of the GDPs of developing countries.

The importance of these taxes in developing countries is generally attributed to the alleged facility with which they can be administered and collected. The fact that imports – as well as exports – are often channelled through a few places (such as ports, airports, border passes) is certainly one of the reasons for their popularity. Musgrave, among others, has maintained that openness – defined as the share of imports and exports in the national income of a country – provides the government with an important tax base or 'handle' that can be used even when the administrative capability of the country is low.[2] He has argued that the collection of these taxes generally requires a lower degree of administrative sophistication than is needed in connection with many internal taxes. Countries with relatively weak administrative capability but with significant foreign trade sectors can thus raise substantial revenues with relative ease especially when the borders are well-guarded and imports are channelled through few points of entries.

Facility of collection, however, is only one of the reasons for the popularity of these taxes.[3] In many cases, it may not be the most important reason. Of, perhaps, equal importance is the fact that tax-payers are less likely to react against the imposition of these taxes than against many others especially when governments justify the use of these taxes with convincing arguments related to the need to levy them in order to achieve various national objectives – employment, industrialization, self-sufficiency and so on. Political and economic reasons thus intermingle with administrative ones to induce the developing countries to rely heavily on import duties.

The decline in the relative importance of import duties and the consequent increase in the relative importance of internal indirect taxes as a result of economic development is now widely accepted in the literature on tax structure change during economic development. Levin and Lewis, for example, provided strong historical support for this decline through their work on Colombia[4] and Pakistan.[5] And Hinrichs,[6] Musgrave,[7] Lewis,[8] and Due[9] have generally backed it with their cross-sectional work.

Table 14.2 provides a convenient summary of the data given in Table 14.1. It gives averages for four groups of countries as well as averages for the whole set of 100 countries. The countries have been grouped according to their income levels. It is thus easy to see how the importance of various taxes changes with the change in the per capita income of the group.[10] Income taxes clearly become more important as the income level rises. At the same time foreign trade taxes become less important. The fall in foreign trade taxes, and in import duties in particular, seems to be accompanied by an increase in the share of domestic taxes on goods and services in GDP.

To test the above hypotheses the share of import duties in GDP (ID/GDP) has been correlated against the per capita income ($\bar{Y}$), the share of imports in GDP (IM/GDP), and the share of domestic taxes on goods and services in GDP (DT/GDP). One would expect that ID/GDP should be negatively correlated with $\bar{Y}$ and DT/GDP and positively correlated with IM/GDP. The regression results are as follows:

$$\frac{ID}{GDP} = 0.2901 \underset{(4.68)}{} -0.0008\bar{Y} \underset{(6.13)}{} + 0.1113 \underset{(9.86)}{} \frac{IM}{GDP} - 0.2291 \underset{(2.96)}{} \frac{DT}{GDP} \quad \bar{R}^2 = 0.532$$

For a cross-sectional regression the results are very good. The $\bar{R}^2$ is quite high and all the t values are significant at the 1 per cent level. Furthermore, all the coefficients have the expected sign. It can thus be concluded that, *ceteris paribus*, the share of import duties in GDP falls with the rise of per capita income. It can also be concluded that there is some trade off between import duties and domestic indirect (that is, sales plus excise) taxes as the level of per capita income rises.

Table 14.1   Developing countries: tax revenue by type of tax (per cent of GDP)

| | GDP per capita (1987 dollars) | Years | | Total taxes | Income taxes | | | |
|---|---|---|---|---|---|---|---|---|
| | | | | | Total | Indiv-idual | Corpo-rate | Other |
| Kuwait | 14870 | 1985 | 1987 | 1.91 | 0.49 | 0.00 | 0.49 | 0.00 |
| Bahamas | 10320 | 1984 | 1986 | 16.80 | 0.00 | 0.00 | 0.00 | 0.00 |
| Netherlands Antilles | 9400 | 1984 | 1986 | 5.59 | 0.00 | 0.00 | 0.00 | 0.00 |
| Bahrain[1,2] | 8530 | 1985 | 1987 | 6.03 | 1.59 | 0.00 | 1.59 | 0.00 |
| Singapore | 7940 | 1984 | 1986 | 16.07 | 7.25 | n.a. | n.a. | n.a |
| Israel[2] | 6810 | 1984 | 1986 | 33.35 | 16.34 | 12.02 | 2.85 | 1.47 |
| Oman | 5780 | 1984 | 1986 | 10.45 | 8.72 | 0.00 | 8.65 | 0.06 |
| Barbados | 5330 | 1983 | 1985 | 24.95 | 9..97 | 3.42 | 6.06 | 0.50 |
| Cyprus | 5210 | 1986 | 1987 | 13.84 | 5.29 | 3.79 | 0.82 | 0.68 |
| Greece[2] | 4350 | 1983 | 1985 | 20.19 | 6.38 | 4.76 | 0.87 | 0.75 |
| Trinidad and Tobago | 4220 | 1979 | 1981 | 34.14 | 28.66 | 4.63 | 22.54 | 1.49 |
| Malta | 4010 | 1984 | 1986 | 25.17 | 9.13 | 4.86 | 4.21 | 0.06 |
| Iran, I.R. of [2] | 3557 | 1984 | 1986 | 9.51 | 2.52 | 0.27 | 2.25 | 0.01 |
| Venezuela[2] | 3230 | 1984 | 1986 | 19.97 | 13.75 | 0.85 | 12.03 | 0.00 |
| Seychelles | 3180 | 1975 | 1977 | 19.34 | 6.21 | 3.82 | 2.40 | 0.00 |
| Portugal | 2890 | 1984 | 1986 | 30.68 | 7.42 | 2.52 | 1.38 | 3.52 |
| Gabon | 2750 | 1983 | 1985 | 27.46 | 18.04 | 1.20 | 16.34 | 0.50 |
| Korea | 2690 | 1986 | 1987 | 14.92 | 4.48 | 2.44 | 2.04 | 0.00 |
| Yugoslavia[2] | 2480 | 1984 | 1986 | 5.58 | 0.00 | 0.00 | 0.00 | 0.00 |
| Argentina[2] | 2370 | 1982 | 1984 | 17.84 | 2.12 | 0.04 | 0.03 | 0.61 |
| Suriname | 2360 | 1984 | 1986 | 20.76 | 9.37 | 5.91 | 3.46 | 0.00 |
| Panama[2] | 2240 | 1984 | 1986 | 21.56 | 6.41 | 0.00 | 0.00 | 6.41 |
| Uruguay | 2180 | 1984 | 1986 | 13.30 | 1.57 | 0.55 | 0.83 | 0.19 |
| Brazil[2] | 2020 | 1984 | 1986 | 22.10 | 4.40 | 0.17 | 1.34 | 2.89 |
| South Africa[2] | 1890 | 1982 | 1984 | 22.85 | 12.39 | 6.48 | 5.61 | 0.29 |
| Mexico[2] | 1820 | 1982 | 1984 | 17.52 | 4.32 | 2.07 | 2.14 | 0.03 |
| Syrian Arab Re. | 1820 | 1984 | 1986 | 12.75 | 5.94 | 0.08 | 5.86 | 0.00 |
| Malaysia[2] | 1820 | 1985 | 1987 | 20.02 | 10.22 | 2.33 | 7.88 | 0.02 |
| Costa Rica[2] | 1590 | 1983 | 1985 | 20.39 | 3.11 | 2.70 | 0.32 | 0.10 |
| Jordan | 1540 | 1984 | 1986 | 18.61 | 3.19 | n.a. | n.a | 0.14 |
| Fiji | 1510 | 1984 | 1986 | 19.13 | 10.47 | 7.69 | 2.51 | 0.26 |
| Mauritius | 1470 | 1985 | 1987 | 19.67 | 2.33 | 1.30 | 1.03 | 0.00 |
| Peru | 1430 | 1984 | 1986 | 14.10 | 2.17 | 0.19 | 3.10 | 0.01 |
| Chile[2] | 1310 | 1984 | 1986 | 20.24 | 3.28 | 1.14 | 2.14 | 0.00 |
| Belize | 1250 | 1983 | 1985 | 20.62 | 5.11 | 3.96 | 1.45 | 0.00 |
| Colombia[2] | 1220 | 1982 | 1984 | 11.41 | 2.58 | 1.50 | 1.06 | 0.00 |
| Tunisia[2] | 1210 | 1982 | 1984 | 23.24 | 4.69 | 2.12 | 2.35 | 0.21 |
| Turkey | 1200 | 1985 | 1987 | 15.04 | 7.34 | 5.22 | 2.11 | 0.00 |
| Ecuador | 1040 | 1983 | 1985 | 13.06 | 7.89 | 0.00 | 6.70 | 1.19 |
| Botswana | 1030 | 1984 | 1986 | 26.36 | 17.56 | 2.07 | 13.57 | 1.92 |
| Paraguay[2] | 1000 | 1984 | 1986 | 8.29 | 1.15 | 0.00 | 1.14 | 0.02 |
| Jamaica | 960 | 1979 | 1981 | 19.21 | 8.38 | 4.46 | 3.92 | 0.00 |
| Cameroon | 960 | 1985 | 1987 | 13.94 | 9.14 | 1.75 | 7.38 | 0.01 |
| Guatemala[2] | 940 | 1985 | 1986 | 6.53 | 0.98 | 0.32 | 0.65 | 0.01 |
| Congo | 880 | 1978 | 1980 | 24.53 | 17.21 | 2.96 | 14.21 | 0.03 |
| Djbouti | 860 | 1984 | 1986 | 24.39 | 4.66 | 2.79 | 1.86 | 0.01 |

| | Domestic taxes on goods and services | | | | Foreign trade | | | | | |
| | General sales, turn-over, | | | | Import | Export | | Social secur- | Wealth and prop- | |
| Total | VAT | Excises | Other | Total | duties | duties | Other | ity | erty | Other |
|---|---|---|---|---|---|---|---|---|---|---|
| 0.27 | 0.00 | 0.00 | 0.27 | 1.11 | 1.11 | 0.00 | 0.00 | 0.00 | 0.04 | 0.00 |
| 2.02 | 0.00 | 0.00 | 2.02 | 13.33 | 12.36 | 0.21 | 0.76 | 1.78 | 0.62 | 1.09 |
| 2.42 | 0.00 | 2.34 | 0.08 | 2.84 | 2.14 | 0.00 | 0.70 | 4.26 | 0.11 | 0.22 |
| 1.23 | 0.00 | 0.09 | 1.14 | 2.96 | 2.96 | 0.00 | 0.00 | 2.52 | 0.17 | 0.00 |
| 3.85 | 0.00 | 1.47 | 2.38 | 1.05 | 1.05 | 0.00 | 0.00 | 0.49 | 2.61 | 0.89 |
| 13.06 | 11.72 | 1.14 | 0.20 | 2.10 | 1.55 | 0.00 | 0.55 | 5.07 | 0.55 | 0.15 |
| 0.32 | 0.00 | 0.00 | 0.32 | 1.18 | 1.18 | 0.00 | 0.00 | 0.23 | 0.00 | 0.00 |
| 7.20 | 4.64 | 0.29 | 2.27 | 4.78 | 4.32 | 0.07 | 0.38 | 4.01 | 1.49 | 2.30 |
| 4.74 | 0.00 | 3.28 | 1.46 | 4.53 | 4.53 | 0.00 | 0.00 | 4.66 | 0.71 | 1.09 |
| 12.73 | 6.79 | 4.83 | 1.11 | 0.34 | 0.34 | 0.00 | 0.00 | 12.15 | 0.74 | 1.91 |
| 1.75 | 0.72 | 0.28 | 0.75 | 2.78 | 2.77 | 0.00 | 0.01 | 0.63 | 0.11 | 0.18 |
| 2.10 | 0.00 | 1.18 | 0.92 | 6.89 | 6.89 | 0.00 | 0.00 | 6.19 | 0.78 | 0.09 |
| 1.39 | 0.13 | 0.38 | 0.88 | 1.94 | 1.87 | 0.00 | 0.07 | 2.46 | 0.37 | 0.13 |
| 1.45 | 0.00 | 1.40 | 0.05 | 4.48 | 1.40 | 0.00 | 3.09 | 1.09 | 0.18 | 0.09 |
| 1.92 | 0.00 | 1.16 | 0.75 | 9.47 | 9.33 | 0.14 | 0.00 | 0.00 | 0.52 | 1.23 |
| 11.60 | 4.93 | 5.26 | 1.41 | 0.89 | 0.89 | 0.00 | 0.00 | 8.48 | 0.58 | 1.71 |
| 2.44 | 1.93 | 0.00 | 0.51 | 6.22 | 5.72 | 0.50 | 0.00 | 0.54 | 0.09 | 0.12 |
| 7.08 | 3.49 | 2.16 | 1.42 | 2.63 | 2.63 | 0.00 | 0.00 | 0.27 | 0.12 | 0.36 |
| 4.27 | 4.27 | 0.00 | 0.00 | 2.58 | 2.58 | 0.00 | 0.00 | 0.00 | 0.00 | 0.00 |
| 7.93 | 2.28 | 3.90 | 1.76 | 2.12 | 0.88 | 1.08 | 0.16 | 2.79 | 1.40 | 0.73 |
| 2.52 | 0.00 | 1.52 | 0.99 | 7.93 | 5.72 | 1.55 | 0.65 | 1.65 | 0.38 | 0.56 |
| 4.38 | 1.63 | 1.85 | 0.90 | 3.07 | 2.79 | 0.24 | 0.04 | 6.19 | 0.46 | 0.54 |
| 9.05 | 5.33 | 3.63 | 0.08 | 2.66 | 1.96 | 0.24 | 0.46 | 5.49 | 0.82 | 0.84 |
| 9.77 | 0.59 | 2.20 | 6.98 | 0.69 | 0.40 | 0.29 | 0.00 | 6.80 | 0.32 | 0.00 |
| 7.43 | 4.52 | 2.43 | 0.47 | 0.83 | 0.79 | 0.04 | 0.01 | 0.34 | 1.55 | 0.30 |
| 9.13 | 0.00 | 2.11 | 7.02 | 2.27 | 0.56 | 1.71 | 0.00 | 2.15 | 0.08 | 0.01 |
| 2.14 | 0.20 | 0.26 | 1.68 | 1.74 | 1.70 | 0.04 | 0.00 | 0.28 | 0.90 | 1.20 |
| 4.58 | 1.45 | 1.79 | 1.34 | 4.70 | 2.85 | 1.85 | 0.00 | 0.18 | 0.11 | 0.41 |
| 6.91 | 3.33 | 3.29 | 0.29 | 4.68 | 2.22 | 2.03 | 0.42 | 5.47 | 0.28 | 0.25 |
| 3.38 | 0.00 | 2.83 | 0.55 | 8.54 | 8.54 | 0.00 | 0.00 | 0.00 | 1.27 | 2.24 |
| 2.96 | 0.00 | 2.28 | 0.68 | 6.61 | 6.61 | 0.00 | 0.00 | 0.00 | 0.09 | 0.25 |
| 4.44 | 1.54 | 1.64 | 1.26 | 11.94 | 9.33 | 2.51 | 0.10 | 1.07 | 0.89 | 0.08 |
| 7.70 | 2.31 | 5.29 | 0.10 | 3.71 | 3.16 | 0.52 | 0.03 | 0.46 | 0.64 | 0.57 |
| 11.81 | 8.74 | 3.03 | 0.04 | 2.82 | 2.62 | 0.00 | 0.19 | 2.21 | 0.44 | 1.76 |
| 2.71 | 0.00 | 1.82 | 0.88 | 11.62 | 10.62 | 0.54 | 0.46 | 0.42 | 0.29 | 0.90 |
| 4.55 | 2.32 | 0.82 | 1.41 | 1.53 | 1.37 | 0.15 | 0.01 | 1.78 | 0.36 | 0.24 |
| 7.18 | 2.06 | 2.75 | 2.37 | 10.10 | 9.88 | 0.22 | 0.00 | 3.20 | 0.70 | 0.44 |
| 5.41 | 2.45 | 0.80 | 0.81 | 1.28 | 1.28 | 0.00 | 0.00 | 0.00 | 0.37 | 0.69 |
| 2.23 | 1.44 | 0.76 | 0.02 | 2.62 | 2.20 | 0.17 | 0.25 | 0.00 | 0.25 | 0.08 |
| 0.55 | 0.38 | 0.00 | 0.17 | 8.21 | 8.18 | 0.03 | 0.00 | 0.00 | 0.04 | 0.00 |
| 2.49 | 0.65 | 1.71 | 0.13 | 1.12 | 0.94 | 0.02 | 0.16 | 1.19 | 0.88 | 1.09 |
| 14.39 | 6.44 | 6.98 | 0.97 | 1.34 | 1.34 | 0.00 | 0.00 | 1.44 | 0.57 | 1.10 |
| 2.60 | 1.24 | 1.12 | 0.23 | 3.50 | 3.01 | 0.45 | 0.03 | 1.10 | 0.39 | 0.25 |
| 0.00 | 0.88 | 0.58 | 0.00 | 0.00 | 0.00 | 0.30 | 0.00 | 0.00 | 0.00 | 0.00 |
| 2.69 | 2.46 | 0.17 | 0.02 | 4.57 | 4.46 | 0.07 | 0.01 | 0.69 | 0.02 | 0.41 |
| 15.39 | 9.13 | 4.08 | 2.18 | 1.65 | 1.62 | 0.03 | 0.00 | 0.00 | 1.50 | 0.54 |

| | GDP per capita (1987 dollars) | Years | | Total taxes | Income taxes | | | |
|---|---|---|---|---|---|---|---|---|
| | | | | | Total | Indiv-idual | Corpo-rate | Other |
| El Salvador | 850 | 1985 | 1987 | 12.23 | 2.51 | 0.91 | 1.36 | 0.24 |
| Thailand[2] | 840 | 1985 | 1987 | 13.77 | 3.14 | 1.72 | 1.42 | 0.00 |
| Nicaragua | 830 | 1984 | 1986 | 28.21 | 4.87 | n.a. | n.a | n.a |
| Honduras[2] | 780 | 1979 | 1981 | 13.12 | 3.70 | 1.29 | 2.39 | 0.02 |
| Cote d'Ivoire | 750 | 1983 | 1985 | 14.98 | 3.10 | 1.62 | 1.20 | 0.29 |
| Dominican Republic[2] | 730 | 1984 | 1986 | 11.43 | 2.34 | 0.90 | 1.50 | 0.00 |
| Papua New Guinea | 730 | 1984 | 1986 | 19.05 | 10.29 | 6.23 | 4.01 | 0.00 |
| Egypt | 710 | 1985 | 1987 | 18.19 | 5.83 | 0.52 | 4.64 | 0.67 |
| Swaziland[2] | 700 | 1983 | 1985 | 25.41 | 6.74 | 3.47 | 2.79 | 0.48 |
| Morocco | 620 | 1984 | 1986 | 20.62 | 4.67 | 2.56 | 1.91 | 0.20 |
| Zimbabwe[2] | 590 | 1983 | 1985 | 27.82 | 12.59 | 7.24 | 4.91 | 0.45 |
| Philippines | 590 | 1984 | 1986 | 9.90 | 2.76 | 0.89 | 1.41 | 0.45 |
| Yemen Arab Rep. | 580 | 1985 | 1987 | 13.72 | 2.27 | 1.43 | 0.81 | 0.03 |
| Bolivia[2] | 570 | 1982 | 1984 | 4.55 | 0.47 | 0.31 | 0.22 | 0.00 |
| Western Samoa | 560 | 1982 | 1984 | 26.24 | 7.01 | n.a. | n.a. | n.a. |
| Senegal | 510 | 1982 | 1984 | 17.38 | 3.88 | 2.31 | 1.02 | 0.55 |
| Indonesia[2] | 450 | 1984 | 1986 | 16.91 | 12.28 | 0.62 | 11.39 | 0.26 |
| Mauritania | 440 | 1981 | 1983 | 17.17 | 5.57 | 3.55 | 1.74 | 0.28 |
| Liberia | 440 | 1984 | 1986 | 18.42 | 7.34 | 5.66 | 1.57 | 0.11 |
| Solomon Islands | 420 | 1985 | 1987 | 20.87 | 7.34 | 4.97 | 2.38 | 0.00 |
| Sri Lanka[2] | 400 | 1984 | 1986 | 18.87 | 3.22 | 0.95 | 2.27 | 0.00 |
| Ghana | 390 | 1985 | 1987 | 11.33 | 2.61 | 1.00 | 1.61 | 0.00 |
| Guyana | 380 | 1983 | 1985 | 36.31 | 14.37 | 4.64 | 9.39 | 0.00 |
| Comoros | 380 | 1984 | 1986 | 12.95 | 1.64 | 0.45 | 1.09 | 0.09 |
| Nigeria | 370 | 1985 | 1987 | 6.49 | 6.34 | 0.01 | 6.08 | 0.24 |
| Lesotho | 360 | 1983 | 1985 | 38.62 | 4.36 | 3.02 | 1.34 | 0.00 |
| Haiti | 360 | 1985 | 1987 | 10.01 | 1.53 | 0.60 | 0.93 | 0.00 |
| Pakistan[2] | 350 | 1984 | 1986 | 12.66 | 1.90 | n.a. | n.a | n.a. |
| Kenya[2] | 340 | 1983 | 1985 | 20.03 | 6.33 | n.a. | n.a | n.a |
| Sudan[2] | 330 | 1980 | 1982 | 9.65 | 1.78 | 0.67 | 1.03 | 0.08 |
| Rwanda | 310 | 1978 | 1980 | 10.63 | 2.17 | 0.82 | 1.24 | 0.11 |
| Benin | 300 | 1977 | 1979 | 13.21 | 2.82 | 0.53 | 1.72 | 0.57 |
| Maldives | 300 | 1984 | 1986 | 15.28 | 0.48 | n.a. | n.a | n.a. |
| Togo | 300 | 1984 | 1986 | 21.97 | 10.20 | 2.24 | 7.17 | 0.78 |
| Sierra Leone | 300 | 1985 | 1987 | 5.52 | 1.61 | 0.62 | 0.99 | 0.00 |
| India[2] | 300 | 1983 | 1985 | 15.52 | 2.07 | 0.87 | 1.14 | 0.06 |
| Somalia | 290 | 1975 | 1977 | 11.86 | 1.02 | 0.92 | 0.09 | 0.00 |
| Niger | 280 | 1978 | 1980 | 10.80 | 3.63 | 0.71 | 2.55 | 0.37 |
| Uganda | 260 | 1984 | 1986 | 11.74 | 0.74 | 0.05 | 0.69 | 0.00 |
| Burundi | 240 | 1979 | 1981 | 12.83 | 2.74 | 1.20 | 1.35 | 0.18 |
| Zambia | 240 | 1986 | 1988 | 21.36 | 5.59 | 1.92 | 2.92 | 0.75 |
| Gambia, The | 220 | 1984 | 1986 | 16.36 | 2.64 | 1.15 | 1.24 | 0.25 |
| Tanzania | 220 | 1983 | 1985 | 17.40 | 5.37 | 1.84 | 3.26 | 0.05 |
| Madagascar | 200 | 1980 | 1982 | 12.61 | 2.56 | 1.38 | 1.18 | 0.00 |
| Mali | 200 | 1984 | 1986 | 9.55 | 1.51 | 0.55 | 0.84 | 0.11 |
| Burma | 200 | 1984 | 1986 | 8.10 | 0.68 | n.a. | n.a. | n.a. |
| Burkina Faso | 170 | 1984 | 1986 | 10.91 | 2.34 | 1.52 | 0.29 | 0.53 |
| Guinea-Bissau | 170 | 1984 | 1986 | 7.22 | 1.64 | 1.64 | 0.00 | 0.00 |

| | Domestic taxes on goods and services | | | Foreign trade | | | | | Wealth and | |
| | General sales, turnover, VAT | Excises | Other | Total | Import duties | Export duties | Other | Social security | property | Other |
| Total | VAT | Excises | Other | Total | duties | duties | Other | ity | erty | Other |
|---|---|---|---|---|---|---|---|---|---|---|
| 4.80 | 2.94 | 1.55 | 0.31 | 4.22 | 1.11 | 3.10 | 0.00 | 0.00 | 0.65 | 0.06 |
| 7.57 | 2.69 | 4.20 | 0.68 | 3.13 | 2.90 | 0.20 | 0.03 | 0.00 | 0.20 | 0.11 |
| 18.05 | 3.38 | 9.90 | 4.77 | 3.57 | 2.21 | 0.02 | 1.34 | 4.03 | 1.31 | 0.41 |
| 3.52 | 0.98 | 2.28 | 0.26 | 5.65 | 3.28 | 2.36 | 0.01 | 0.00 | 0.11 | 0.14 |
| 4.49 | 2.23 | 0.96 | 0.49 | 7.62 | 5.23 | 2.38 | 0.00 | 1.39 | 0.73 | 0.05 |
| 4.34 | 0.00 | 3.87 | 0.47 | 3.92 | 3.35 | 0.36 | 0.21 | 0.48 | 0.10 | 0.15 |
| 2.99 | 0.00 | 2.70 | 0.30 | 5.36 | 4.74 | 0.59 | 0.04 | 0.00 | 0.01 | 0.40 |
| 4.33 | 0.00 | 4.01 | 0.32 | 5.39 | 5.27 | 0.12 | 0.00 | 5.40 | 0.36 | 2.31 |
| 1.00 | 0.70 | 0.00 | 0.30 | 17.21 | 17.20 | 0.01 | 0.00 | 0.00 | 0.35 | 0.11 |
| 10.08 | 6.19 | 3.08 | 0.81 | 4.01 | 3.75 | 0.24 | 0.02 | 1.25 | 0.61 | 1.24 |
| 9.55 | 6.35 | 2.93 | 0.26 | 4.51 | 4.46 | 0.00 | 0.04 | 0.00 | 0.89 | 0.20 |
| 4.24 | 0.97 | 2.34 | 0.93 | 2.63 | 2.29 | 0.20 | 0.14 | 0.00 | 0.08 | 0.21 |
| 1.94 | 0.00 | 1.53 | 0.41 | 7.13 | 7.13 | 0.00 | 0.00 | 0.00 | 0.24 | 2.13 |
| 2.01 | 0.22 | 0.89 | 0.24 | 0.95 | 0.73 | 0.01 | 0.21 | 0.95 | 0.11 | 0.08 |
| 4.10 | 0.00 | 3.80 | 0.30 | 14.96 | 13.83 | 0.14 | 0.99 | 0.00 | 0.09 | 0.08 |
| 5.40 | 3.72 | 1.36 | 0.32 | 7.19 | 7.06 | 0.11 | 0.01 | 0.98 | 0.45 | 0.12 |
| 3.45 | 2.11 | 1.01 | 0.34 | 0.81 | 0.73 | 0.08 | 0.00 | 0.00 | 0.21 | 0.11 |
| 2.82 | 0.67 | 1.58 | 0.19 | 8.56 | 6.17 | 0.00 | 0.00 | 0.00 | 0.14 | 0.06 |
| 4.99 | 0.39 | 2.23 | 2.37 | 5.52 | 5.47 | 0.03 | 0.02 | 0.00 | 0.15 | 0.42 |
| 0.58 | 0.00 | 0.15 | 0.43 | 12.98 | 9.96 | 3.01 | 0.01 | 0.00 | 0.00 | 0.14 |
| 7.85 | 5.73 | 1.99 | 0.13 | 7.15 | 4.86 | 2.29 | 0.00 | 0.00 | 0.33 | 0.00 |
| 3.31 | 0.69 | 2.57 | 0.05 | 5.39 | 2.36 | 3.02 | 0.01 | 0.00 | 0.01 | 0.01 |
| 13.96 | 10.23 | 2.59 | 1.14 | 4.62 | 1.74 | 0.18 | 2.70 | 6.42 | 0.83 | 0.29 |
| 1.11 | 0.93 | 0.00 | 0.17 | 9.91 | 7.59 | 2.08 | 0.23 | 0.00 | 0.23 | 0.07 |
| 0.86 | 0.00 | 0.86 | 0.00 | 1.65 | 1.63 | 0.02 | 0.00 | 0.00 | 0.00 | 0.01 |
| 4.15 | 3.50 | 0.13 | 0.52 | 29.90 | 29.43 | 0.47 | 0.00 | 0.00 | 0.01 | 0.19 |
| 4.84 | 1.75 | 2.67 | 0.42 | 2.81 | 2.38 | 0.43 | 0.00 | 0.04 | 0.22 | 0.57 |
| 5.54 | 0.99 | 4.55 | 0.00 | 5.18 | 4.98 | 0.13 | 0.07 | 0.00 | 0.04 | 0.00 |
| 8.67 | 5.83 | 1.97 | 0.88 | 4.35 | 4.01 | 0.34 | 0.00 | 0.00 | 0.56 | 0.11 |
| 2.33 | 0.00 | 2.06 | 0.18 | 5.46 | 5.12 | 0.35 | 0.00 | 0.00 | 0.02 | 0.06 |
| 2.12 | 0.00 | 2.11 | 0.01 | 6.06 | 3.18 | 2.88 | 0.00 | 0.51 | 0.12 | 0.15 |
| 2.30 | 0.75 | 1.10 | 0.45 | 9.34 | 8.58 | 0.29 | 0.47 | 1.57 | 0.04 | 0.25 |
| 3.87 | 0.00 | 0.00 | 3.87 | 10.49 | 9.52 | 0.04 | 0.93 | 0.00 | 0.00 | 0.44 |
| 2.72 | 2.13 | 0.31 | 0.28 | 8.77 | 6.93 | 0.25 | 1.58 | 1.83 | 0.23 | 0.07 |
| 1.40 | 0.00 | 1.14 | 0.26 | 2.63 | 2.52 | 0.11 | 0.00 | 0.01 | 0.00 | 0.06 |
| 9.69 | 0.13 | 4.95 | 4.61 | 3.16 | 3.10 | 0.04 | 0.03 | 0.00 | 0.18 | 0.00 |
| 3.19 | 0.00 | 1.78 | 1.40 | 5.38 | 5.11 | 0.27 | 0.00 | 0.00 | 0.25 | 0.87 |
| 2.61 | 1.69 | 0.81 | 0.10 | 4.70 | 4.04 | 0.55 | 0.11 | 0.62 | 0.35 | 0.06 |
| 2.74 | 2.17 | 0.43 | 0.14 | 8.26 | 1.03 | 6.64 | 0.59 | 0.00 | 0.00 | 0.00 |
| 3.59 | 0.00 | 3.43 | 0.16 | 5.24 | 3.64 | 1.60 | 0.01 | 0.44 | 0.97 | 0.07 |
| 8.20 | 5.14 | 2.95 | 0.11 | 7.41 | 3.90 | 3.13 | 0.38 | 0.09 | 0.07 | 0.01 |
| 1.25 | 0.00 | 0.60 | 0.65 | 12.31 | 11.40 | 0.91 | 0.00 | 0.11 | 0.00 | 0.05 |
| 10.20 | 10.04 | 0.00 | 0.16 | 1.37 | 1.32 | 0.02 | 0.04 | 0.03 | 0.12 | 0.32 |
| 5.99 | 3.44 | 1.43 | 1.12 | 3.62 | 3.15 | 0.47 | 0.00 | 1.87 | 0.31 | 0.13 |
| 4.56 | 3.05 | 1.33 | 0.19 | 3.62 | 2.39 | 1.16 | 0.06 | 1.05 | 0.42 | 1.30 |
| 5.40 | 4.76 | 0.01 | 0.63 | 2.02 | 2.02 | 0.00 | 0.00 | 0.00 | 0.00 | 0.00 |
| 2.36 | 0.97 | 0.83 | 0.56 | 5.01 | 4.36 | 0.27 | 0.26 | 1.43 | 0.16 | 0.87 |
| 2.10 | 0.00 | 2.10 | 0.01 | 3.04 | 1.76 | 0.33 | 0.95 | 0.31 | 0.11 | 0.95 |

| | GDP per capita (1987 dollars) | Years | | Total taxes | Income taxes | | | |
|---|---|---|---|---|---|---|---|---|
| | | | | | Total | Indiv-idual | Corpo-rate | Other |
| Bangladesh[2] | 160 | 1983 | 1985 | 7.30 | 0.94 | 0.93 | 0.01 | 0.00 |
| Zaire | 160 | 1984 | 1986 | 22.98 | 7.67 | 3.88 | 3.78 | 0.00 |
| Malawi[2] | 160 | 1984 | 1986 | 18.02 | 7.43 | 2.57 | 4.86 | 0.00 |
| Nepal | 160 | 1983 | 1985 | 7.11 | 0.71 | 0.53 | 0.18 | 0.00 |
| Chad | 150 | 1984 | 1986 | 5.26 | 1.24 | 0.83 | 0.35 | 0.00 |
| Ethiopia[2] | 120 | 1979 | 1981 | 15.84 | 4.07 | 1.37 | 2.08 | 0.61 |

1. Year 1986.
2. General Government.

Source:  International Monetary Fund, *Government Finance Statistics Yearbook* XII, 1988; World Bank, *Atlas*, 1987.

*Table 14.2   Developing countries: tax revenue by type of tax and group of countries (per cent of GDP)*

| Per capital income (dollars) | | Total taxes | Total | Income taxes | | |
|---|---|---|---|---|---|---|
| Range | Average | | | Indiv-idual | Corpor-ate | Other |
| 0–349 | 234 | 13.04 | 3.08 | 1.25 | 1.77 | 0.23 |
| 350–849 | 549 | 17.96 | 5.27 | 2.33 | 2.83 | 0.23 |
| 850–1699 | 1171 | 17.49 | 6.00 | 2.56 | 3.73 | 0.26 |
| 1700 or more | 4502 | 18.02 | 7.25 | 3.27 | 4.85 | 1.05 |
| All countries | 1692 | 16.61 | 5.39 | 2.29 | 3.29 | 0.45 |

## Import duties and resource allocation

### Import duties for the protection of domestic production

Countries that have embarked on a course of industrialization through import substitution have often levied these taxes not just for revenue but also for the encouragement of the local production of particular products. The main theoretical rational for this policy is provided by the infant industry argument that maintains that a country might have a comparative advantage in particular industries once they are established and are allowed to reach a certain size. In other words, it is often assumed that an industry has to be in existence for a certain period of time and reach a certain size before it can produce at internationally competitive costs. In the meantime the government will, thus, have to help this industry.[11]

| Total | Domestic taxes on goods and services | | | Foreign trade | | | | Social secur-ity | Wealth and prop-erty | Other |
| | General sales, turn-over, VAT | Excises | Other | Total | Import duties | Export duties | Other | | | |
|---|---|---|---|---|---|---|---|---|---|---|
| 2.49 | 0.90 | 1.57 | 0.03 | 3.53 | 2.63 | 0.14 | 0.76 | 0.00 | 0.18 | 0.16 |
| 5.27 | 3.92 | 1.29 | 0.05 | 9.14 | 5.64 | 3.49 | 0.01 | 0.59 | 0.01 | 0.53 |
| 6.37 | 5.39 | 0.69 | 0.29 | 4.10 | 3.72 | 0.38 | 0.00 | 0.00 | 0.02 | 0.10 |
| 3.58 | 1.99 | 1.09 | 0.50 | 2.25 | 2.16 | 0.09 | 0.00 | 0.00 | 0.55 | 0.02 |
| 0.51 | 0.19 | 0.10 | 0.08 | 2.75 | 2.69 | 0.04 | 0.01 | 0.06 | 0.16 | 0.37 |
| 4.47 | 1.43 | 2.70 | 0.34 | 6.49 | 3.25 | 3.23 | 0.00 | 0.00 | 0.66 | 0.12 |

| Total | Domestic taxes on goods and services | | | Foreign trade | | | | Social secur-ity | Wealth and prop-erty | Other |
| | General sales, turn-over, VAT | Excises | Other | Total | Import duties | Export duties | Other | | | |
|---|---|---|---|---|---|---|---|---|---|---|
| 4.15 | 2.99 | 1.47 | 0.65 | 5.40 | 4.12 | 1.08 | 0.24 | 0.40 | 0.21 | 0.27 |
| 5.08 | 2.59 | 2.57 | 0.62 | 6.95 | 5.95 | 0.74 | 0.23 | 0.80 | 0.29 | 0.36 |
| 5.54 | 3.08 | 2.33 | 0.66 | 4.86 | 4.19 | 0.73 | 0.09 | 1.06 | 0.51 | 0.61 |
| 4.96 | 3.21 | 1.87 | 1.40 | 3.50 | 2.97 | 0.50 | 0.25 | 2.88 | 0.56 | 0.58 |
| 4.89 | 2.95 | 2.04 | 0.85 | 5.19 | 4.31 | 0.79 | 0.21 | 1.34 | 0.39 | 0.44 |

The help to the industry can come either in the form of outright budgetary subsidies, which would cover or at least reduce the difference between total costs and total revenues, or in the form of tariff protection against foreign competitors. This protection could be provided by a tax levied on those imported goods that compete with the goods produced by the industry that the government wishes to protect. Between these two alternatives governments have normally chosen protection. The reasons for this choice may be obvious: when tariffs are used there is no budgetary disbursement but, on the contrary, the government is likely to receive some revenue. Furthermore, the government can claim that it is pursuing national objectives while it collects additional revenues. If there are taxes that appear painless, here they are. Furthermore, those who actually bear the final burden of these taxes may not even be aware of them since they are legally collected from importers who will be able, most of the time, to shift these taxes on the consumers.

A very high tariff might give a high level of protection but not much revenue. This will happen if the price elasticity of demand for the product is high so that the tariff will excessively reduce imports. A low tariff, on the other hand, could do the opposite. Thus, the level of tariff that may maximize revenue might be either too high or too low with respect to the desired level of protection.[12] *Mutatis mutandis,* the level of tariff that is desired for protection may not be optimal for revenue. We thus find an example of an instrument attempting to achieve two not necessarily consistent objectives.

When protection is expanded from particular 'infant' industries to most of the industrial sector, as it has often been the case in developing countries, the countries are *de facto* abandoning the principle of comparative advantage in international trade, even with the amendment of the infant industry argument, and are pursuing more autarkic policies of import substitution. Through these policies they have hoped to become less dependent on the rest of the world and more immune to cyclical fluctuations; they have also hoped that the ensuing industrial growth will facilitate the modernization and development of their economies.

Through the pursuit of import substitution policies, the developing countries have thus tried to stimulate their industrial sector especially in connection with industrial goods which were not considered non-essential. But this sector needed capital goods and intermediate products which were available only from the industrialized countries. To facilitate the importation of these products the governments of many developing countries thought it desirable to maintain an overvalued exchange rate. This was done by deterring imports in general but especially by limiting as far as possible the importation of those final goods which were not considered necessities. These goods, normally called non-essential, or luxury, goods have been levied with much higher import duties aimed at discouraging their domestic production. Thus, at least in the intention of the policy-makers, import duties were used partly to encourage domestic production and partly to discourage domestic consumption of the taxed products.

In recent years it has become customary to discuss protection not in nominal but in effective terms. Balassa, Corden, Johnson and others developed and popularized the concept of effective protection. This concept is essentially based on the belief that we cannot get a full measure of protection by looking at nominal tariffs on commodities but we need to look at tariffs on processes and on industries.[13] Only when we consider effective protection (or the effective protective tariff rate) are we able to get a full idea of the resource-allocation effect of a tariff structure. The fact is that in a market economy resources are allocated by enterprises and these enterprises in most cases do not produce the full value contained in a product but use inputs that they buy from other enterprises or import from abroad.

The nominal tariff on the import of automobiles, for example, may tell us little about the degree of protection afforded to the automobile industry if that industry adds only, say, 20 per cent of the final value of the cars and buys the remaining 80 per cent from foreign suppliers. If these inputs can be imported duty free while an assembled car has to pay a 10 per cent nominal tariff, then the effective protection for the resources invested in the car industry will not be 10 but 50 per cent.[14] This means that the value added generated by the local automobile industry (and thus its cost of production) can exceed by 50 per cent the value added at world prices. On the other hand, a concentration on nominal protection would indicate that the price of a locally produced car could exceed by only 10 per cent the world price. Given the value added per unit of output, the rate of effective protection is thus positively related to the nominal tariff on the product but it decreases with the increase in the nominal tariff on inputs.[15]

From empirical evidence based on the concept of effective protection for several developing countries, the following conclusions can be drawn:

1. As in most of these countries the restrictions imposed on the importation of intermediate inputs are generally lower than those imposed on final goods, the protection given to domestic value added in the production process is almost always greater than that granted to final goods.
2. There are substantial variations in the degree of protection afforded to various sectors.
3. Furthermore, there are a few activities for which effective protection is actually negative. This implies that the tariff structure is such that a net tax is imposed on some domestic activities.
4. This negative effective protection is generally associated with agricultural and mineral-producing sectors but it is also found in connection with particular manufacturing sectors.

*Import duties to discourage imports of non-essential goods*
The high nominal import duties levied on 'non-essential' or 'luxury' goods have often been justified in terms of equity or ability to pay of tax-payers as these goods, especially at the initial stages of economic development, and especially in those countries where per capita incomes are low and unevenly distributed, are consumed mainly by those with relatively high incomes.

Import taxes levied for equity reasons may be useful when a country is at a very early stage of economic development and when its production is mostly limited to agricultural products, mining and non-traded goods such as construction and services. Under these circumstances, and in view of the inevitable limitation in the administrative capability of the country's tax collectors, the taxation of imports will be a useful and relatively easy way to raise needed revenues without unduly distorting the allocation of domestic resources. At this level of economic development the country is not able to produce or even to assemble locally the more technologically advanced imported products; consequently, no reallocation of resources is likely to be induced by these taxes.[16]

Eventually, however, the country will reach a level of economic development and a degree of technological sophistication (aided often by foreign interests) when some of the manufactured products that were hereto imported can be locally produced or at least assembled. At this later stage taxes on imports are normally levied not only to provide revenues but also to protect specific domestic industries against foreign competition especially during the period of infancy. It is at this stage that the issues concerning the allocation of resources become particularly significant since some of the protection provided by the duties will be wanted but some will not be.

An import duty on a given commodity is equivalent to an *ad valorem* tax on the local consumption of that commodity together with an equal *ad valorem,* subsidy to the local production of that commodity. It follows that the higher is the import duty, the higher will be the tax on consumption but also the higher will be the implicit subsidy to the local production of that commodity. When we look at tariffs from this perspective, we can easily realize that import duties, from a theoretical point of view, are inferior instruments for pursuing a policy of domestic intervention.[17] In fact even if, for example, a strong case should exist for assisting the initial development of a new domestic industry, this case might justify a subsidy to the production of that industry or even a subsidy combined with a tax on local consumption. It would, however, be a rare coincidence that the desired policy would be one justifying an *ad valorem* subsidy to production combined with an equal *ad valorem* tax on consumption. But this is exactly the result of the imposition of an import duty.

*Mutatis mutandis* it is unlikely that in trying to discourage the import of a given non-essential commodity the government would ever wish to give an equal *ad valorem* subsidy to the local production of that commodity. But this is again exactly what happens through the use of import duties. As for equity reasons, the governments of the developing countries have often imposed high import duties on luxury and other 'non-essential goods', the net result has been the granting of a high (implicit) subsidy to the local production of these goods. Thus, while the importation of these goods has been discouraged, their local production has been encouraged. Consequently, the allocation of resources has been biased toward those non-essential goods. The more advanced a country becomes the more sensitive will its resource allocation be to these stimuli. Foreign investment, together with the technology introduced by multinational corporations, can and often does accelerate these trends.

**Revenue aspects**

The above discussion has been outlined in terms of allocation of resources. However, it has also revenue implications. As already stated, 'non-essential' products generally carry much higher import duties than those classified as 'essential' and which include capital goods and intermediate products including raw materials. Under these circumstances, several developments are likely to take place whenever the final products are levied with high nominal tariffs. First and immediately, there will be some shift in the composition of imports away from those products with higher duties: more imports of the so-called essential product can be expected. This shift will inevitably be accompanied by deadweight losses which will represent a net cost to the economy. Since the demand curves for specific products are likely to be more elastic over the long run – since tastes have time to adjust – this shift will become progressively stronger as time passes. Second, there will be increasing pressures from various groups for exemptions especially for intermediate products from these duties for particular circumstances which, if successful, will have allocative as well as equity implications. Third, as the domestic industry begins to produce these products under the stimulus of the protection provided by the high duties, revenues from import duties will fall further. If, in response to these developments, the rates on the commodities subject to duties are increased to compensate for the revenue losses, more smuggling is likely to take place.

These developments are not unrelated among themselves. The more successful is the first – that is, the more the composition of imports changes – the weaker will be the pressures for exemption for particular circumstances. Equally, and perhaps more importantly, the more successful are the pressures for exemptions, the greater will be the resentment on the part of those who are not so favoured and, thus, their willingness to buy the products from smugglers or to carry on some of this activity themselves. Of course, the accompanying increases in the rates of import duties will themselves provide a strong incentive to smuggling.[18] This is a situation not too different from that which develops with income taxes when evasion is easy and goes unpunished. Evasion leads to higher nominal rates and the increase in these rates is seen by many tax-payers as a tax on honesty. Thus, citizens who under normal circumstances would not have evaded their taxes may come to feel that they have a right to do so, which of course leads to further increases in the nominal rates.[19]

These developments will bring about losses in revenue – which can be substantial in view of the relative importance of import duties – unless the governments take some corrective steps. It is imperative that at this stage internal commodity taxation be introduced to replace import taxation so that if a country wants to discriminate against the consumption of non-essential products, it can do so regardless of whether these products are locally produced or are imported.

In this way the country may also succeed in maintaining its total tax revenues and not see them eroded by the reallocation of resources.

The natural progression from import duties to internal commodity taxation is now part of a 'conventional wisdom'. The progression shows what has happened historically. However, it is far better, if possible, to apply the internal commodity taxes before the reallocation of resources takes place in order to prevent the distortions discussed above.

### Administrative aspects[20]

A few words should now be added about the administration of these taxes. It is often argued that these taxes are easy to administer and that this is the reason for their popularity in developing countries. If by 'easy to administer' it is meant 'easy to raise substantial revenue', there cannot be any issue with that argument. If, however, it is meant that these taxes can be administered fairly, then there *is* an issue.

The major difficulties customs administrators are faced with are in the areas of accounting for imports (establishing effective control over import shipments), duty assessment, and combating smuggling.

### *Accounting*

Establishing effective control over incoming goods, until they are given an authorized destination (such as home consumption, transit, warehousing, temporary admission and temporary deposit), often proves difficult. The main difficulties are:

1.  The large volume of cargo arriving in ports and airports which are ill-equipped to handle them. Insufficient unloading and storage facilities do not allow for adequate surveillance. Thus, they make substitution and theft easy and often result in loss of shipments.
2.  Controlling and keeping track of goods released under suspensive systems (temporary importations, transit, bonded warehouse and deposits). The documentary control schemes are usually in place but are ineffective due to lack of training, negligence in following up on shipments that have left customs, poor discipline, lack of supervision and internal auditing. Goods may thus enter the domestic market without paying customs duties.
3.  Containerization, which largely complicates customs control. The effective clearance of containers, that is clearance systems minimizing the risk to revenue while at the same time allowing for rapid delivery of goods to their destination, requires special arrangements which developing countries have often been slow in making. Without such arrangements (special examination bays and/or container stations, unloading and checking at the importer's premises, mobile verification units) a substantial share of imports may go unchecked, incorrect declarations may be accepted and revenue may be lost.

*Duty assessment*

As regards duty assessment, its major elements are the determination of the applicable duty rate (tariff classification), the value (valuation) and in case discriminatory or preferential tariffs apply, the origin. All three represent difficulties, especially in developing countries where qualified personnel are scarce.

*Tariff classification.* Tariffs in most countries are specialized and duty rates may differ widely within the same category or class of goods depending on such things as their composition (which materials and in which proportions?), degree of processing or assembly capacity (machinery, instruments), power source, use. Most countries, including the majority of developing countries, use international classification systems, in particular the Customs Cooperation Council Nomenclature (CCCN) and now increasingly the Harmonized System (HS). These nomenclatures are extensive and exhaustive and the rules for classification are complicated. The classification of the great variety of manufactured imports in the tariff schedule is often a difficult matter, requiring well-trained verifiers or import specialists, professionals well trained in goods technology and classification rules. In the absence of specially trained customs officers, importers and brokers can take advantage of the situation and have their goods classified under more favourable tariff headings and thus not pay the full duty.

*Valuation.* While valuation is a difficult matter in general, in customs it is a problem in virtually every single importation. Checking whether the declared value of a shipment complies with the country's customs value standard and making the necessary adjustments is usually a difficult task. Valuation systems are usually based on internationally accepted codes based on the GATT principles of non-arbitrariness and fairness and the use of actual commercial facts in determining the value. The application of acceptable valuation practices, while at the same time protecting the interest of the Treasury, is especially difficult in developing countries. These countries are short of qualified officers and are limited in their ability to obtain price information. Furthermore, there are strong incentives for importers to declare low values, in view of the generally high tariffs and prevailing import restrictions.

Transfer price practices have further complicated the work of customs valuators. The use of specific duties instead of *ad valorem* duties or the use of administrative values (minimum values) would be adequate means to avoid the problems of valuation and protect revenue. Such methods, however, have to be discarded on tax policy grounds and/or because they are inconsistent with GATT principles regarding free trade. There is no easy solution to the difficult problem of valuation and especially in developing countries it will remain one of the most difficult aspects of duty assessment as long as tariffs are high and administrations weak.

*Origin.* Determination and verification of origin can be a complicated administrative task, principally because the sources of information lie in other countries.

In addition, with respect to duty assessment, it is important to keep in mind that customs duties and taxes are paid on a transaction basis (as opposed to periodical income and sales taxes). The large number of import transactions and the urgency quickly to nationalize the goods puts a heavy pressure on the administration (as opposed to the open-ended review of periodic tax returns) and adds a degree of difficulty to the administration of import taxes.

## Smuggling

As regards smuggling, a distinction needs to be made between outright smuggling (illegal border crossing of goods) and technical smuggling (documentary fraud).

The problem of outright smuggling may be more or less severe depending on the height of the tariff, the restrictiveness of the import regime, the geography of the country and other factors. Smuggling is generally difficult to combat since borders cannot be controlled permanently over their full length. Modern means of transportation (containers) and the high volume of shipments in international trade make smuggling more difficult to detect. The number of shipments that can be physically examined is becoming an increasingly small portion of total shipments. The organization of an effective and reliable border surveillance system and selective container checking systems, giving a reasonable deterrent against contraband and fraud, is difficult to achieve, especially in developing countries. Low pay and poor working conditions, moreover, may result in lax and easily corruptible officials. Furthermore, often governments do not take sufficiently forceful action against smuggling even when contraband goods abound in their market.

Technical smuggling is practised mainly through misrepresenting the value or the description of the goods. With respect to value it may occur in many different forms, such as the non-inclusion in the declared value of certain dutiable charges (such as the full transportation cost, buying or other commissions, payments to third parties, compensation deals); deduction of higher discounts than actually obtained; incorrect declaration of payment terms; non-declaration of relationship (related companies); and misrepresentation of the quality of the merchandise. Fake invoices sometimes are made out by the seller's representative in the importing country or by the buyer himself using forms carrying the heading of the exporting firm and the falsity usually is difficult to prove.

With respect to the description of the merchandise, making use of the intricacies of the tariff classification system, the lack of knowledge or inquisitiveness of customs officials or the absence of adequate means for customs to examine and analyse the goods, the importer may misrepresent their technological characteristics, composition, use and so on, and classify them in incorrect tariff headings to lower his duty liability. Without well-trained and honest verifiers and appropriate means to ascertain the real nature and characteristics of the goods, many developing countries are prone to this kind of technical fraud.

In most countries technical smuggling is more important as a revenue leakage than outright smuggling. It is less risky than outright smuggling as the importer can usually claim ignorance when it is discovered. Moreover when the administration is lax in applying penalties, there may be virtually no risk at all.

In conclusion, foreign trade taxes are an easy means to raise revenue. Their administration, however, is fraught with more difficulties than is generally realized. Effective administration of foreign trade taxes hinges on sound basic control systems and well-trained officials. When these conditions are not fulfilled, the effective administration of forcign taxes will be difficult to achieve.

## Notes

1. Most public finance textbooks completely ignore these taxes while they dedicate a lot of space to taxes that are of marginal importance in an international context. International trade specialists have paid more attention to these taxes.
2. Richard Musgrave, *Fiscal Systems*, New Haven, Yale University Press, 1969.
3. One must distinguish between facility of collection and facility of administration. As it will be discussed below (pp. 220–25), the fair administration of these taxcs is not as easy as is generally supposed.
4. Jonathan Levin, 'Effects of economic development on the base of a sales tax: a case study of Colombia', *IMF Staff Papers*, March 1968.
5. Stephen R. Lewis, 'Revenue implications of changing industrial structure', *National Tax Journal*, December 1967.
6. Harley H. Hinrichs, *A General Theory of Tax Structure Change During Economic Development*, Cambridge, Harvard Law School, 1966.
7. Richard A. Musgrave, *Fiscal Systems*, New Haven, Yale University Press, 1969.
8. Stephen R. Lewis, Jr, 'Government revenue from foreign trade: an international comparison', *Manchester School of Economic and Social Studies* XXXI, January 1963.
9. John F. Due, *Indirect Taxation in Developing Economies*, Baltimore, Johns Hopkins University Press, 1970.
10. For a detailed analysis of these trends, see Tanzi 'Quantitative characteristics of the tax systems of developing countries' in David Newbery and Nicholas Stern (eds), *The Theory of Taxation for Developing Countries*, Oxford University Press, 1987:205–41.
11. US economic history has often been taken as a proof of the validity of this argument. A very good discussion of the infant industry argument and of the other conditions that may justify a departure from a policy of free trade can be found in I. Little, T. Scitovsky, and M. Scott, *Industry and Trade in Some Developing Countries*, Oxford, Oxford University Press, 1970, Chap. 4. Robert E. Baldwin has convincingly argued that the case for infant industry protection has been oversold since four principal infant industry cases are invalid. See his 'The case against infant industry tariff protection', *Journal of Political Economy* 77, 3, May/June 1969. Thus, Baldwin shows that the above-mentioned theoretical justification is valid for very few cases. However, his argument rests on the implicit assumption that a well-working capital market is in existence.

12.    This tariff would be such as to bring about an internal price for the imported product at which the price elasticity of demand is one. This would be the optimal tariff from the revenue point of view as long as it does not stimulate internal production.

13.    Bela Balassa, 'Tariff protection in industrial countries', *Journal of Political Economy* December 1965; W.M. Corden, 'The structure of a tariff system and the effective protective rate', *Journal of Political Economy*, June 1966; H.G. Johnson, 'The theory of tariff structure with special reference to world trade and development', *Trade and Development*, Institut Universitaire des Hautes Etudes Internationales, 1965. Corden refers to the paper by C.L. Barber, 'Canadian tariff policy', *Canadian Journal of Economics and Political Science* 21, 1955, as the pioneering contribution to the subject. The concept though not the terminology was also clearly used in United Nations, *World Economic Survey*, 1963, New York, United Nations, 1964:186, especially note 16.

14.    There are alternative ways of measuring the effective protective tariff rate. In the example above the rate of effective protection is calculated by subtracting from the tariff rate on the product (that is, the 10 per cent import duty on automobiles), the average tariff rate on inputs (which was zero in the example), and by dividing this by the value added per unit of output (that is, 20 per cent). See H. Robert Heller, *International Trade, Theory and Empirical Evidence*, Englewood Cliffs, NJ, Prentice-Hall, Inc., 1968:154-5; for a more complex method that adjusts for the overvaluation of the exchange rate, see Corden's article cited above (n. 13). For a review, see Little, Scitovsky, and Scott, op. cit., pp.169–74.

15.    From the above discussion it follows that it is effective and not nominal protection that determines the allocation of resources; however, it is nominal rather than effective protection that determines the allocation of consumer expenditure.

16.    Also the differences between effective and nominal protection are likely to be much less great since products are either totally locally produced (that is, no imported inputs) or are totally imported.

17.    There is a growing literature that deals with the theory of optimal intervention and optimum subsidy. In particular, see Jagdish Bhagwati and V.K. Ramaswami, 'Domestic distortions, tariffs and the theory of optimum subsidy' in Robert E. Baldwin *et al.*, *Trade, Growth and the Balance of Payments*, Chicago, Rand-McNally and Company, 1965:3-34; Robert A. Mundell, 'El papel de los impuestos a la exportación y importación en la economia del Peru' in OAS–IDB, Programa Conjunto de Tributación, *Estudio Fiscal del Peru*, Washington, OAS, 1969, prepared under the direction of Milton C. Taylor. For a critical comment on this literature, see Donald B. Keesing, 'Public finance considerations in tariff theory for developing countries', *Public Finance* XXIX, 2, 1974.

18.    The economic consequences of smuggling have been extensively analysed in a book edited by Jagdish N. Bhagwati. See *Illegal Transactions in International Trade, Theory and Measurement*, Amsterdam, North-Holland Publishing Company, 1974.

19.    For an example of the erosion of revenues connected with the changes discussed above, see Stephen R. Lewis, 'Revenue implications of changing industrial structures: an empirical study', *National Tax Journal* XX, 4, December 1967.

20.    I wish to thank Adrien Goorman for assistance with this section.

# 15  Export taxes in developing countries

## Introduction

Export taxes are not such important revenue sources as import duties. They generate about 5 per cent of total taxes and less than 1 per cent of GDP for all developing countries combined (see Tables 14.1 and 14.2). Still they raise considerable revenue in several developing countries. These taxes are generally levied on the exports of particular products – and especially of agricultural crops, such as grain, coffee, bananas, rice, cocoa. At times, however, they have been imposed on all exports especially when a large devaluation presumably led to excessive temporary profits for exporters or when there were stringent revenue needs.

The potential of export taxes for causing serious misallocation of resources is considerable even when the rate of the tax is relatively low. It is often ignored that since export taxes are applied to the gross value of the exported product, they are likely to represent a much higher share of the net added value contributed by the export sector. Unless one has a clear knowledge of the relationship between net value added and total (gross) value of output, the effective rate is generally higher and sometimes much higher than the nominal rate. The higher is the share of inputs in the value of the exported product, the higher is the effective tax rate. Furthermore, this effective export tax rate is increased even more when, as is often the case, the exporters have to cede the foreign exchange earned to the government at the official and overvalued exchange rate.

In this chapter the reasons advanced by various countries to justify the imposition of export taxes are first outlined. Then the distortions that are likely to be generated by these taxes are analysed. The chapter concludes with a case study of the taxation of coffee exports in Haiti.

## Reasons for the imposition of export taxes

Regardless of the numerous official pronouncements for levying export taxes, the main reason must probably be found in what one might call the cynical law of taxation. Simply stated, this law says that governments will follow the path of least resistance and will levy those taxes which politically as well as administratively are easiest to impose and collect. Exports are generally channelled through few points; have often a weight that in relation to their value is high so that there is some discouragement to smuggling; involve few and, in the case of agricultural products, homogeneous commodities; and have a value that is generally, though not always, known to customs officials. Because of these reasons, it is generally assumed that these taxes are even easier to collect than taxes on imports. Thus, Musgrave's 'tax handle' approach provides part of the 'non-official' reason for the imposition of these taxes.

The governments of the developing countries that have imposed these taxes have at times advanced various reasons for doing so.

1.  Several countries have put taxes on the export of particular commodities (such as rice, sugar, meat) with the declared intention of keeping down the internal prices of those products (for example, rice in Thailand and meat in Uruguay and Argentina). This was done with products that are important in the consumption basket of the industrial workers or of the lower-income classes; thus, the ultimate official justification for taxing the exports of the particular products has been the promotion of industrialization or of income redistribution in favour of urban workers.

2.  Other countries have taxed the exports of particular agricultural commodities (such as cocoa, coffee, wool) or raw materials in order to stimulate the local production and/or export of more elaborate products which use these commodities as inputs.[1] Thus, a country may tax the export of cocoa but not that of candies or chocolates (for example, Ecuador) or that of coffee beans but not that of instant coffee (for example, Brazil).

3.  Some countries have used differentiated export taxes to induce producers to produce better crops whenever several qualities or grades of the same product can be produced (for example, Arabica, Robusta and so on). In these cases lower quality exports are taxed more heavily than higher quality.[2] In other cases differentiated export taxes have been used to stimulate exports from less-developed regions (such as exports of bananas in Ecuador).

4.  Some countries have imposed export taxes on a sliding scale with the objective of stabilizing exporters' earnings and supposedly national income (for example, Burundi with coffee). In these cases there is generally a basic price, which is supposed to provide the producers with a basic income, at which no tax is levied. Above that price, the difference between the export price and the basic price is levied at progressively larger rates so that, given the export volume, the net-of-tax earnings of the exporters is expected to fluctuate by less than the prices.

5.  In some countries export taxes are earmarked totally or partially for specific purposes. For example, coffee-producing countries have Coffee Institutes that are supposed to promote the interests of the coffee industry (for example, Colombia). These institutes are financed by export taxes on coffee.

6.  Finally, the governments of several countries have considered the export taxes as substitutes for land or income taxes. In some cases, the taxes on

exports are final taxes; in others (such as export of fishmeal, sugar and wool in Peru) the export taxes have been considered advance payments for income taxes.

In addition to the above-mentioned 'official' reasons for the imposition of export taxes, we shall outline briefly two non-official uses for export taxes. A full discussion of them is not possible here because of their complexity and also because we would be straying too far from fiscal policy which is our major concern.

The literature on developing countries has often emphasized the difficulties encountered by these countries in exporting manufactured produce. It is often maintained that one of the major obstacles to the exports of these products is the existing rate of exchange; this rate is largely determined by the countries' comparative advantage in the production of raw material and traditional non-manufactured products and is assumed to be much too high to make possible the export of manufactured products. It has then been argued that these exports can be stimulated either through the use of export incentives or through what has been called compensated devaluation. Two alternative forms of such devaluation were proposed some years ago by Daniel M. Schydlowsky and by the General Secretariat of the Organization of American States (OAS). For Schydlowsky

> compensated devaluation consists of a simultaneous and offsetting adjustment of the financial exchange rate and the trade restrictions such that all the commodity exchange rates for imports and traditional exports stay unchanged. The only net change takes place in the financial rate and in the nontraditional export rate.[3]

Thus, he does not seem to contemplate the use of export taxes. An alternative form of compensated devaluation which does specifically rely on export taxes was made in one of the papers prepared by the OAS General Secretariat for the III Inter-American Conference on Taxation held in Mexico City.[4] That paper suggested that the developing countries could devalue their exchange rates enough to make the products of their manufacturing sector competitive in world markets. This devaluation, however, would give windfall profits (measured in local currencies) to the exporters of traditional products who would receive more units of local currency for each unit of foreign exchange. It was consequently suggested that export taxes could be imposed on the latter on a sliding scale to eliminate or reduce these excessive profits. It was also suggested that these export taxes could be differentiated among the traditional export sectors to equalize the gains among them.[5]

The other justification for export taxes relates to the export of commodities (such as oil, tin, copper) which by their own nature are exhaustible. Thus, one may justify taxes on the export of minerals on the ground that the financial cost of production would not include the cost to the country associated with the depletion of that non-replaceable resource. Obviously, this is an argument for the payment of royalties related to production rather than to export of the commodity. But if the commodity is mostly exported, export taxes can be used as substitutes for royalties.

### Incidence and economic effects of export taxes
#### Who bears the export taxes?

Export taxes are collected from the exporters as long as the trading of the exported commodity is not carried out by a marketing board which monopolizes the export of the particular commodity. The exporters may be either independent dealers or the producers themselves. This distinction becomes important when one wants to analyse the true (as distinguished from the legal) incidence of the export tax.[6] In other words, who bears the tax? Or better, whose real income is decreased by the levying of an export tax? There are several alternative possibilities:

1. The tax might, first of all and at least in the short run, be completely or partly shifted on foreign consumers. This will normally require either that the country has a monopoly over the production of the particular product or that its production is a very large proportion of the world output and that the price-elasticity of supply on the part of other producers is not high.[7] In this particular case the increase in the world price that accompanies the imposition of the tax will not stimulate the production of the same product (or close substitutes) in other countries. In cases in which close substitutes exist, the price elasticity of demand for the product will be high so that no or very little shifting will be possible.

   It should be realized that to the extent that a country succeeds in shifting the export tax on foreign consumers, the increase in the world price of the product will sooner or later encourage new producers to enter that particular industry or line of activity so that in the long run the price elasticity of the supply will increase. As an example, the heavy taxation of coffee exports for past years on the part of the world's largest and probably most efficient producer of coffee (Brazil) stimulated production elsewhere so that the share of world exports accounted for by Brazil shrank.[8]

   In most cases the 'small-country hypothesis' can safely be accepted. This hypothesis postulates that 'the country in question is not sufficiently big to have any important degree of influence over the world market prices.[9] Whenever this hypothesis holds, 'countries that are considering export duties should regard them primarily as taxes on their own producers and traders rather than as a means of taxing foreigners'.[10] Of course if many small countries can organize an efficient cartel, complete shifting might be possible in the short run. An example of this was provided by the oil cartel of the OPEC countries.

2.  As a second possibility, the tax might be borne by the producers. This will depend on different factors. First, it will depend on the strength of the bargaining positions of the groups within the country. If producers are many (while the exporters are few), if they own and work the land themselves,[11] if the particular output requires the use of highly specialized resources which, in the short or medium run, cannot easily be shifted to other lines of activities or other crops (as it is the case with trees), and if the yield of the next best use is relatively low, then it can be safely concluded that the producers will bear the burden of the tax. As will be shown below (pp. 233–9), this is the situation which most likely has prevailed in the coffee sector in Haiti.

3.  As a third possibility, one can assume that the exporters are also the owners of the specialized factors of production required to produce the particular exportable commodities. In this case they may hire local labour. If this labour is highly specialized and immobile and if the wage rate is above the subsistence wage, some shifting backward might be possible in the form of lower wages. This, of course, requires that the workers are not organized and that social legislation (minimum wage) does not prevent the shifting from happening.

The preceding discussion makes clear that, in general, the answer to the question of who bears the burden of the export tax is not a simple one since it depends on the particular situation. However, it may be worthwhile to emphasize that as long as the tax is not fully shifted to foreign buyers, there will be serious internal distortions caused by it. These are discussed below.

*Economic effect of export taxes*
In the discussion that follows the small-country hypothesis is accepted; thus, no shifting of the tax on to foreign consumers is assumed. The world price is given to the country. This assumption, which obviously is not always valid, facilitates the analysis of distortions associated with the imposition of an export tax on a particular product.

To understand clearly the economic effects of an export tax on a given product, we shall assume, first, that the product is completely exported and that, even at a lower price, there would not be any domestic demand forthcoming. This might, for example, be the case with uranium produced by a small agricultural country. This situation would also be approximated with respect to several mineral or even agricultural products when the actual *and potential* share of total production which is domestically consumed is so small as to be insignificant (for example, tin in Bolivia or copper in Zambia). Next, we shall relax this assumption and assume that the domestically consumed share of total production is not insignificant. We shall see that, in this second alternative, the potential of export taxes for creating distortions and welfare losses is far greater.

If the product is totally exported and if there is no potential domestic demand forthcoming at lower prices, the export tax is equivalent to a production tax so that its effects are identical to the latter's. The tax will reduce the net price that the exporters receive and if they are also the producers or if they shift the tax to the producers, the returns to the factors of production in the export activity will be reduced. If these factors have alternative uses, as they often do, and if these alternative activities are not taxed, or are taxed at lower rates, it is likely that at the margin there will be some shifting of resources away from the export sector toward other sectors.[12] Only if the resources are so specialized that they cannot be used elsewhere (that is if the elasticity of supply is zero), will the sector not be affected. The main point, however, is that in this situation an export tax will have no costs, or no distortions, that do not exist also with a production tax.[13]

Let us now assume that the product is also consumed within the country. This is the case when an export tax has really the potential for creating distortions which go far beyond those which exist with production taxes. Obviously, some of these distortions may be intentional if not in their magnitude at least in their direction. In theory, a tax on the export of a product is equivalent to two different components. One is an equal *ad valorem* tax imposed on the production of the product, the other is an equivalent *ad valorem* subsidy to the local consumption of that product.[14] Consequently, the higher is the export tax, the higher is the implicit production tax and the implicit subsidy to the local consumption of the product. The result of this is that while production is discouraged by the implicit tax, the local consumption of that product is encouraged by the implicit subsidy.[15]

The actual reaction of domestic consumption and production to these effects depends on the elasticities of the domestic demand and supply schedules. If domestic demand for the product is highly elastic, the diversion of production towards local consumption might be substantial so that exports might be significantly affected. On the other hand, if this elasticity is very low or zero, there would be little or no diversion. Equally, if the factors of production which are used are highly specialized, the effect on production may be small. Over the longer run, both of these effects (that is, on consumption and production) are likely to be more important.

The problem is essentially that the implicit subsidy to local consumption is always equal, *ad valorem,* to the production tax. Therefore, only under the particular circumstances when the government wants to subsidize the internal consumption of the exportable product at a rate exactly equivalent to the implicit product tax, will an export tax be a theoretically efficient instrument *vis-à-vis* the stated objective. If, however, the government wants to subsidize consumption by more than it taxes production (as, for example, for basic necessities), or if it wants to subsidize it by less than it taxes production (as with non-necessities or luxury products), the taxes on exports are not efficient instruments.

Their efficiency, however, can be increased if export taxes are integrated with excise taxes. Thus, for example, if a basic necessity (say, rice) was already levied with an excise tax, then a reduction in this tax combined with the imposition of the export tax would have the net effect of subsidizing local consumption by more than it taxes production.[16] And, if an export tax is combined with an excise tax on a luxury product, the net effect would be a subsidy to local consumption which is less than the tax on production. Thus, the combination of export taxes and excise taxes would allow a country to pursue objectives which could not be achieved by the use of either alone.

Finally, the removal of an export tax, which has been in existence for some time, will have effects opposite to those discussed above. In other words, such a removal would amount to an equivalent *ad valorem* subsidy to production, coupled with an equivalent *ad valorem* tax on consumption. These effects, of course, are in relation to the *status quo ante* rather than in relation to a situation where no tax existed.

The analytical framework discussed above can be used to speculate about the equity and employment aspects of export taxes. The issue of equity, in a partial equilibrium framework, essentially boils down to who pays the tax and who gets the (implicit) subsidy in the form of a reduced price for the local usage of the product. Obviously, if the producers are large landowners (beef producers in Uruguay?) while the users belong to lower income groups, the redistributional impact of the tax will be in (what is for most observers) the right direction.[17] On the other hand, if the producers are very poor (as is the case with coffee producers in Haiti) while the users are either the whole population or the wealthier sectors, the tax may be considered inequitable.

Often, as mentioned above, export taxes have been used specifically to lower the domestic price of the product in order to either subsidize the consumption of industrial workers (beef in Uruguay, rice in Thailand) or to reduce the input cost for industrial activities (instant coffee in Brazil). To the extent that, as it is often believed, the industrial sector is less labour intensive than the agricultural sector, the net effect of discouraging agricultural production and of encouraging industrial production is likely to be negative as far as employment is concerned. But, of course, in concrete experiences, the net effect will depend on the labour intensity of the specific crop that is taxed and on that of the specific industrial sector that is being stimulated.

## A case study: coffee production and taxation in Haiti[18]
Coffee plays a very important role in the economy of Haiti. As a source of foreign exchange, its importance is overwhelming, generating between one third and one half of total export earnings. Coffee is also very important as a source of

livelihood for a large proportion of the population. In 1968, for example, at least 374,000 people out of a population of about four million, were reported to be involved directly in the production of coffee; about 16 per cent of the total area under cultivation was used for the production of this crop. For these reasons, what happens to this sector has a very significant effect on the economy.

A United Nations mission that went to Haiti in 1949, in its discussions of the taxation of coffee, wrote that:

> The...tax on coffee exports...should be reconsidered with a view to its early repeal, as it unduly burdens the coffee production...There is need, in fact, for a reform of the whole coffee export-tax structure. Until other revenue sources have been developed in sufficient degree to allow doing away with it entirely, a single and gradually lowered tax – flat or progressive – should be substituted for the three or four separate export taxes now encumbering the coffee production.[19]

Over the next quarter of a century, the taxes on coffee exports were not repealed but, on the contrary, became progressively heavier. The number of separate export taxes increased to at least nine for each type of coffee. As one would expect from the theoretical discussion, production and exports suffered. Exports started showing a rather accentuated downward trend and 1963 was the last year in which the export quota allotted to Haiti was filled. From that year to 1972, the total combined shortfall of exports in relation to the final adjusted quota was 777,565 60-kilo bags.[20] This represents a total loss of foreign exchange of around US$38 million. This figure is of the same order of magnitude as the total taxes collected from coffee over the same period of time. Thus, if one should make the assumption, or reach the conclusion that the heavy taxation of coffee was the main cause of this shortfall, one could state that, *gross modo,* there was about one dollar of foreign exchange lost for each dollar of tax collected. This is, indeed, a heavy price to pay for a country in great need of foreign exchange.

Obviously, this calculation should not be taken too literally since other factors besides taxes may have affected production. There were, for example, some destructive hurricanes over the period which took their toll of coffee output.[21] But hurricanes were not exactly a novelty to the area. Therefore, we shall hold to the hypothesis that taxation was, over the longer run, probably the most important factor.

In 1973 a 60-kilo bag of unwashed Arabica was subjected to a total tax of 87.07 gourdes (or US$17.4); a bag of washed Arabica was levied at the somewhat lower but still high total tax of 68.32 gourdes (US$13.7) and a bag of 'brokens' was levied at 88.32 gourdes (or US$17.7). These taxes were about a third of the export price of coffee.[22]

The differential tax rates by quality of coffee were originally applied with the objective of discouraging the production of low-grade coffee (unwashed and 'brokens') in favour of high quality (washed) exports. Such a discriminating treatment was already in existence at the time of the United Nations mission to Haiti quoted above but it has not had the desired effect and no significant shifts have occurred toward higher grades of coffee. Unwashed Arabica continued to account for about 90 per cent of total coffee exports.

Taxes of this magnitude on the export of a product cannot fail to have important economic repercussions. Some of these effects exist in connection with any export tax; others are associated with the particular circumstances which surround the production and marketings of coffee in Haiti. In this context, the issue of who bears the tax – that is, the issue of the incidence of this tax – is of paramount importance.

The first question to ask is whether the incidence is on the domestic economy or whether the tax is exported by being shifted forward to the foreign consumers. Obviously, in this case this question is easy to answer since Haiti's share in the world's production and export is relatively minute. There is no doubt that the burden of the tax falls on the domestic economy. The second and more interesting question then is whether the producers or the merchant–exporters are the ones who actually bear the taxes on coffee. This question requires a brief digression on the 'industrial organization' of this sector.

Typically, the Haitian producers of coffee sell their products to middlemen–buyers called *speculateurs* who in turn make the coffee available to the exporters. Given the fact that coffee is, at least within each grade, a fairly homogeneous product, if these three groups were all large in number, one could argue that they all would share in bearing the coffee taxes.[23] In reality, the situation approaches very much the model of an oligopsony in the textbooks on price theory: the power is all on one side. According to the Haitian Institute for the Promotion of Coffee, there are in fact only 24 exporters in Haiti. In 1971, the three largest ones accounted for 45.16 per cent of total exports and the ten largest ones for 77.85 per cent. In addition, they are all members of a Federation of Coffee Exporters.

Between the exporters and the producers, there are somewhere between 1,500 and 2,000 *speculateurs*. These have often been reported to be the middlemen who supposedly buy from the producers and sell to the exporters. But this is only partly true, since about 80 per cent of these *speculateurs* are *engagés* (hired); in other words, they are on the payroll of particular exporters. Furthermore, they also have more credit to advance to the peasants since they receive these funds from the exporters who in turn borrow them from banks.[24] The 20 per cent of the *speculateurs* who are *libres* – independent – are free to sell to any of the 24 exporters. But they do not have the financial resources available to those who work for the exporters since the banks are less willing to advance money to them than to the exporters. Furthermore, because of geographical limitations, the producers normally sell to the local *speculateur* and the latter normally sells to the exporter who is most important in that area.

The picture cannot be complete without a description of the producers. As already said, in 1968, the only year in which this information is available, there were 374,000 people producing coffee on some 140,000 hectares. As Table 15.1 shows, the holdings on which coffee was produced were very small providing to the majority of the producers, who in most cases own and work the land themselves, barely a subsistence standard of living.[25]

*Table 15.1    Coffee holdings by size (hectares or percentages)*

| Size of Holdings (Hectares) | Percent of Holdings |
|---|---|
| 0 to 0.6 | 15.0 |
| 0.6 to 1.3 | 19.4 |
| 1.3 to 2.6 | 30.6 |
| 2.6 to 6.0 | 23.9 |
| over 6.0 | 11.1 |

Source: Census of 1959.

The 'industrial organization' of the coffee industry in Haiti should leave little doubt on the question whether the tax falls most heavily on the merchant–exporters or on the producers. Both theoretical and practical considerations support the conclusion that it falls on the latter. The exporters face a buyers' market. They all have the power and the means and, given their small number, they are unlikely to compete very actively with one another.[26] The producers, on the other hand, depend on the small quantities of coffee that they produce for their meagre livelihood and often have to borrow against future crops at high interest rates.[27] Once they do this, they are committed to specific buyers. Not knowing about world prices, they normally accept whatever price is paid to them. It is reported that they receive the same price regardless of the quality of the coffee.[28]

The coffee tax thus amounts to a very high proportional tax on the income of the coffee producers. It has generally been equivalent to an average income tax rate of 25–40 per cent depending on the price of the product. This makes this group by far the most heavily taxed group in Haiti. Considering that most of its members are among the poorest in Haiti, this raises a serious equity issue.

Table 15.2 throws some additional light on the issue. The table incorporates the assumption about shifting accepted above (pp. 230–31); that is the tax is assumed to fall on the producers. The table shows, for the 1950–71 period, the distribution of the returns from coffee exports among the government, the merchant–exporters and the producers. The already mentioned sharp increase in the taxation of coffee is evident. The share accruing to taxes doubled between the early 1950s – when, as argued by the United Nations report cited above, taxes were already too high and were already discouraging production–and the 1960s. The tax per average 60-kilo bag rose from US$9.8 in 1950 to US$16.3 in 1971.[29]

Table 15.2   Distribution of returns from coffee exports (values in dollars per
60-kg bag and percentages)

| Fiscal Years | FOB Export Price | Taxes Amount | Taxes Shares | Intermediaries Amount | Intermediaries Taxes | Procedures Amount | Procedures Shares |
|---|---|---|---|---|---|---|---|
| 1950 | 61.2 | 9.8 | 16 | 7.0 | 11 | 44.4 | 63 |
| 1952 | 62.4 | 10.1 | 16 | 7.9 | 12 | 44.4 | 72 |
| 1953 | 64.8 | 10.4 | 16 | 10.6 | 16 | 43.8 | 68 |
| — | — | — | — | — | — | — | — |
| 1964 | 48.0 | 15.5 | 32 | 8.5 | 18 | 24.0 | 50 |
| 1965 | 50.4 | 16.1 | 32 | 13.9 | 28 | 20.4 | 40 |
| 1966 | 51.0 | 16.1 | 32 | 13.9 | 27 | 21.0 | 41 |
| 1967 | 47.4 | 16.1 | 34 | 12.1 | 25 | 19.2 | 41 |
| 1968 | 44.3 | 16.1 | 36 | 9.7 | 22 | 18.5 | 42 |
| 1969 | 43.5 | 15.9 | 37 | 10.6 | 24 | 18.5 | 42 |
| 1970 | 56.4 | 16.3 | 29 | 12.8 | 22 | 27.3 | 49 |
| 1971 | 52.2 | 16.3 | 31 | 11.5 | 22 | 24.4 | 47 |

Sources:   Based on information available from the Ministry of Finance and Economic Affairs,
Customs Administration and the Haitian Institute for the Promotion of Coffee.

This increase is obviously made more burdensome by the fall in the price of
coffee up to the end of the period covered in this study.

Table 15.2 indicates that the share accruing to the merchant–exporters also
increased sharply (as did their actual charge per bag exported) in spite of the fact
that, according to the Coffee Institute, there has been no improvement in the
services that they provide. They still export mainly the unwashed variety that
requires little elaboration.Thus it appears that the producers had to bear not only
the higher taxes but the higher chargers on the part of the intermediary. These
higher charges are just like additional taxes as far as the producers are concerned.
Thus, the total burden per bag of coffee exported rose from US$16.8 in 1950 to
a high of US$30.0 in 1965–6. This burden stood at US$27.8 in 1971.

Coffee prices dropped from the early 1950s to the 1960s. This accentuated the
effects of the increase in taxes and in marketing commissions. In fact, because
of the combination of lower prices and higher charges for taxes and intermediaries, the average price per bag exported received by the producers fell from
US$44.4 in 1950 to a low of US$17.0 in 1968. A fall of such magnitude cannot
fail to have important economic effects. The next section analyses some of these.

**Some conclusions on the economic effects of the Haitian coffee exports tax**
Faced with the situation described above, a first defence mechanism that has
been available to the coffee producers has been switching from the production
of coffee to that of other non-taxed crops.[30] This kind of switch obviously takes
a long time and is bound to affect some lands sooner than others. It also takes
place only after the coffee producers have come to feel that the fall in their net
income is not transitory but permanent. The peasants have been understandably
reluctant to cut coffee trees, which require several years to grow, in order to

produce other crops. But with the lowering of the price of coffee over the period analysed in this chapter –1960–72 – and, perhaps more importantly, with the increase in the tax (and in the charges by the intermediaries) the pressure to do so must have increased. In such cirumstances, the longer is the period considered, the more likely it is that the theoretically anticipated shift to other crops will actually take place.

At a subsistence level of income crop failure may have disastrous conse-quences for a peasant family.Consequently, the lower income received by the coffee producers can be expected to increase their aversion toward taking risks. The net result of this is that some land will be shifted toward the production of non-taxed and relatively riskless subsistence products. This shift, however, while understandable and, perhaps, justified from the point of view of the individual, is very costly to the country since it involves a loss in its expected real income. What it means, in fact, is that the country's resources are used less productively. The fall in production is shown quite clearly in Table 15.3. Coffee production fell from a yearly average of 611,000 bags for the 1960–64 period to 520,000 bags for the 1969–72 period.[31]

As theory tells us, the high tax on the export of coffee can be expected to stimulate sales to the local market or direct consumption on the part of the producers. As was stated in the theoretical section of this chapter (see pp. 228–9), an export tax can be broken down into a tax on the production of that product and an equivalent subsidy to its local consumption. The higher the export tax, the higher the implicit subsidy to its local consumption. In other words, at the same time that production is discouraged, local consumption is encouraged. That such a shift may in fact have been taking place is supported by the evidence that over the 1960–72 period, while production and exports fell, local consumption increased both relatively and absolutely in spite of the fact that there was hardly any growth of national income over the period.

Table 15.3 shows some of these effects. Average yearly consumption of coffee rose from 181,000 bags for the 1960–64 period to 205,000 bags for the 1969–72 period. Over the same period average yearly exports declined from 430,000 to 313,000 bags a year.

The lowering of taxes on coffee exports would appear to be a necessary condition for stimulating the production and the export of this product. A shift from this form of taxation to either taxes on incomes, which account for almost no revenue, or on general sales would be supported from both an efficiency and from an equity point of view. In the particular situation of Haiti, however, there is a question as to whether it would also be a sufficient condition. The basic question here is the following: given the above-described structure of the coffee sector, would the lowering of this tax be reflected in equivalent higher prices paid to the producers? Or would it rather result in part or perhaps even largely in higher profits for the merchant–exporters? This is, indeed, a difficult question to answer.

*Table 15.3   Production, consumption, and exports of coffee, 1960–72 (thousands of 60-kg bags and percentages)*

| Fiscal Years | Production | Exports | Consumption | As a Percent of Production Exports | Consumption |
|---|---|---|---|---|---|
| 1960 | 690 | 476 | 214 | 69 | 31 |
| 1961 | 463 | 273 | 190 | 59 | 41 |
| 1962 | 762 | 545 | 217 | 71 | 29 |
| 1963 | 531 | 425 | 106 | 80 | 20 |
| 1964 | 583 | 364 | 219 | 62 | 38 |
| 1965 | 600 | 383 | 217 | 63 | 37 |
| 1966 | 612 | 408 | 204 | 67 | 33 |
| 1967 | 509 | 283 | 226 | 56 | 44 |
| 1968 | 576 | 325 | 251 | 56 | 44 |
| 1969 | 545 | 308 | 237 | 56 | 44 |
| 1970 | 450 | 275 | 175 | 61 | 39 |
| 1971 | 544 | 358 | 186 | 66 | 34 |
| 1972 | 540 | 311 | 229 | 57 | 43 |

Sources:  For 1960–69 data from the Haitian Coffee Institute; for 1970–72 data from the National Bank of Haiti.

Under the present institutional set-up and given the relative economic power of the peasants–producers and the exporters there is really no mechanism that guarantees that the producers are actually the ones who would benefit from a tax reduction.

## Notes

1.   The export tax legislation of many countries has had the explicitly stated objective of discouraging exports of raw and non-elaborated materials and of encouraging that of elaborated products. In other words, these taxes have had the announced objective of reducing the relative export prices of more elaborated products *vis-à-vis* those of primary products.

2.   Such differentiation has been used, for example, in Burundi, Ecuador and Haiti with respect to coffee.

3.   Daniel M. Schydlowsky, 'Latin American trade policies in the 1970s: a prospective appraisal', *The Quarterly Journal of Economics* LXXXVI, 2, May 1972:23. This article should be consulted for the details of the proposal.

4.   See Secretaria General de la OEA, 'La politica tributaria en cuanto determinante del nivel y estructura de las exportaciónes', in OAS, *La Politica Tributaria Como Instrumento del Desarrollo*, Mexico, III Conferencia Inter-americana sobre Tributación, 3–8 September 1973.

5.   The reader should consult the original paper as well as the two comments on that paper (by Felipe Pazos and Christopher K. Clague) for details and for a discussion of the OAS proposal.

6.   For another discussion of this question, see R. Goode, G.E. Lent, and P.D. Ojha, 'Role of export taxes in developing countries', *IMF Staff Papers*, XIII, 3 November 1966.

7.   It will also require that before the imposition of the tax the country's exporters were not taking full advantage of their monopoly situation. If, before the tax, the price was already a monopoly price, the tax will not be shifted or, if it is, the country will not maximise its foreign exchange revenues.

8.   In Brazil coffee exports have not been levied by an export tax but, implicitly, by the obligation

of coffee producers to sell their coffee to a public agency (Instituto Brasiliero do Café) at prices that have often been far below the world price.

9.   A. Harberger, 'Tax policy as a determinant of the level and structure of export', *III Inter-American Conference on Taxation*, Mexico, 3–8 September 1972:2.
10.  R. Goode, G.E. Lent, P.D. Ojha, op. cit., p. 465.
11.  Most export taxes, excluding royalties which are strictly not export taxes, fall on crops so that the agricultural sector is the one most affected.
12.  In many developing countries the shift will often not be toward other cash crops but toward subsistence crops which are not likely to be taxed at all.
13.  The same conclusions arise if the producers are forced to sell their output to a government agency that acts as a monopoly and then exports the product or sells it at the same (export) price in the internal market.
14.  If the local consumption of the product is levied with an excise tax, the effect of the export tax can be obtained by an *ad valorem* tax on production with an equal *ad valorem* reduction in the excise tax on the local consumption. In this case, no cash subsidies would need to be paid.
15.  It will be in the interest of producers to sell in the local market as long as they can do it at a price that is greater than the f.o.b. export price less the export tax.
16.  Obviously, if this basic necessity is not taxed internally, this option would not be available.
17.  In a general equilibrium framework, the situation would be more complex because it would have to include at least the use of the tax on the part of the government as well as the employment effects associated with the disincentive to production.
18.  This section is based on Tanzi, 'Export taxation in developing countries: taxation of coffee in Haiti', *Social and Economic Studies* 1, March 1976.
19.  *United Nations, Mission to Haiti*, United Nations Publications, 1949 II B 2, Chapter XI:310–11.
20.  Data from the Haitian Institute for the Promotion of Coffee.
21.  Furthermore one can argue that the lands no longer used for producing coffee may have been used to produce other commodities which may have been exported. But this does not seem to have happened.
22.  The average price for a 60-kilo bag was around $50.
23.  See discussion of this possibility in Goode, Lent, and Ojha, op. cit., p. 465. See also Eliezer B. Ayal, 'The impact of export taxes on the domestic economics of underdeveloped countries', *The Journal of Development Studies* 1, July 1965.
24.  The exporters were reported in 1973 to pay 8–9 per cent for these loans. These rates are far lower than would be paid by a coffee producer assuming that he were ever able to qualify for a direct loan.
25.  From Table 15.1 one can easily calculate the relatively small income of producers by realizing that the productivity per hectare averages about 270 kilos. Many producers do not produce more than one or two 60-kilo bags per year.
26.  Of course it does not mean that they do not compete at all.
27.  The exporters are likely to make a profit also on the differential between the rate of interest that the banks charge to them and the rate they charge the producers.
28.  Illiteracy, which must be close to 100 per cent among the coffee producers, is given as the main reason for this.
29.  As shown above, it was still higher in 1973.
30.  High taxes on the export of sugar, coupled with very low prices paid to farmers for the production of sugar-cane, have meant that the coffee producers could not shift to the production of this other important cash crop.
31.  It should be recalled that throughout much of this period the quota for Haiti under the International Coffee Agreement exceeded exports so that there would have been no difficulty in disposing of a greater output.

# Index